Betsy BEADS

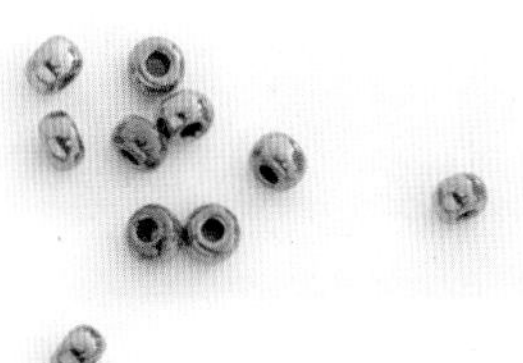

BETSY BEADS

PUBLISHER
Alexis Yiorgos Xenakis

EDITOR
Elaine Rowley

MANAGING EDITOR
Karen Bright

TECHNICAL EDITOR
Rick Mondragon

INSTRUCTION EDITORS
Sarah Peasley
Ginger Smith

GRAPHIC DESIGNER
Natalie Sorenson

PHOTOGRAPHER
Alexis Xenakis

PRODUCTION DIRECTOR & COLOR SPECIALIST
Denny Pearson

BOOK PRODUCTION MANAGER
Greg Hoogeveen

TECHNICAL ILLUSTRATOR
Carol Skallerud

CEO
Benjamin Levisay

MARKETING
Lisa Mannes

First published in the USA in 2012 by
XRX, Inc., PO Box 965, Sioux Falls,
South Dakota 57101-0965

ISBN 13: 978-1-933064-25-3

BOOKS

605-338-2450
Visit us online — knittinguniverse.com

Printed in China.

BETSY BEADS

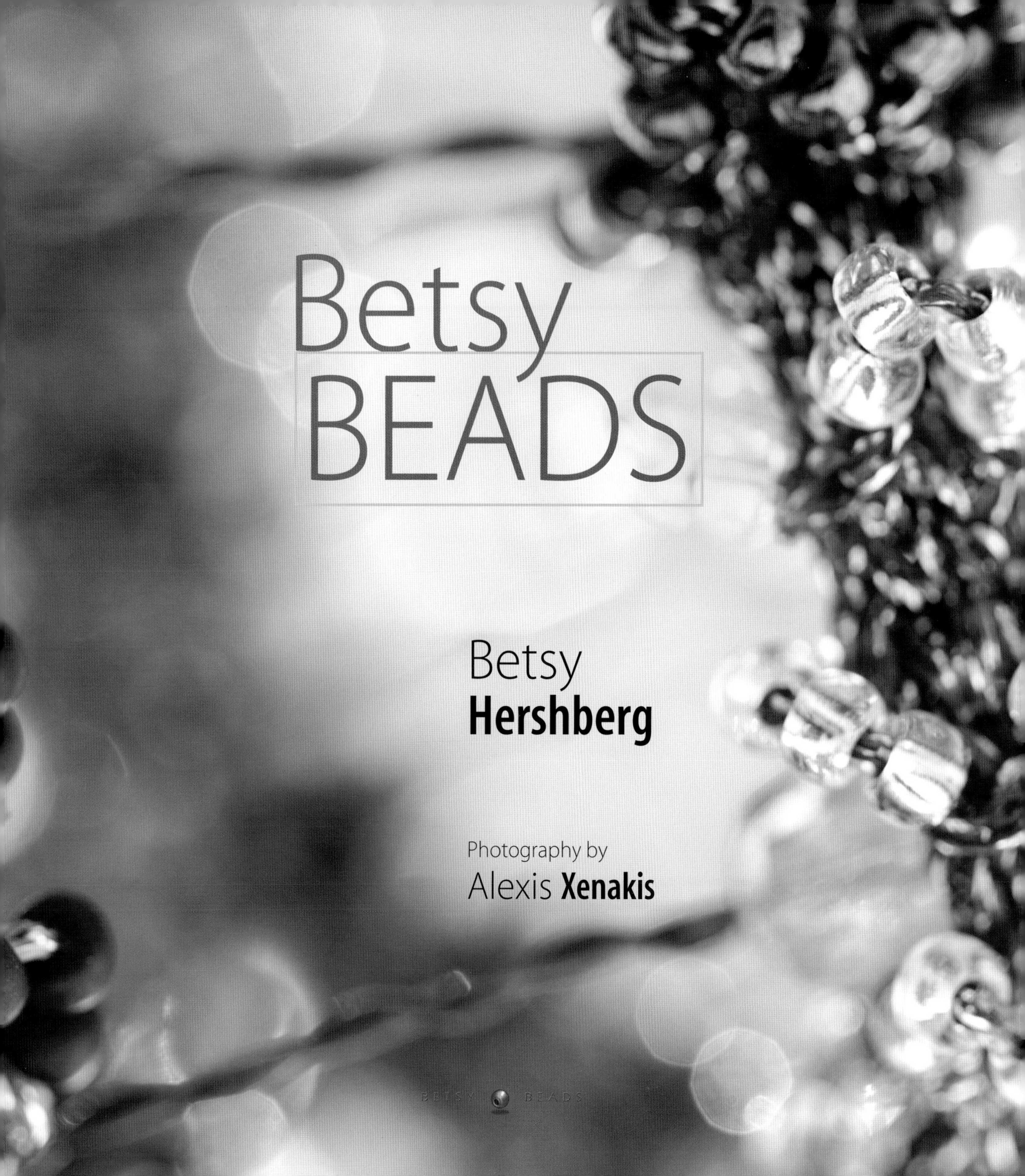

Betsy BEADS

Betsy **Hershberg**

Photography by

Alexis **Xenakis**

BETSY BEADS

Contents

Introduction VI

How to use the book VIII

Beading basics 2

Essays

Getting started X

Waiting for inspiration 10

What if... creativity 40

Coloring inside the lines 68

Technically speaking... 100

Finishing the hat... 138

Struggling with the 'A' words 156

Techniques 160

Resources 164

Colophon 166

I-cord

Tech trials 12

KISS: Keep it simple spiral *necklace* 16

Star light, star bright *necklace* 20

Over the rainbow *necklace* 24

Twofers *bracelet* 28

Ladder 72 *bracelet* 32

Chiaroscuro *belt* 36

Tubes and straps

Tech trials 42

Twilight *necklace* 46

Wineberry *necklace* 50

Precious hoops *earrings* 54

Double play *bracelet* 58

Bunch bands *bracelets* 62

Stash buster *belt* 66

Stitch pattern embellishment

Tech trials 70

Color it yours *scarf* 74

It's elementary *suspenders* 78

Disco 'spenders *suspenders* 82

Infinity I *necklace* 84

Infinity II *necklace* 88

Faux Louboutin *evening bag* 92

Marge's yarmulke 96

Knit beads

Tech trials 102

Four seasons *earrings and necklace* 106

Silver orbits *earrings* 112

Wrap and roll *necklace* 116

Beads by the barrel *necklace* 120

Links and loops *Golden links necklace and Fruit loops bracelet* 124

All wrapped up *Christmas ornaments and Easter eggs* 130

Welts and hems

Tech trials 140

Wired for wow *bracelet* 142

Granite cuff *bracelet* 146

Bead warmers *earwarmer and scarf* 148

Girly pearls *necklace* 152

For my mother.

I tried it. And look what happened!

left-brained (lĕft´brānd´) adjective: related to or displaying the characteristics normally associated with the left half of the brain, e.g. logical, verbal, organized, analytical, rational, sequential, mathematical, cautious.

Confessions of a left-brained knitter…

For most of my life, I happily described myself as a traditional knitter. I was possessed of classic left-brained character traits, content to focus on expanding my technical expertise, always seeking out projects that could teach me something new. I also loved modifying existing patterns, but the idea that in doing so I was being creative in any way never occurred to me. My comfort with altering patterns was simply a trait I owed to my first knitting teacher: my remarkable mother. She possessed great technical knowledge, but more importantly she encouraged me to be what I now recognize as a fearless knitter. I would often ask what she thought of one of my prospective alterations and, although she may never have said these exact words, the implication was always: "Just try it and see what happens!" It is only now, so many years later, that I understand the power of those words.

Over the last ten years, as a result of a newfound passion for bead knitting, I have discovered that I have a creative capacity for knitting that for the first 50 years of my life I did not know existed. If you are interested, you can read about some of the events that triggered this discovery in the Colophon at the end of this book. My years of teaching

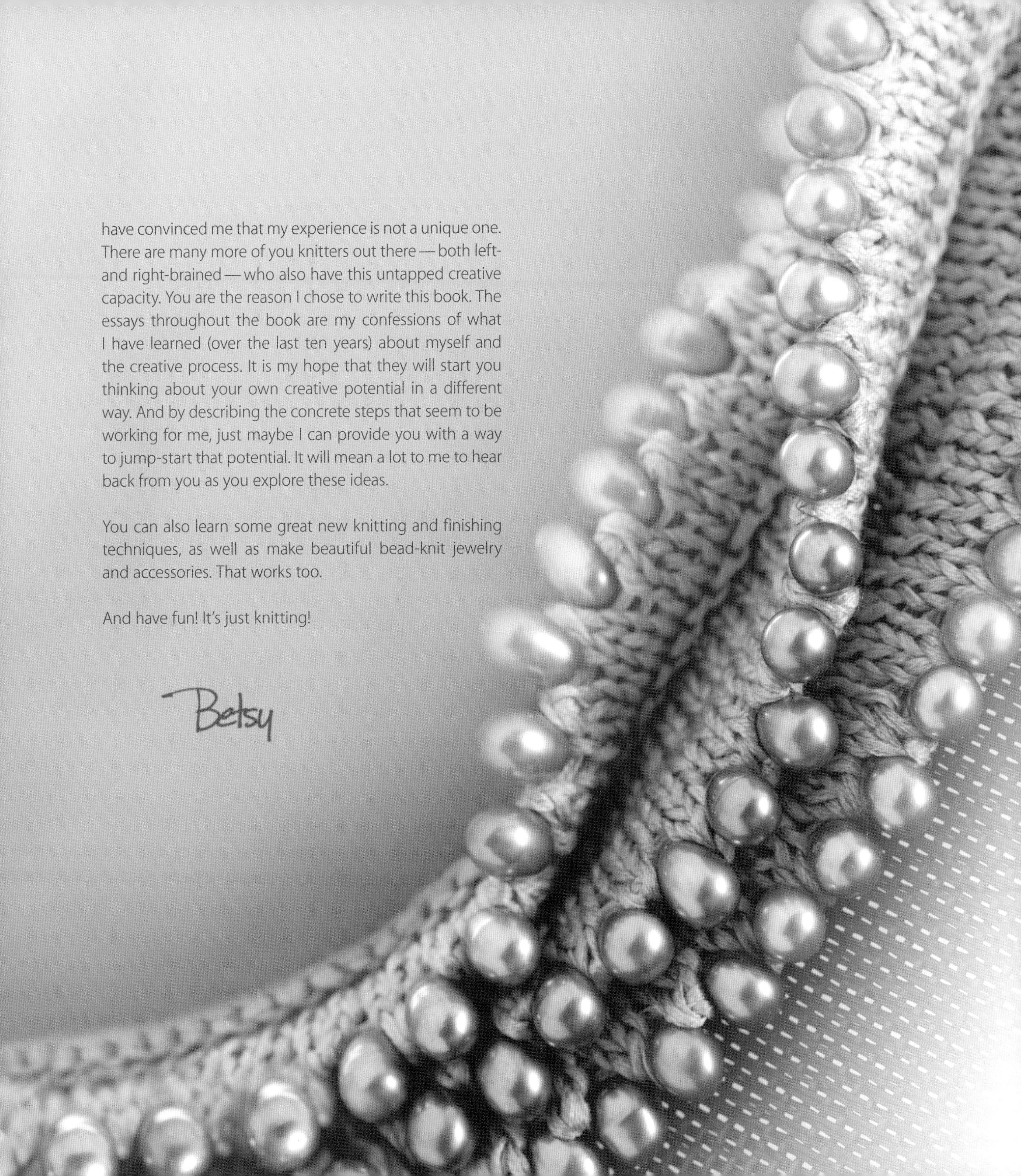

have convinced me that my experience is not a unique one. There are many more of you knitters out there — both left- and right-brained — who also have this untapped creative capacity. You are the reason I chose to write this book. The essays throughout the book are my confessions of what I have learned (over the last ten years) about myself and the creative process. It is my hope that they will start you thinking about your own creative potential in a different way. And by describing the concrete steps that seem to be working for me, just maybe I can provide you with a way to jump-start that potential. It will mean a lot to me to hear back from you as you explore these ideas.

You can also learn some great new knitting and finishing techniques, as well as make beautiful bead-knit jewelry and accessories. That works too.

And have fun! It's just knitting!

Betsy

How to use the book

The following section, Beading Basics, provides fundamental information about bead-knitting techniques, tools, and materials. Each section of the book—and the targeted Tech Trial that precedes it—focuses on a specific component or technique used in the projects in that section.

Small and manageable Tech Trials give you the opportunity to learn and practice these techniques with yarns and beads you may already have at home. If you don't, you should be able to acquire them with minimal trouble and expense. No local bead store? The Resource section at the end of the book can help you find the beads, findings, and tools used.

The Tech Trials are often a sequence of small variations on a theme, each of which can stand on its own, but combining variations can result in an even greater impact. Think of them as building blocks. Something new can evolve with each round of play; the newest iteration may provide one answer while also giving rise to the next question. For those of you who take comfort in a less fearless approach, these Trials allow working the technique—and gaining confidence—before deciding to invest in making one of the related projects. The process may also stir an idea or two for an original project of your own!

I hope you allow yourself time to become familiar with any of these techniques that are new to you. If you feel confused, take a moment to breathe and look again. And it's okay to allow yourself to put down whatever it is that is frustrating you and come back to it later. Remember that much of the knitting you do so comfortably now may have been a challenge at first.

And most of all, I hope that by sharing what I am learning along my journey, I will inspire you to begin a journey of your own—one small step, one small change, at a time.

The project

Betsy introduces the project, highlighting her design process.

Twilight

At first look, people assume that the technique used to create this bead-knit tube is anything BUT what it actually is. The guesses include I-cord, bead crochet, even Kumihimo, the Japanese braiding technique. Nope! None of the above. It is simply a wide, rectangular piece of bead-knit stockinette fabric with all of the beads placed on the purl side. And what does stockinette fabric want to do? Curl! All I had to do was exploit this natural tendency and then find a way to join the cast-on and bound-off edges together seamlessly. I lost count of my attempts to figure that out, but I can be pretty stubborn and finally worked out what I now call a Zipper Graft. This seamless, bead-knit tube is one of my favorite components and surely one of the most versatile.

FIESTA YARNS Gelato
100 yds in Onyx

48 BETSY BEADS

Specifics for the yarn, colors, and yardage used in the project (and occasionally an alternative) shown life-size.

Special **technique illustrations** serve as at-a-glance reminders. For more detail, refer to Beading Basics or Techniques.

For same finished measurements, match **gauge**. Exact gauge is often not critical, but firm tension usually is.

Prepare

With beading needle, string 440 beads: primarily A beads, with B beads strung at random intervals.

Knit

Leaving an 8" tail and using a long-tail cast-on, cast on 89.

Begin chart: Row 1 (RS) P1, **[SB, p2]** to end—44 beads.
Row 2 K1, **[SB, k2]** to end.
Rows 3–8 Repeat Rows 1 and 2.
Row 9 Repeat Row 1.
Bind off in pattern, placing beads as in Row 2.
Cut yarn, leaving a 30" tail.

Finish

With RS facing, tapestry needle, bind-off tail, and using Zipper Graft, join cast-on and bound-off edges. Use cast-on and bind-off tails to sew on clasp. Weave tails inside the tube and trim.

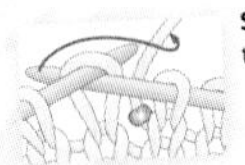

SB Slide bead close to last stitch worked.

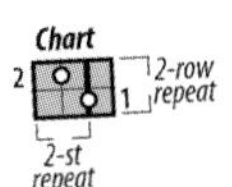

Stitch key
Purl on RS, knit on WS
SB, p1 on RS
SB, k1 on WS

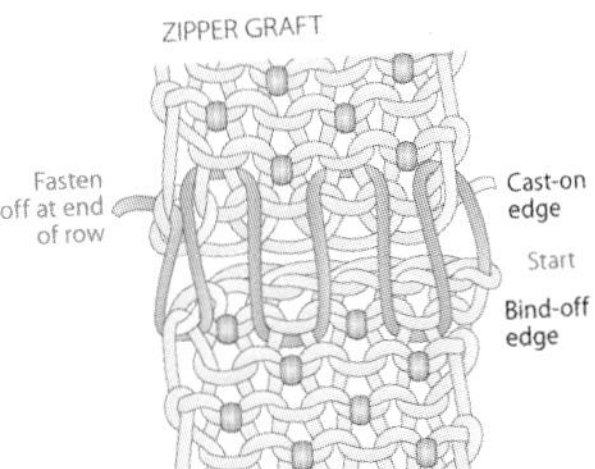

gauge
6 stitches = 1" over pattern
finished length 15¼" closed, including clasp; knitted piece measures 14½"

yarn
medium weight
100 yds ribbon tape

beads
465 size 6º Japanese seed beads, shown in 2 colors

needles
2.75mm/US2, 60cm (24") long

and...
beading needle
tapestry needle
single-strand clasp

Generic description for yarn and beads; yardage and number of beads to allow for waste.

Suggested **needle size** only; use the size you need for firm tension.

NOTES: easy

See page 160 for knitting abbreviations and techniques, and page 2 for beading basics.

Crystal beads are added at random as the beads are strung. How many to use is knitter's choice. The sample used about 33 crystal beads out of 440 total beads.

To lengthen or shorten circumferen... necklace: for every 2 additional stitc... per row, string 10 more beads.

WHAT IF...

The design possibilities for bead-color combinations and placement on this kind of bead-knit tube are truly endless. The entire tube does not have to be beaded—you can leave sections where the yarn shows through. When considering beading patterns for a tube like this, make sure to remember the continuity required—you'll want the pattern to continue seamlessly when cast-on and bind-off edges are grafted together.

Think of using this kind of tube as a decorative handle for a purse, as a belt, or even as an applied trim or embellishment.

Specifics for the beads, colors, and amount used in the project.

"**What if... ?**" offers other ways to think about the project — how to wear it, how to simplify the construction, even an option for using the technique differently. Think of them as idea seeds!

Suggested **skill level**

Easy fairly straightforward

Intermediate usually involves one of the more challenging elements

- multiple colors of beads to be strung
- more complex finishing
- multiple knitting or assembly/ construction techniques in one project
- more complex shaping, chart reading

Advanced several of the above in one project

For more help refer to Techniques or review Beading Basics.

Getting started

Why is it always so much easier to do something else rather than to start that new thing? Why? Because we are creatures of habit. That something else is usually something familiar, and familiar is comforting. When we work on something we know how to do, we feel competent and anticipate success. On the other hand, starting that new thing is risky. Before we have written the first word, cast on the first stitch, drawn the first line, in our minds we are already miles down the creative road, fearful of land mines that may or may not exist, and anticipating negative criticism which we know will break our hearts.

Borrowing the well-known slogan of sports advertising, what if we could "Just do it?" Do it because we have an idea. Do it because we are curious. Do it without grand expectations. Do it because we just enjoy the doing.

Shortly after committing to do this book, I had what could be described as a mild panic attack. What had I gotten myself into? I was the ultimate impostor. How had I tricked these trusting souls into believing I could produce a book? I didn't have the first idea of how to get started. I shared my fears with my smart and creative daughter, who magically advised the following: "Mom! You don't have to get up out of your chair and run a marathon. Just start by wiggling your creative fingers and toes." Small steps. Fingers and toes. Knitting because it calms me down and focuses me. Altering the stitches or the beads, one small change at a time, because I'm curious. Knitting without the expectation that my first creation will end up in the Metropolitan Museum of Art.

Knitting just because I love to knit. Writing because there is something I really want to share.

Not a bad place to start!

Morning Glory *necklace (2010)*
Glass beads, fiber
Taking the time to notice the beauty that surrounds us, like the morning glories in my garden, is a good way to get started.
Technique link: All purl I-cord

Beading basics

Beading basics Index

3-needle bind-off with beads	***page 45***
Attaching clasp	***page 123***
Bead stringing	***page 6***
Beaded cast-on	***page 9***
Beaded bind-off	***page 9***
Beaded overcast seam	***page 31***
Cinch wrappers	***page 102***
Knit bead left (KBL)	***page 8***
Knit bead right (KBR)	***page 8***
Knit paillette	***page 83***
Place bead with crochet hook	***page 147***
Slide bead (SB)	***page 7***
Stop bead	***page 6***
Zipper graft	***page 49, 61***

There have already been books written on the broad topic of Bead Knitting. (The two I recommend are *Knit One, Bead Too* by Judith Durant and *Knit and Crochet with Beads* by Lily Chin.) As a result, I will deal primarily with the materials and techniques necessary to complete the projects in this book.

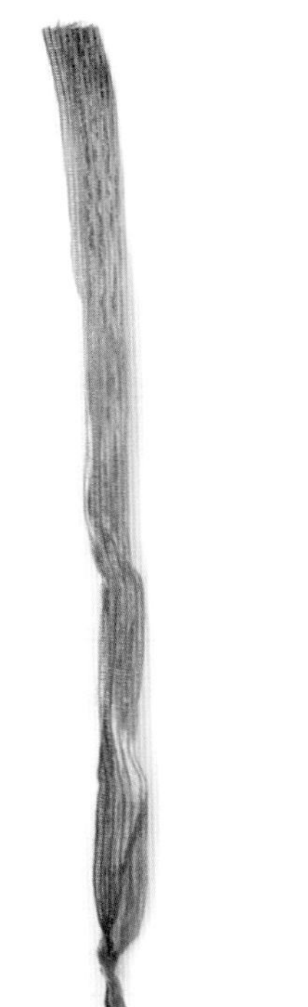

MATERIALS

I always suggest that, wherever possible, you patronize your local yarn or bead store when you need project materials. If you don't, the next time you seek out the store it may not be there. My personal thanks go to all of the local store owners who work so hard to bring us the goods and services that allow us to pursue our passions.

I know that many knitters feel most comfortable using the same yarns and beads specified in a project. If availability, expense, or personal preference dictates, please do not hesitate to try the projects with other yarns or beads, bearing in mind that the weight of the yarn and the size of the bead must be similar if you expect to achieve a similar end result. I also really hope that at some point you will feel free to experiment with alterations to the existing patterns.

Yarns

Having grown up in an era that offered a much more limited choice of materials with which to knit, synthetic fibers were few and we called everything "yarn." In this book the term is used generically, referring to any and all of the fabulous fibers available to today's knitters. When choosing a yarn for bead knitting, there are several factors to be considered.

Whichever bead-knitting technique is employed, at some point in the process the yarn used to secure the bead to the knitted fabric will have to fit through the opening in the bead, so smooth yarns are usually best. Textural yarns — with slubs, flags, eyelash, etc. — are often problematic or completely unworkable. They can also work against the desired visual effect of the beads. However, they can be used quite effectively as embellishment yarns on a bead-knit project.

If the project calls for stringing beads onto the yarn prior to knitting, the yarn must be strong enough to withstand the abrasion caused by the repeated sliding of beads up and down the yarn. Many fine luxury yarns will break from both the abrasion and the weight of the beads, and are ill-suited to bead knitting. If the yarn you want to use can't be pre-strung, you can still add beads to a project by stringing them on a lighter weight carry-along yarn and knitting it together with your main yarn.

For many of my jewelry projects, I find that choosing a yarn that already has some of the qualities of traditional jewelry — a natural sheen, a metallic thread, or a smooth reflective surface — can really enhance the look of the finished piece. I am particularly fond of tubular ribbon yarns and chainette yarns in rayon, viscose, and/or polyester (with or without metallic threads), silk thread or ribbon, and lightweight cording. This is not to say that fine wools cannot also be used. They can be used and I do use them — they just create a different look.

The aftercare required by the yarn or the finished project must also be considered. Once beads have been added to a project the care options are more limited. For example, I never recommend that beads be added to a project that must be dry cleaned, as the processes and chemicals used can damage the finish of the beads. If a fiber must be dry cleaned, it is not a good choice for bead knitting. If a fiber tolerates gentle hand washing, then it should be usable for bead knitting from the perspective of care.

The specific yarns used in each of the projects in this book were chosen because I liked them and felt they worked well for the overall effect I was trying to achieve, but also because at the time they were used, they were readily available. If we knew at the time of publication that a project yarn had been discontinued, an alternative has been offered.

Yarns (from left to right): 2 tubular chainette ribbons, flat ribbon, metallic, cord

Threads

For knitting

I love knitting with what would normally be considered sewing or embellishment threads — embroidery floss, silk or metallic threads, etc. If patience and eyesight allow, and if you can get past any fears of working with teeny tiny needles, give this a try. The color range and textural variety available with these threads is often too tempting to resist. Just know that there is little to no stretch in most sewing fibers, so keeping a firm and consistent tension is a must.

For finishing

There are projects that require the use of something other than the project yarn for finishing or embellishment, sometimes because of the size of the bead being used or the need for a stronger fiber. These finishing threads are most important for stringing the components of a project or attaching a clasp or other closure. For this usage, I recommend one of the available monofilament-type threads, such as WildFire or FireLine, or a braided cord for a heavier project. They come in several colors and varying weights (I like the 12 lb, .008" WildFire or the 6 lb, .008" Size D Fireline). These threads promise little or no stretch (thus maintaining the desired length of the strung elements) and are strong enough to resist being cut by the sometimes-sharp edges of some glass and metallic beads or the shanks of some clasps.

Beads

I love the description, "Anything with a hole through it can be considered a bead." Thinking this way can help expand the range of things you consider adding to knit fabric. For the purposes of this book, however, my palette of beads is narrower. There are projects that incorporate pearls, sequins and very long bugle beads, but most projects use glass seed beads of moderate size: 5º, 6º and 8º (the bigger the number, the smaller the bead).

As you are working on the technique samples, you should feel free to use whatever brand of seed bead you wish. When it comes to the full projects, however, I almost always recommend using Japanese seed beads. While they are slightly more expensive, they are also more consistently shaped, meaning you will have fewer unusable beads in a tube. The size of the hole is larger relative to the circumference of the bead than in Czech beads. This means you will be able to string a wider range of fibers through Japanese beads than through other beads.

The three major Japanese manufacturers of glass beads are Miyuki (my favorite), Matsuno, and Toho. The profile of each maker's seed bead is slightly different. Miyuki beads tend to be fractionally larger and really round. To my eye they appear like puffy doughnuts. Matsuno beads often have a slightly square look, while Toho beads are fractionally smaller than both Miyuki and Matsuno. They each make beads that are similar in color and finish, but also offer beads that are unique.

Japanese bead profiles

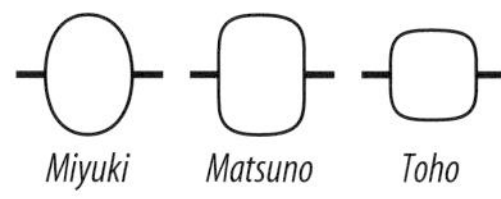

Relative hole sizes

Japanese *Czech*

Top-drilled bead

I do also use Czech beads. The randomness of their sizing can be a design feature. And occasionally I am lucky enough to come across a stash of vintage Czech glass beads. The shapes and finishes on those older beads are often unique and can truly make a design.

When purchasing beads for any project, it is always best to purchase them from a local supplier so you can take your chosen yarn with you and make sure of 2 things: ***1*** You should check to make sure you can thread your yarn through the beads. ***2*** It is helpful to string a bead or two to make sure the color and finish of the bead is going to give you the effect you want. Beads strung ON yarn may have a very different look than beads held NEXT to yarn. This is especially true of beads with any translucency, where the color of the yarn will be slightly visible through the bead and can sometimes dramatically alter the look of the bead. If you don't have a local store and decide to purchase beads on the Internet, make sure the seller allows beads to be returned if they turn out to be the wrong color or size.

You should always purchase significantly more beads than the project calls for to account for unusable beads. With Japanese beads, the waste will be small; with Czech beads, significantly higher. Because methods of packaging differ, it is difficult to offer a set number of tubes or other containers to purchase. Most retailers should be able to provide the weight of the beads in the containers they use. The approximate bead counts shown here allow you to estimate the number of seed beads you are purchasing.

Bead counts

SIZE	APPROXIMATELY
5°	**6 per gram**
6°	**11 per gram**
8°	**36 per gram**
11°	**90 per gram**

HINT: *When I first started working with beads, I looked for and purchased inexpensive odd lots of beads on EBay. I was able to experiment with a wide range of beads — different sizes, different materials, different shapes — without a huge investment.*

I can't emphasize enough the importance of counting your beads — more than once! — after stringing them and before starting your knitting, especially when multiple colors or different sizes and types are being used. Replacing missing beads is occasionally doable but never fun and often takes more time than it takes to reliably count your beads at the start. Extra glass beads present less of a problem as they can be removed from the yarn by breaking them with a strong, small pliers.

Tools

In addition to basic knitting supplies, there are a few other tools necessary for basic bead knitting, and a few that are required for specific projects in this book.

Beading needles

For those projects for which beads are strung on the yarn in advance, a beading needle or something similar is required. Here are some options:

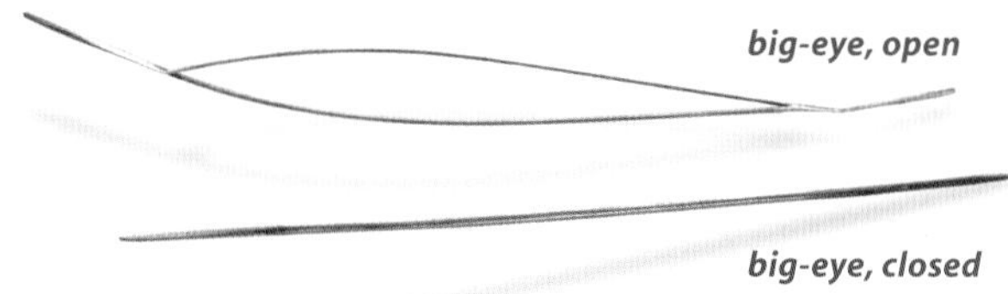

Big-eye beading needles These needles are basically two fine pieces of stainless steel that have been welded together on both ends. The middle of the needle can be opened, making it easy to thread a wide range of fibers of almost any size or weight. The needle is fairly stiff with very sharp points on either end, so it may also be used for light sewing or for bead weaving, always with care not to split your yarn due to the sharpness of the points.

Twisted-wire needles These needles, available in varying lengths and degrees of fineness, are made from a single piece of wire that is twisted back on itself after a small loop, the eye of the needle, is created at one end. This needle is very, very flexible. The yarn is easily threaded through the eye, but then the loop collapses as it passes through the hole of the bead being strung. This type of needle is able to pass through holes that are even smaller than those a big-eye needle can pass through, although the flexibility of this needle makes it slightly more difficult to pick up beads for stringing, and unsuitable for any sewing or bead-weaving tasks. And you will have to reopen the eye/loop with a larger sewing or tapestry needle or the tip of a knitting needle before it can be rethreaded.

Plastic dental floss threaders An inexpensive alternative to metal needles are the plastic dental floss threaders available at drug stores. They won't pass through the smallest beads, but are a great option for medium or large beads.

Other needles

Tapestry and darning needles Blunt-tipped tapestry needles and sharp-tipped darning needles are needed for much of the finishing work. The decision of whether to use a blunt or sharp tip is primarily a function of the weight and construction of the yarn used and how easily it splits. With finer yarns, and definitely with silk threads, a finer point is easier to work with. A blunt tip is recommended for plied yarns or fibers like chainette or cording, where the construction of the fiber presents lots of small threads that could be caught by a sharp tip.

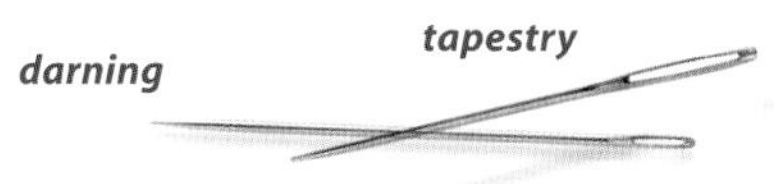

Stole or upholstery needles There are finishing techniques that require a needle to pass through a long tube or strap, and for such tasks a stole or upholstery needle is the ideal tool. These are long, blunt-tipped needles and range in length from 6-12". I consider them invaluable.

Bead mat

When working with beads, place some type of fabric that has a little nap on your work surface. This can be the small rectangle of blanket fleece sold by many bead stores or just a plain piece of felt or a terry washcloth you have around the house. The goal is to provide a slightly rough surface that will keep the beads from rolling away, possibly onto the floor. Your pets may enjoy the tiny new toys, but trust me — crawling around to retrieve missing beads gets old very quickly.

Needle-nose pliers or bead crimper

Ocassionally you may wish to remove an extra or unwanted bead from a string of beads. A needle-nose pliers or bead crimper can be used to break the bead. Make sure to first cover the bead, protecting your eyes and skin from any shards of flying glass.

Findings

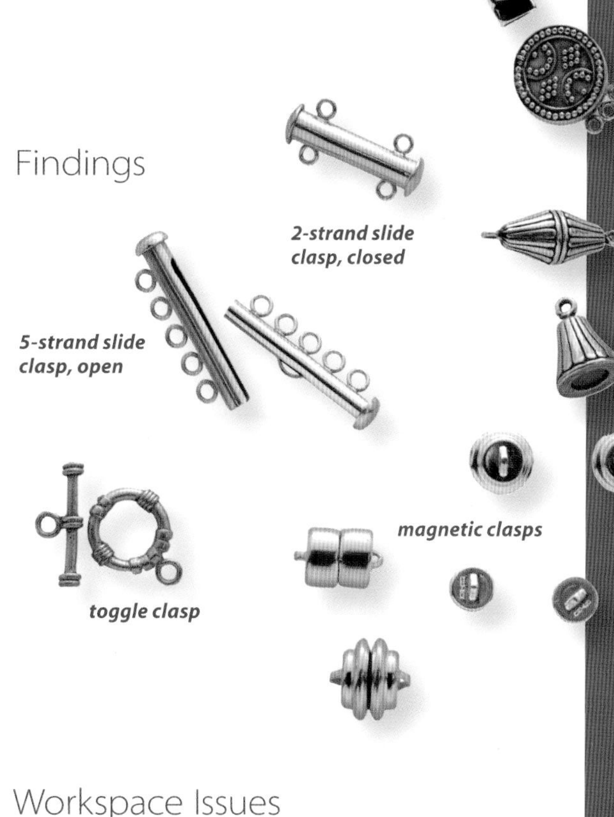

Workspace Issues

Clearly you should work in the space and the way that's most comfortable for you, but know that you don't have to sit at a table to do bead knitting. Here are my suggestions for making your bead knitting experience easer and most productive:

- Sit in your favorite knitting chair.
- I'll assume this chair has the best light available to you. You need great light!
- Find a tray with sides (MUST have sides!) and place a piece of napped fabric on the surface of the tray — blanket/polar fleece or felt is ideal, but a wash cloth or dish towel will also do. You just want to have a surface that keeps your beads from rolling around.
- Place all the containers of beads you think you'll want to work with on the tray along with your chosen yarn and knitting needles. You'll want to pour the beads out onto the fleece in order to string or count them.
- Keep all the small tools you might possibly want to use either on the tray or very close by — small sharp scissors, beading and tapestry needles, tape measure, etc.

Sit down, place this portable workspace in your lap, RELAX and go to work! (Keep breathing....)

Knitting Chart

End knitting

12, 10, 8, 6, 4, 2 →

← 11, 9, 7, 5, 3, 1

Start knitting

→ *Direction of knitting*

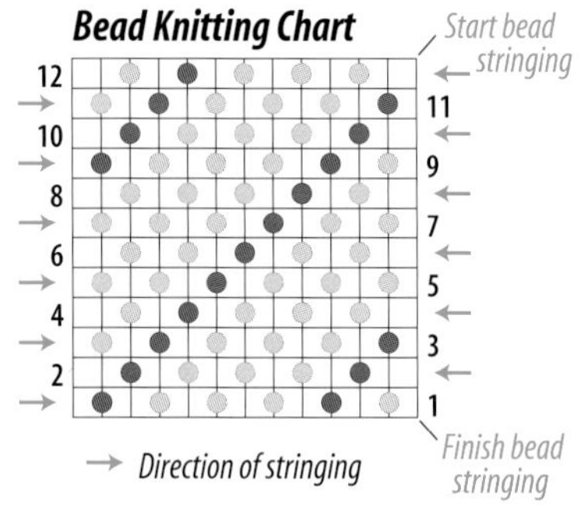

Stringing sequence:

66 beads total

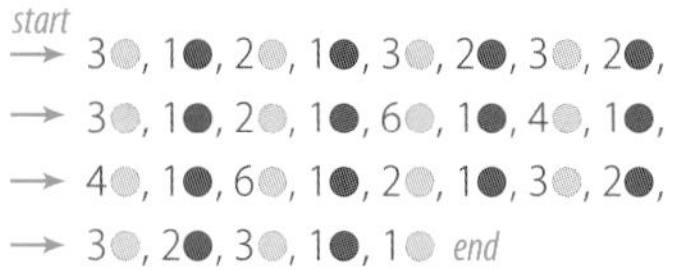

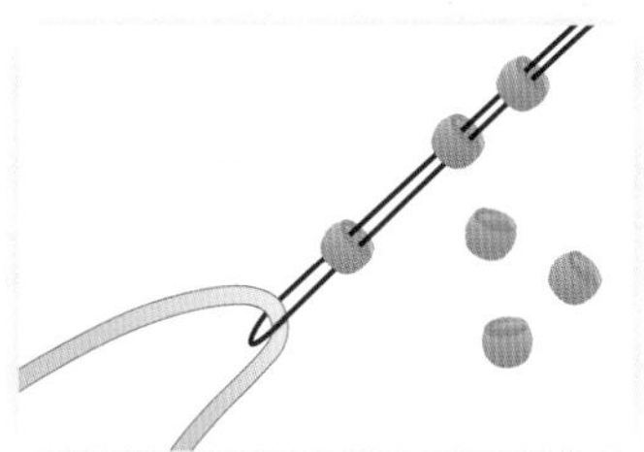

TECHNIQUES

Bead stringing

Using one of the beading needles, the actual stringing of beads is a simple task. If the beads are of uniform color, shape, and size, you just string as many beads onto the yarn as the pattern calls for. It becomes a more complex task only when beads of a different color, shape, or size need to be strung in a specific order to ensure their correct placement in a project. The easiest way to present such a pattern is in chart form, much like those used for intarsia or Fair Isle color work, in which each block of the chart represents a knit stitch. When beads are added to a chart, the beads are either shown on the line between 2 blocks (when a bead is knit *between* 2 stitches) or inside a block (when the bead is knit *through* and *onto* a single stitch). These 2 bead-knitting techniques are described in detail below.

A standard knitting chart starts at the bottom right corner of the chart with Row 1, worked from right to left. Row 2 is then worked from left to right. The rest of the rows are worked in the same way: odd-numbered rows from right to left and even-numbered rows from left to right (see Knitting Chart).

When a project includes beads as part of the chart, the beads must be strung in **reverse order** from the way the chart is read while knitting. This is because the **first** bead strung on the yarn is closest to the ball of yarn and will be the **last** bead worked into the knitting. The **last** bead strung will be the **first** bead worked. Before you begin stringing any beads, figure out which is the last stitch to be knit with beads, and begin stringing there (see Bead Knitting Chart and Stringing Sequence).

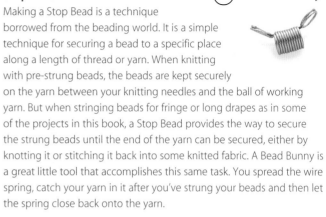

Stop Bead ***Bead Bunny***

Stop Bead

Making a Stop Bead is a technique borrowed from the beading world. It is a simple technique for securing a bead to a specific place along a length of thread or yarn. When knitting with pre-strung beads, the beads are kept securely on the yarn between your knitting needles and the ball of working yarn. But when stringing beads for fringe or long drapes as in some of the projects in this book, a Stop Bead provides the way to secure the strung beads until the end of the yarn can be secured, either by knotting it or stitching it back into some knitted fabric. A Bead Bunny is a great little tool that accomplishes this same task. You spread the wire spring, catch your yarn in it after you've strung your beads and then let the spring close back onto the yarn.

Bead knitting techniques

There are many, many ways to include beads in knitting. Several require pre-stringing beads, while another allows you to add beads with a crochet hook rather than actually knitting them into the fabric. I also love using embellishments such as weaving beads into knit fabric and sewing beads into the project as part of the finishing process. For the projects in this book, I have used my two favorite pre-stringing techniques and a few different embellishments.

Gauge considerations Beads do take up space and therefore will alter the stitch gauge of your knit fabric, making it wider than plain knitting. If large beads are used, or if small beads are used in great enough numbers, they can also increase the weight of the fabric, and that can alter row gauge. Swatches for projects that include beads must also include beads in order to determine an accurate gauge.

Pre-stringing techniques

Slide bead between stitches (SB)

This is my absolute favorite way to knit with beads. It is the easiest and perhaps affords the most versatility.

One important thing to know about bead knitting: Beads **want** to be on the purl side of knitting, kind of like the slubs that seem to gravitate to the purl side of stockinette fabric. Something about the architecture of the knit stitch allows beads to slip more easily to the purl side. If you want beads to be visible on the knit side of stockinette, you have to trap them there. So I figure — why swim upstream? Let beads go where they want and figure out a way to best exploit their natural

SLIDE BEAD BETWEEN STITCHES (SB)

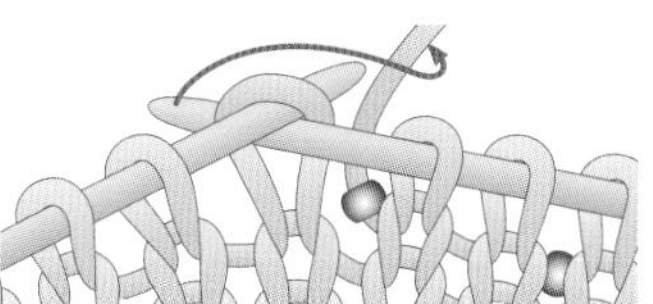

1 Slide bead on working yarn close to last stitch before working next stitch. Drawing shows sliding beads while knitting.

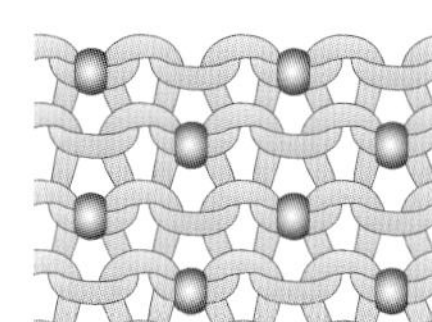

Beads show between stitches on purl side. Drawing shows beads staggered every row.

preferences. Because purl stitches appear on both sides of garter stitch fabric, you can place beads on **either** or **both** sides of garter stitch. When working in stockinette, it turns out to be very easy to place beads on the purl side of the fabric while working either a knit row **or** a purl row. This makes it possible to place beads on every row and create a wonderfully dense field of beads if desired.

Here's how it works: To knit a bead between stitches while working either a knit or a purl row, work a stitch, slide a bead up snug against your needle, and then simply work the next stitch. The bead will end up in a horizontal orientation (with the hole going east-west) on the bar of yarn between the stitches. And because the working yarn is always held to the purl side of the work (to the back while knitting and to the front while purling), the bead will be visible where purl stitches are visible — on the reverse-stockinette side of stockinette fabric or on either side of garter-stitch fabric.

When placing beads between stitches on every row of reverse stockinette, do not stack the beads directly above those in the row below — they will crowd and push each other in random directions. Instead, stagger the beads to give each enough room to stay where it is intended to be.

When placing beads between stitches and on only one side of garter stitch fabric, beads are placed every other row, providing enough room to either stagger the beads or stack them.

Knit beads onto stitches

This technique — knitting beads onto stitches — is one way to place beads on the knit side of stockinette fabric and is also known as **True Bead Knitting**. **Beaded knitting** is the generally accepted name for all other bead-knitting techniques. **True Bead Knitting** is the technique used to create the beautiful bead-knit bags of the Victorian era. When used as an all-over technique, beads are the only things visible on the face of the fabric created. The yarn on which the beads are strung is visible only on the back (non-public) side of the fabric. With this technique, beads can be knit onto either leg of the V-shaped knit stitch.

I use a part of this technique in some of the projects in this book, but none of the projects require the use of the quite complex technique necessary to create the all-over beaded look of those Victorian bags. The projects in this book limit the use of this technique to knitting a bead onto a stitch only while working a knit row, so the basic technique for placing beads in this way can be learned and understood. It is a 2-step process, and a different technique is used to place the beads on either the left or right leg of the knit stitch.

Beads between stitches on reverse stockinette stitch

Top, beads placed directly above each other, distorting design

Bottom, beads staggered to create all-over design

Beads between stitches on garter stitch

Top, beads placed directly above each other with enough room maintain design

Bottom, beads staggered to create less dense all-over design

Bottom, beads knit through stitches onto stockinette

Blue on left leg of stitch, Red on right leg of stitch

KNIT BEAD ON LEFT LEG (KBL)

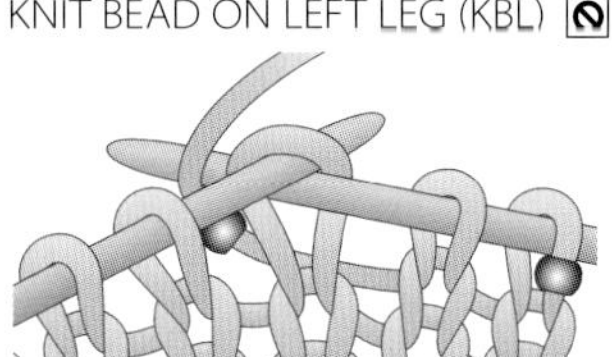

1 Position bead on working yarn and wrap as a standard knit (front to back, counter-clockwise).

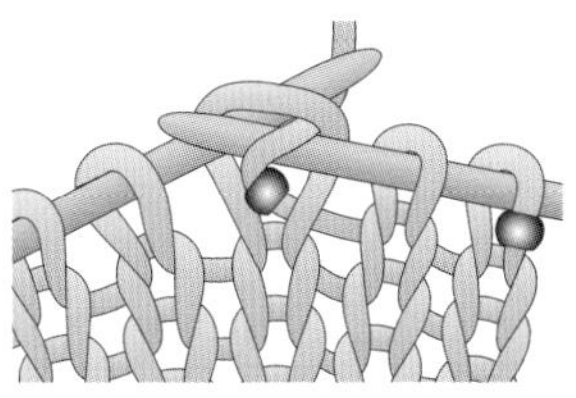

2 Knit, bringing bead through stitch and making sure bead comes to front of work.

3 On next row, purl through back loop above bead.

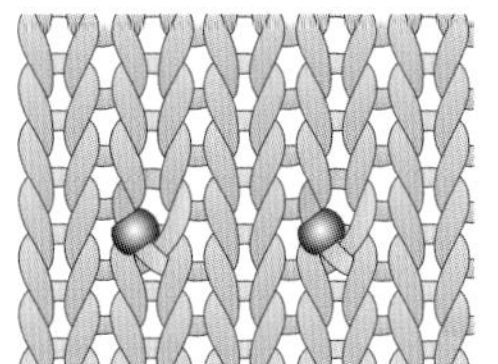

Stitch is twisted, with bead on left leg of the twisted stitch.

Knit bead on left leg (KBL)

Step 1 To place a bead on the **left** leg of a knit stitch, slide a bead up the working yarn as you wrap it around the right needle to create a new stitch.

Step 2 As the new stitch is being pulled through the old stitch on the left needle, make sure the bead passes **through** that stitch as well. When the new stitch is completed and on the right needle, the bead should be **on** that stitch and able to be moved easily to either the front or the back of the work.

Step 3 On the return purl row, when you come to a stitch with a bead on it, push the bead away from you to the knit side of the work, then purl that stitch through the back of the loop (tbl), making sure the point of the needle enters the stitch **above** the bead. Working through the back of the loop twists the stitch holding the bead and secures the bead on the **left** leg of the twisted stitch.

Knit bead on right leg (KBR)

Step 1 To place a bead on the **right** leg of a knit stitch, slide a bead up the working yarn as you wrap the yarn in reverse (clockwise) around the right needle to create a new stitch.

Step 2 As the new stitch is being pulled through the old stitch on the left needle, make sure the bead passes through that stitch as well. When the new stitch is completed and on the right needle, the bead should be **on** that stitch and able to be moved easily to either the front or the back of the work.

Step 3 On the return purl row, when you come to a stitch with a bead on it, push the bead away from you to the knit side of the work, then purl that stitch, making sure the bead passes through the stitch. Because you have worked the stitch by using a reverse wrap, the stitches with beads on them can be purled in the front of the loop and still be twisted. This method secures the bead on the **right** leg of the twisted stitch.

KNIT BEAD ON RIGHT LEG (KBR)

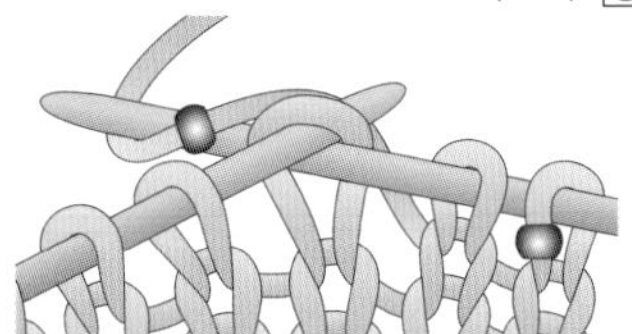

1 Position bead on working yarn, but wrap yarn around needle in reverse (back to front, clockwise).

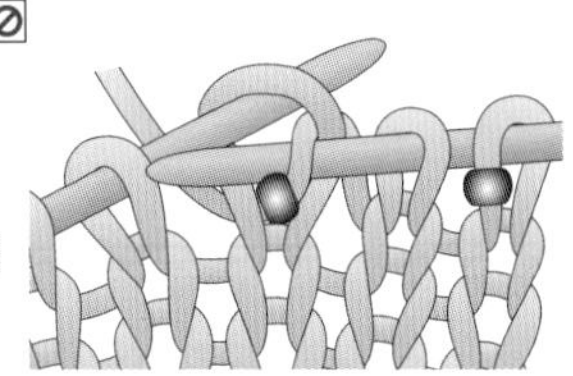

2 Knit, bringing bead through stitch making sure bead comes to front of work.

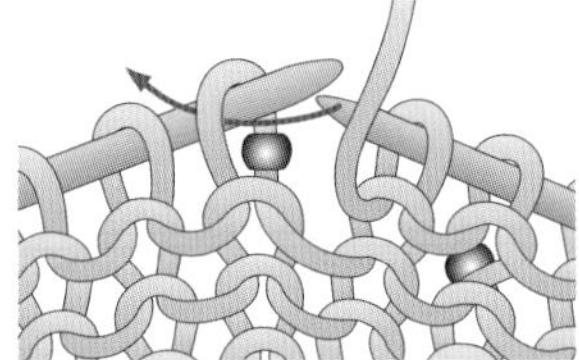

3 On next row, purl.

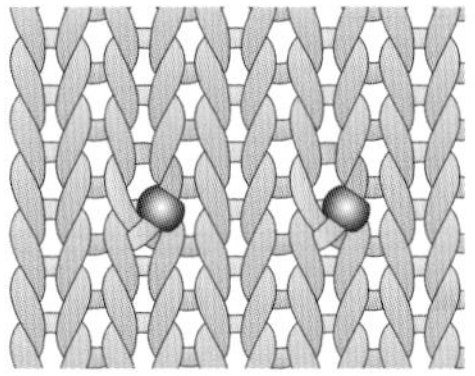

Stitch is twisted with bead on right leg of the twisted stitch.

Beaded cast-on

String the desired number of beads onto the yarn. Using a long-tail cast-on, and making sure to keep the beads between the cast-on needle and the ball of working yarn (**not** on the cast-on tail), cast on as many or as few beads as you wish and at whatever interval you wish. You can even cast on multiple beads for different effects, such as a beaded picot edge or a beaded loop (see illustration). When you wish to place beads along the cast-on edge, slide them up to the needle before casting on that stitch. The working yarn with beads on it may be held to the front **or** back of the cast-on needle; however, the beads will appear more prominent on the side of the finished work from which they are cast on. This placement is purely a matter of the individual knitter's preference.

BEADED LONG-TAIL CAST-ON

1 String beads onto yarn. Make a slipknot, leaving a long tail (1 to 1½" for each stitch to be cast on, and keeping strung beads between needle and ball of yarn.

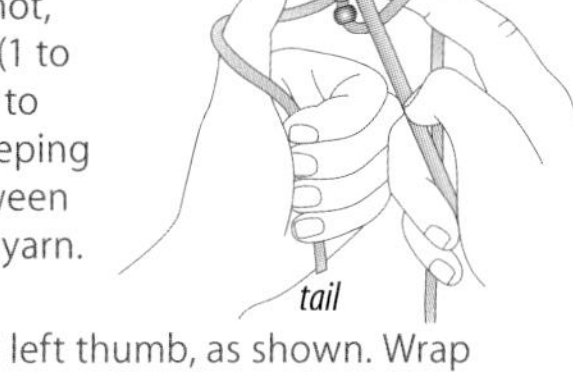

2 Wrap tail around left thumb, as shown. Wrap yarn over right index finger, slide one bead up very close to needle and secure strands.

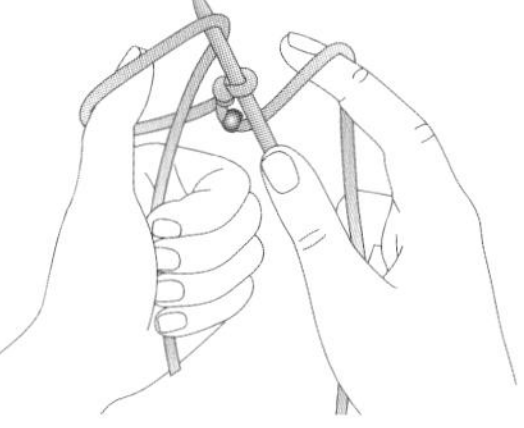

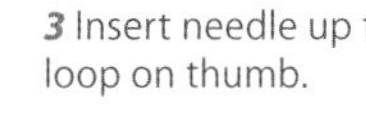

3 Insert needle up through loop on thumb.

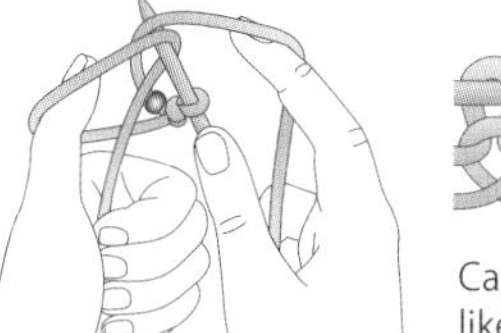

4 Wrap yarn over needle knitwise. Bring yarn through thumb loop to form a stitch. Use thumb to adjust tension on the new stitch. Make sure bead stays tight up against the needle. Repeat Steps 2–4 for each additional stitch.

Cast-on will look like this from WS.

WITH MULTIPLE BEADS

Work as for Beaded Long-tail Cast-on EXCEPT:

Slide required number of beads up very close to needle. Space as desired.

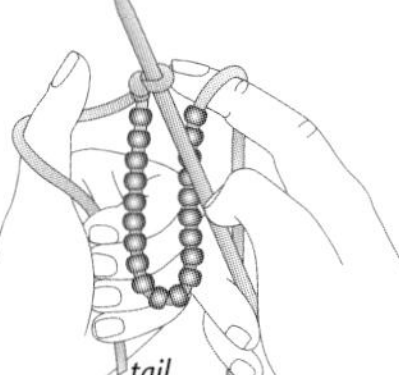

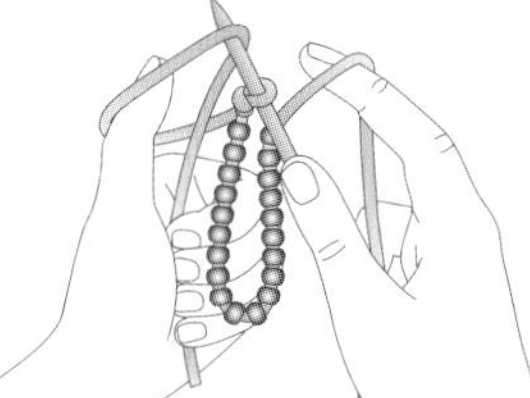

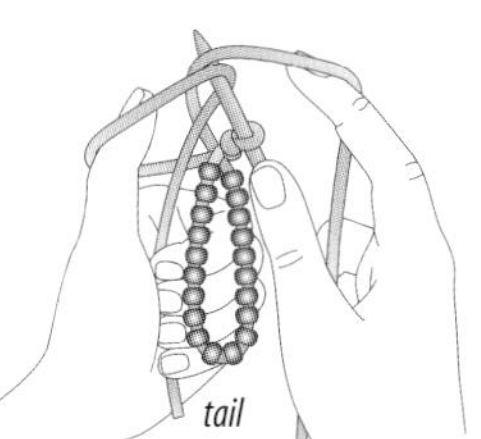

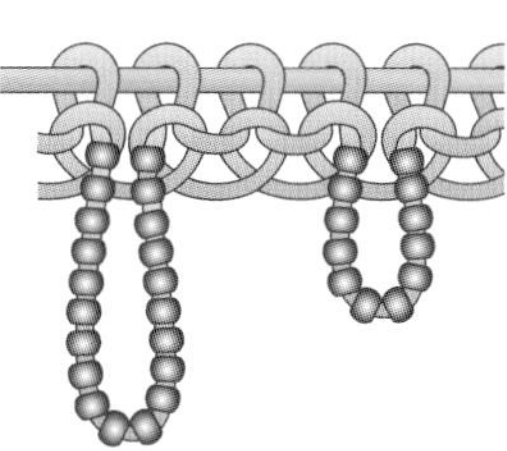

Beaded bind-off

A beaded bind-off requires that beads are pre-strung, and that each bead is knit **through** a stitch. Beads may be knit into every stitch or in whatever numbered pattern is desired. Once a bead is knit through a stitch and the stitch is on the right needle, the bead should be **on** that stitch and able to be moved easily to either the front or the back of the work. Before binding off a stitch with a bead on it, the bead may be pushed to the **front** or the **back** of the work, depending on the desired look. Pushing the bead to the back causes the bead to appear to stand up along the bound-off edge. Pushing the bead to the front causes the bead to appear to sit along the edge rather than on top of the edge. When binding off stitches, it is important to remember to pass the stitch you are binding off over both the stitch ahead of it and over any bead on that stitch.

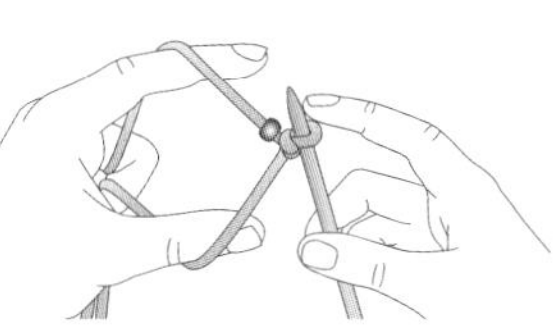

If you are more comfortable working long-tail cast-on with both yarns in one hand (shown in detail on page 160), use that method to cast on with beads..

BEADED BIND-OFF, UPPER

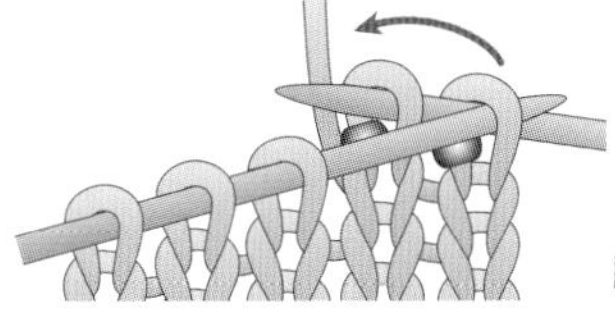

1 Knit 2 stitches each with a bead on the left leg. *2* With left needle, pass first stitch on right needle over second stitch…

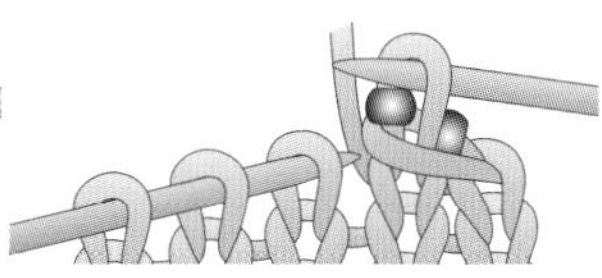

…and off needle (see above).
3 Knit one more stitch with a bead to left leg.
4 Pass first stitch over second. Repeat Steps 3–4.

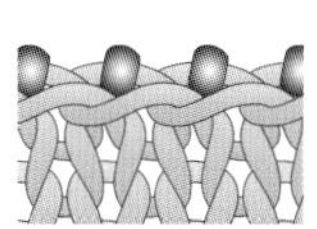

Beads will lie on upper edge of bind-off.

BEADED BIND-OFF, LOWER

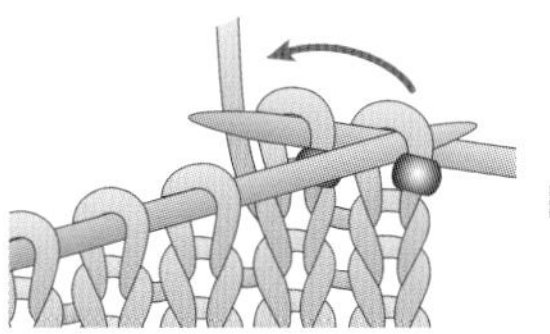

1 Knit 2 stitches, each with a bead on the right leg.
2 With left needle above bead, pass first stitch over second stitch and bead…

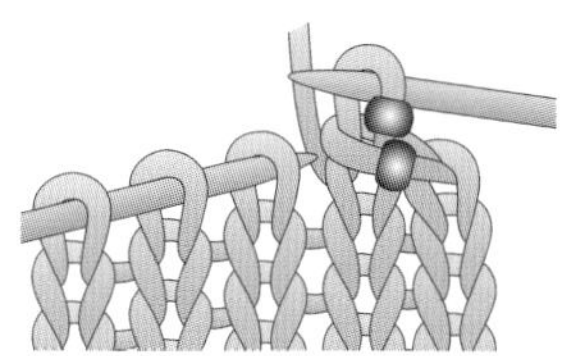

…and off needle (see above).
3 Knit one more stitch with a bead on the right leg.
4 With left needle above bead, pass first stitch over second. Repeat Steps 3–4.

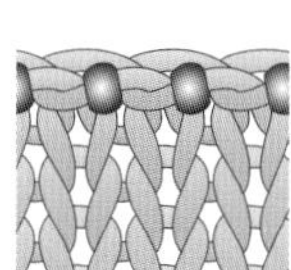

Beads will lie on lower edge of bind-off.

Waiting for inspiration

Waiting for inspiration. Now there's a thankless task if ever there was one. Kind of like sitting in an open field, waiting for lightening to strike you. Not such great odds.

So what is this elusive thing called inspiration? Where does it come from? How do you find it? Do you really need it in order to create things you can love and be proud of? Here is what I believe. Inspiration is EVERYWHERE, and often where least expected, but it comes differently to different people. For some, it's driven by a grand purpose, such as educating others about a compelling political or social objective. For others, the materials with which they choose to work or the subject matter on which they choose to focus propels their creative choices. And still others simply love and remain fascinated by the process of the work they do, joyfully creating whatever results from that process. But I think there is something that all creative people have in common. Rather than passively waiting for creative lightning to strike, they make active choices. They make them in a variety of ways and for a variety of reasons, such as economic necessity, or personal beliefs or experiences. But at some point they decide on what to focus their energy and then continue to make choices that dictate how they realize their creative vision. They take action. They don't wait.

But which comes first, inspiration or creativity? Does inspiration drive creativity, or does being engaged in a creative process open the mind to inspiration? I don't think there is one right answer to this question. The right answer is the one that works for you.

The work that led to this book has taught me that my inspiration grows from actively observing the world and the work around me and being committed to and engaged in a process I love. For me, ideas come most often from work rather than the work coming purely from ideas. I choose the next evolution based on what has come before, try it and see what happens. This book invites you to work in the same way. Try some of the things offered here, decide what pleases you, make choices, and then perhaps make different choices. Just get to work. What are you waiting for?

PS. What a wonderful, quirky affirmation it was when I realized that all the letters needed to spell the word active are contained in the word creative. Duh!

***Silver ribs** bracelet (2007)*
Glass beads, fiber, sterling silver clasp
Beaded silver welts against a black background provide eye-popping dimension to this chunky bracelet.
Technique link: Beaded welt.

I-cord

TECH TRIALS

While I-cord was the simple, early introduction to knitting for many (remember those red wooden mushrooms with the 4 nails on top?), it is a hugely versatile technique, adaptable for use in all kinds of knitting projects. After a review of the basic technique, take time to try your hand at the Tech Trials to learn what happens when you make one or more small changes to the basic I-cord technique.

Basic I-cord

Knit all stitches

To work basic knit I-cord, cast a small number of stitches (usually from 4 to 6) onto a double-pointed needle (dpn). Knit across. Then, instead of turning the work, slide the stitches back to the right end of the needle, bring the working yarn around behind the needle, and work the next row, which is really a round. Repeat this sequence for each round, never turning the work, for the desired length. The resulting fabric will be a hollow tube, inside of which you could actually insert a knitting needle, pencil, etc.

5 stitches

4 stitches

Purl all stitches

Working I-cord in all purl stitches instead of knit stitches causes the cord to spiral, a terrific effect otherwise almost impossible to produce naturally.

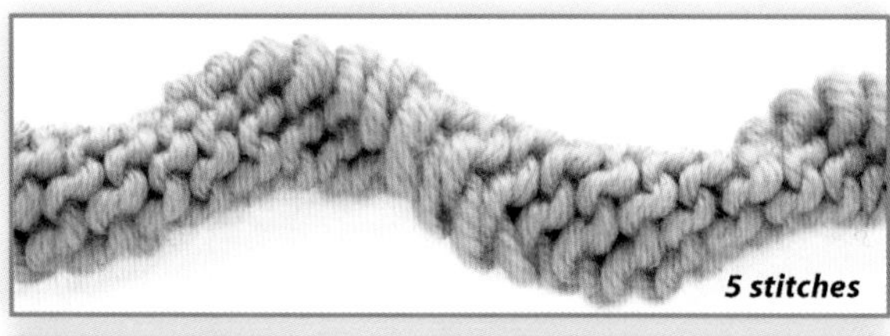

5 stitches

4 stitches

Mixed-stitch I-cord

The 4 samples below are only some of the variations possible when you mix the knits and purls while working your I-cord. With these variations, there will be a difference between the front and the back of the cord, with both still being usable. The k1-p3-k1 cord is flat, more strap-like.

Knit 5 rounds, purl 1 round

Knit 1 round, purl 1 round

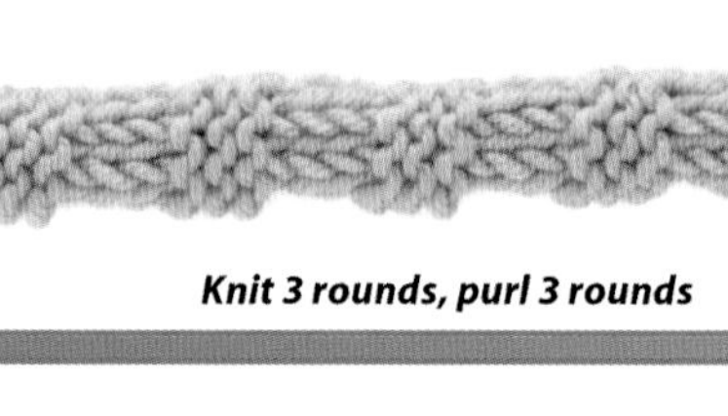

Knit 3 rounds, purl 3 rounds

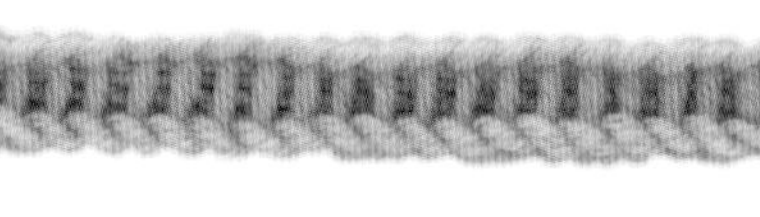

Each round: K1, p3, k1

Self-striping and self-patterning sock yarns

When worked as I-cord, these yarns produce some terrific effects that can be exploited for embellishment or used as integral parts of garment or accessory design.

Color-controlled I-cord

Allowing the color changes of a variegated yarn to determine when you change your stitches alters the look of the I-cord in interesting and often unanticipated ways.

Knit all dark stitches, purl all light stitches

Knit all light stitches, purl all dark stitches

Variegated yarn

Working I-cord with variegated yarns often highlights the color changes *and* the stitch patterns.

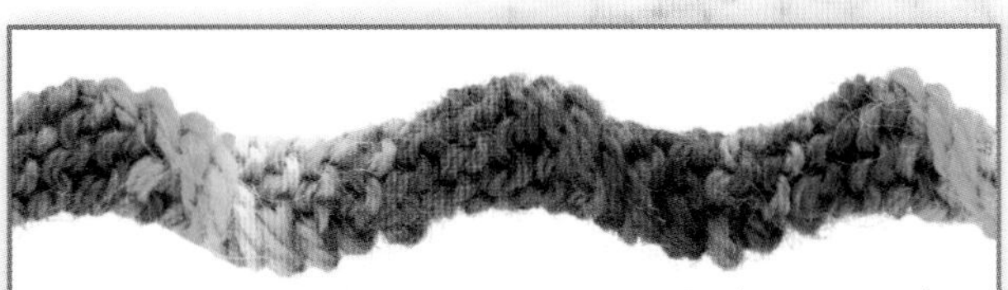

Purl every round

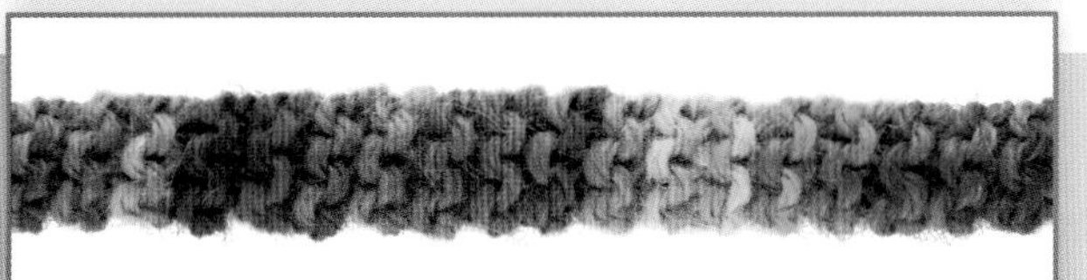

Knit 1 round, purl 1 round

Beaded I-cord

TECH TRIALS

NOTES

See page 160 for knitting abbreviations and techniques, and page 2 for beading basics.

Tighten the second stitch as you work each beaded round.

WHAT YOU NEED

Any size 6° beads

Smooth sock- to DK-weight wool or wool-blend yarn in a solid, light color

2 double-pointed needles (dpn) in a size you would normally use for the yarn (usually 3.25–3.72mm/US3–5)

Beading needle

Stringing beads before working your I-cord expands the design possibilities exponentially! Here are just a few:

With beading needle, string 60 beads. Using a dpn, cast on 4 stitches.

Pattern A

Round 1 Knit.

Round 2 P1, **[SB, p1]** 3 times.

Round 3 Knit.

Round 4 Purl.

Work Rounds 1–4 a total of 10 times.

Pattern B

Work Rounds 1–2 a total of 10 times.

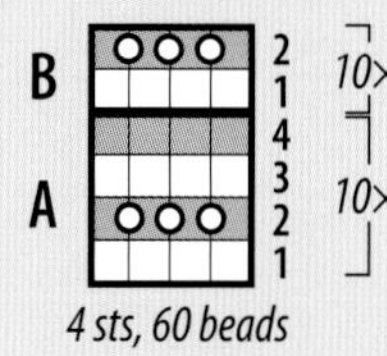

Knit 1 round, purl 1 round
2 beading patterns: A (bottom), B (top)

Knit 5 rounds, purl 1 round

With a beading needle, string 50 beads. Using a dpn, cast on 5 stitches.

Rounds 1–5 Knit.

Round 6 **[P1, SB]** 5 times.

Work Rounds 1–6 a total of 10 times.

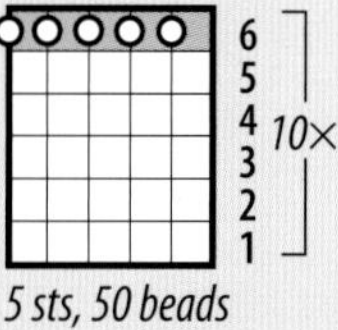

Stitch key

- *Knit on RS*
- *Purl on RS*
- *SB, p1*
- *SB, k1*
- *KBL with standard wrap. On next round, knit stitch tbl with bead to RS of work.*
- *KBR with reverse wrap. On next round, knit stitch through front loop, stitch twists because of reverse wrap.*

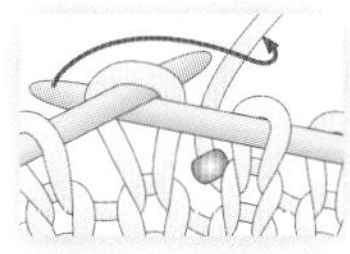

SB Slide bead close to last stitch worked.

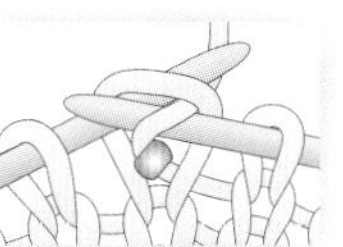

KBL in the round
Knit bead through stitch with standard wrap. On next round, knit stitch through back loop.

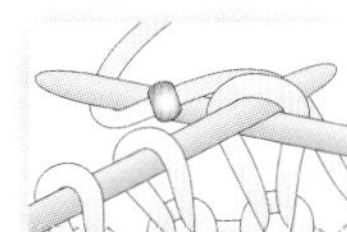

KBR in the round
Knit bead through stitch with reverse wrap. On next round, knit stitch in front loop — stitch twists because of reverse wrap.

Multi-stitch rounds, front

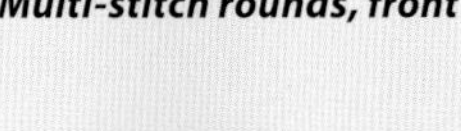

With a beading needle, string 40 beads. Using a dpn, cast on 5 stitches.
Round 1 K1, p1, **[SB, p1]** 2 times, k1.
Round 2 K1, p3, k1.
Work Rounds 1–2 a total of 20 times.

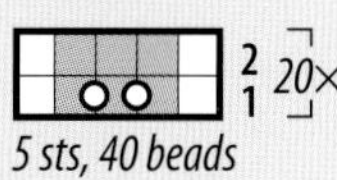
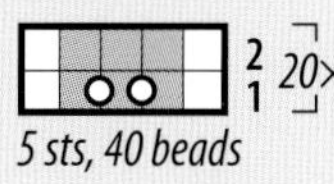

5 sts, 40 beads

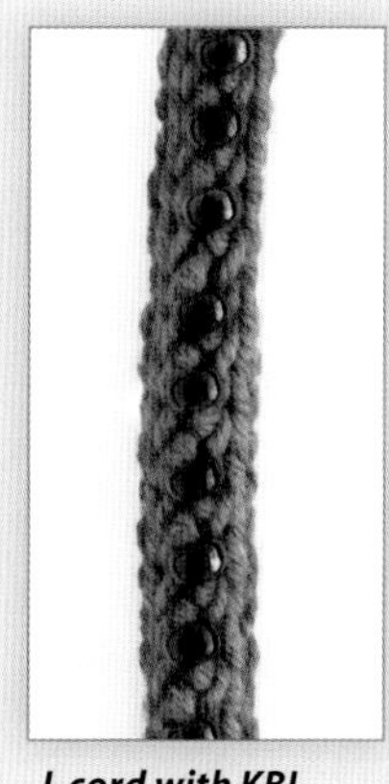

I-cord with KBL, Pattern A

With beading needle, string 16 beads: 4 each of 2 colors, alternating colors; then 8 same-color beads.
Using a dpn, cast on 5 stitches.

Pattern A
Round 1 Knit.
Round 2 K2, KBL, k2.
Round 3 K2, k1tbl with bead to the front of the stitch, k2.
Work Rounds 2–3 a total of 8 times.

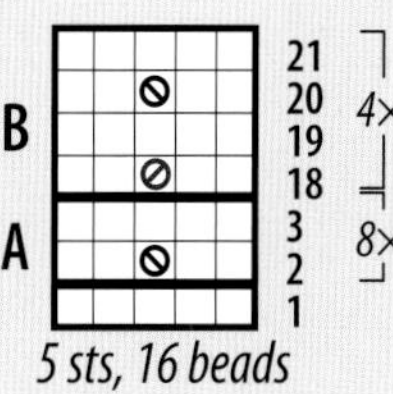

5 sts, 16 beads

Multi-stitch rounds, back

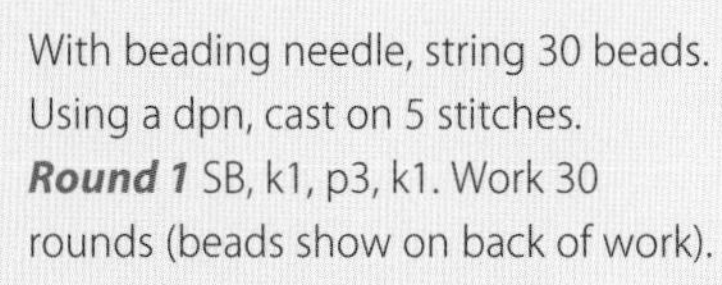

With beading needle, string 30 beads. Using a dpn, cast on 5 stitches.
Round 1 SB, k1, p3, k1. Work 30 rounds (beads show on back of work).

5 sts, 30 beads

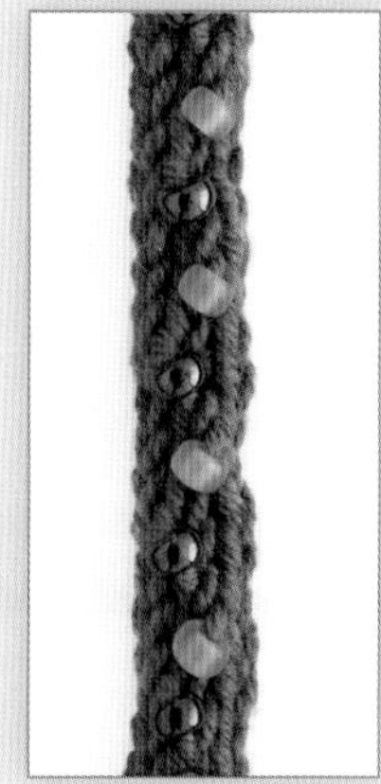

I-cord with KBL and KBR, Pattern B

Pattern B
Round 18 K2, KBR, k2.
Round 19 K2, k1 with bead to front of stitch and right needle above bead, k2.
Round 20 K2, KBL, k2.
Round 21 K2, k1tbl with bead to front of stitch, k2.
Work Rounds 18–21 a total of 4 times.

KISS: Keep it simple spiral

BETSY  BEADS

KISS: Keep it simple spiral

Calling this first project simple and straightforward makes me smile, because the first thing you notice about this colorful bead-knit necklace is that, while it is simple to knit, it is anything but straight. I've offered it as the first pattern in the book because it illustrates one of my favorite "Eureka!" knitting moments ever, and is a great example of what this newfound creative process has taught me.

I struggled for years to find a way to make some kind of knit cord that would hold a spiral on its own — all to no avail — so I settled for twisting straight cording before joining the ends with a clasp. It looked like a spiral, but of course it untwisted the moment you undid the clasp. Then one day, while playing around with I-cord, I decided to see what would happen if I purled instead of knit the stitches. After about 20 rounds, the cord began to twist and spiral — on its own! The final purl stitch in every round was slightly elongated and created a sort of spine that traveled around the cord, providing the perfect place to knit a bead that could highlight the spiral even more. As a child of the 60s, I have to say that this was such a Zen moment — recognizing that what you are looking for can often be found only when you stop looking.

PRISM YARNS Tencel Tape
50 yds in Garden

MIYUKI Size 6° glass seed beads
150 in 149F Matte Transparent Capri Blue

Prepare

With beading needle, string 150 beads (1 bead per round).

Knit

Leaving an 8" tail, cast on 5.

Begin I-cord: All rounds SB, p5.

Work 150 rounds (approximately 17"). Do not bind off.

Finish

Cut yarn, leaving an 8" tail. With tapestry needle, thread tail through all 5 stitches, remove knitting needle, gather, knot tightly, and weave tail inside cord. Gather other end, threading tail through cast-on stitches. With beading needle and thread or filament, sew clasp to ends of I-cord.

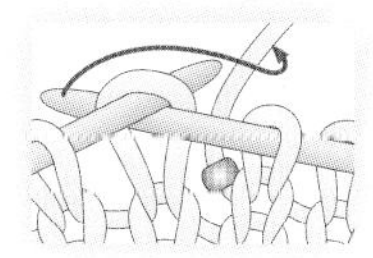

SB Slide bead close to last stitch worked.

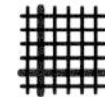

gauge

9 rounds to 1"
finished length 17", including clasp

yarn

light weight
50 yds tencel tape

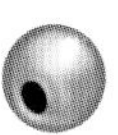

beads

160 size 6º Japanese glass seed beads

needles

2 4mm/US6

and…

beading needle
tapestry needle
small amount of nylon thread or beading filament
11×11mm silver-plated magnetic clasp

NOTES: easy

See page 160 for knitting abbreviations and techniques, and page 2 for beading basics.

Tight tension is important when working this design — especially on the second stitch of each round — to encourage the natural spiral of the I-cord.

WHAT IF…

For a bracelet, simply work a shorter version of the necklace, or a very long version that can be wrapped around your wrist several times before fastening the clasp.

You can use almost any weight of smooth yarn as long as the beads you use can be strung onto the yarn. Consider using a solid-colored yarn and a random assortment of different colors of beads, or a chunky yarn with large, brightly-colored plastic or glass pony beads.

Fun!

Star light, star bright

Star light, star bright

A gorgeous metallic fiber makes this necklace perfect for a special occasion. And because hundreds of beads are needed to complete the design, the choice of a smaller-sized bead keeps the necklace incredibly light in weight and easy to wear. Believe it or not, the beaded loops that give this I-cord necklace so much texture were another accidental discovery. When working on a piece of bead-knit I-cord, I accidentally slid too many beads up the yarn between 2 purl stitches and they made this wonderful little picot-like loop. Well, that's kind of cool! How would it look with the entire cord covered in them? And Star Light, Star Bright was born.

TRENDSETTER Toreador
75 yds in 101 Silver

OR

TAHKI SELECT Star
75 yds in 003

TOHO Size 8º glass seed beads
60 in 222 Bronze (A)
168 in 367 Pink/Dark Gray (B)

MIYUKI Size 8º glass seed beads
144 in 701 Silver-lined Crystal (C)
192 in 401F Matte Black (D)

Prepare

With beading needle, string beads as follows (12 beads per round):

96 D (8 rounds)
84 B (7 rounds)
72 C (6 rounds)
60 A (5 rounds)
72 C (6 rounds)
84 B (7 rounds)
96 D (8 rounds)

SB Slide *1* bead close to last stitch worked.
S4B Slide *4* beads.

Knit

Leaving an 8" tail, cast on 6.

Begin I-cord: Rounds 1–3 Knit.

Round 4 P1, S4B, p2, S4B, p2, S4B, p1—12 beads.

Repeat Rounds 1–4 until all beads have been used. Knit 3 rounds without beads. Bind off, leaving an 8" tail.

Finish

With tapestry needle, thread bind-off tail through bound-off stitches, gather, sew to clasp, and weave tail inside cord. Repeat at other end, threading cast-on tail through cast-on stitches.

gauge
11 rounds = 1"
finished length 17", including clasp

yarn
fine weight
75 yds metallic yarn

beads
600 size 8° Japanese glass seed beads, shown in 4 colors

needles
2 2.75mm/US2

and...
beading needle
tapestry needle
toggle clasp

NOTES: intermediate

See page 160 for knitting abbreviations and techniques, and page 2 for beading basics.

When stringing beads, make sure to check the number and color of beads several times before changing to the next color.

Tighten the second stitch as you work each beaded round.

WHAT IF...

For a more casual look, choose a non-metallic yarn and beads with less shine—maybe solid-colored opaque beads or some with a matte finish.

Think about spacing the beaded rows farther apart to allow a wonderful yarn choice to show through.

Over the rainbow

I often describe myself as being pathologically symmetrical. The comfort I find in the balance of symmetry is classically left-brained. But every now and then I wish I could find a way to break out of my comfort zone and be less organized, less controlling in my design choices. When I discovered New York, the wonderful variegated rayon ribbon yarn from Interlacements, I decided to give up control and let the colors of the yarn guide the placement of the beads. The different dye patterns of each colorway result in different beading patterns for each strand of the necklace, and yet when strung together they form an unexpectedly balanced whole.

INTERLACEMENTS New York
30 yds each in 132 Yellow/Brown (A), 116 Poppy Fields (B), 302 Taiga (C), AND 305 Bachelor Buttons (D)

I-CORD
Leaving an 8" tail, cast on 4.
Plain rounds K4.
Bead rounds **[K1, SB]** 4 times — 4 beads
Work I-cord to length indicated, placing beads as desired. Do not bind off. Place stitches on hold.

gauge
10 rows = 1"
finished length 23", including clasp

yarn
light weight
30 yds each in 4 colors of tubular chainette ribbon

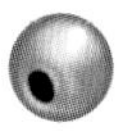
beads
420 size 6° Japanese glass seed beads

needles
2 2.75mm/US2

and...
beading needle
tapestry needle
4-strand bar clasp

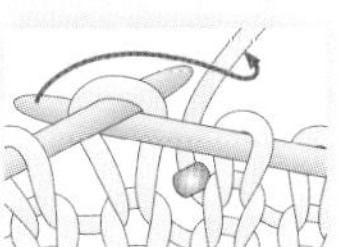
SB Slide bead close to last stitch worked.

Prepare
With beading needle, string each color of yarn with at least 100 beads.

Knit.
Cord 1 With A, work 15" I-cord.
Cord 2 With B, work 18" I-cord.
Cord 3 With C, work 20½" I-cord.
Cord 4 With D, work 22½" I-cord.

Finish
Adjust lengths of cords if desired by removing or adding rounds. Cut yarns. Working with short cord, with tapestry needle, thread tail through stitches on hold, gather, sew to 1 hole of the clasp, and weave tail inside cord. Repeat at other end of cord, threading cast-on tail through cast-on stitches. Repeat for remaining cords.

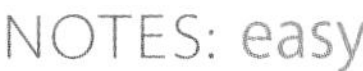

NOTES: easy
See page 160 for knitting abbreviations and techniques, and page 2 for beading basics.

Bead placement for this project is dictated by the color changes in the yarn. Choose one color in each variegated yarn and knit the beads into the I-cord whenever that color is being worked.

WHAT IF...
Try using just one color of yarn, but vary the color of beads on each strand.

Using multiple strands of I-cord for a necklace or bracelet is lots of fun. Think about braiding or twisting the cords together for a very different look.

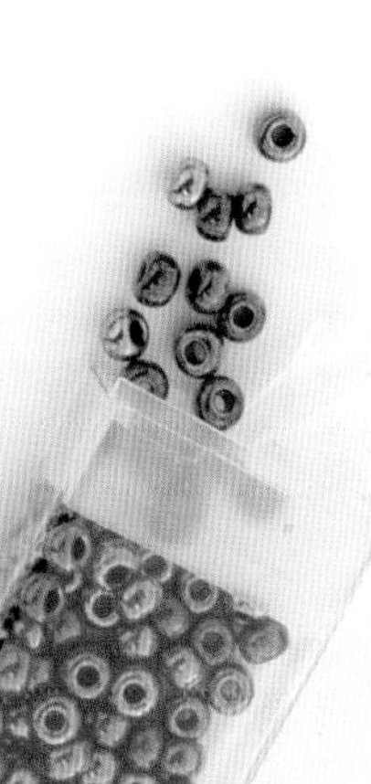
MIYUKI Size 6° glass seed beads
400 in 462 Metallic Gold Iris

Twofers

ELLEN'S HALF PINT FARM 100% Merino Sock
30 yds each in Spring Pansy (A) AND Blues (B)

Twofers

This bracelet design is the result of asking myself "What if…?" about the first bracelet I ever knit. Looking for a way to turn I-cord into jewelry, I decided to simply sew the cords together, with each overcast stitch holding a single bead. No actual bead knitting was involved! Using I-cords worked in 3 different colorways, I made a 3-sided bracelet that could be rotated to show 2 colors at a time—a convertible bracelet of sorts. This updated design uses 4 lengths of I-cord sewn together with both plain and beaded seams. Again, no actual bead knitting, but the bracelet is now completely reversible! The 3-strand slide clasp helps make this possible.

WHAT IF…

I used a wonderful bead mix and just 2 yarns for this version of the bracelet—one solid and one variegated—but with 4 cords to knit and 4 seams to stitch, the possibilities for yarn and bead combinations are plentiful.

The beaded focal piece on the original 2004 bracelet (photo to the left) used a bead-weaving technique called peyote stitch to hide the place where I stitched the ends of the cords into a circle, but joining the ends with a clasp works just as well.

Knit

I-cord *MAKE 4: 2 IN A AND 2 IN B*

Leaving an 8" tail, cast on 6. Work 6-stitch I-cord for 60 rows, or desired length. Do not bind off. Cut yarn, leaving a 20" tail. Place stitches on hold.

MIYUKI Size 8º glass seed beads
360 in 23 Circus Mix

Finish

1 Join 2 A I-cords: With tapestry needle and B, and using a somewhat loose overcast stitch, begin at cast-on ends and sew under 1 full edge stitch of each cord, leaving approximately ¼" of overcast stitch showing.

2 Join 2 B I-cords with A.

3 Lay both sets of joined I-cords flat, side by side, with cast-on ends aligned. With beading needle and B, and using an overcast stitch, begin at cast-on ends and join cords as above, threading 3 beads onto the yarn before each stitch, and leaving 2 full stitches showing on the front and back of each I-cord. When you reach the end, adjust the lengths of the cord if necessary by removing or adding rounds.
Bind off across each pair of cords.

4 Fold along beaded seam and join opposite side in same manner.

5 With tapestry needle and cast-on and bind-off tails, sew on clasp. Weave tails inside cord and trim.

gauge

8½ rounds = 1"
finished length 7½", including clasp

yarn

fine weight
100 yds each in variegated and solid sock yarn

beads

380 size 8º Japanese glass seed beads

needles

3.25mm/US3

and...

beading needle
tapestry needle
small stitch holders
3-strand slide clasp

NOTES: easy

See page 160 for knitting abbreviations and techniques, and page 2 for beading basics.

Lengths of I-cord are joined together with 4 overcast seams: 2 with yarn and beads and 2 with yarn only.

Using a slide clasp allows the bracelet to be truly reversible.

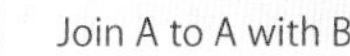

1 Join A to A with B.

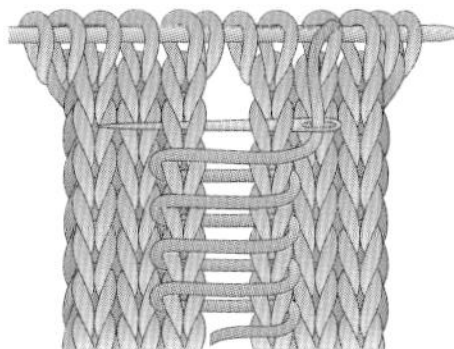

2 Join B to B with A.

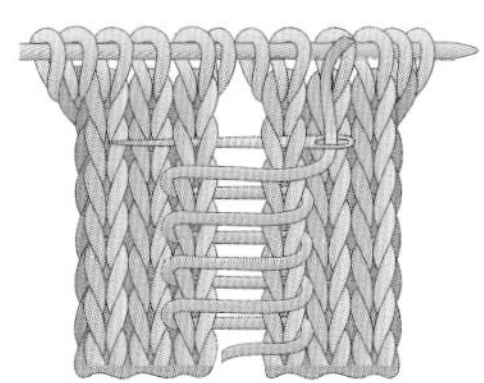

3 With wrong sides together, join A to B with beaded overcast seam.

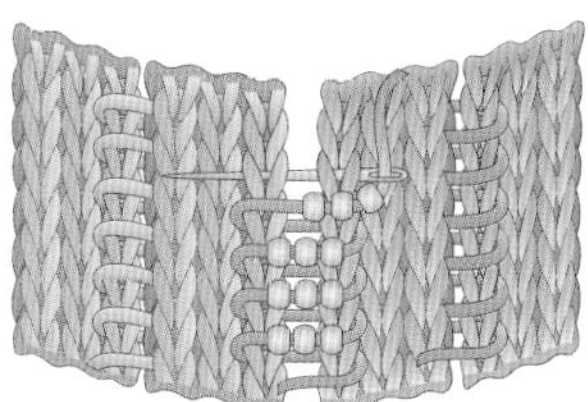

4 Repeat beaded overcast seam on opposite side.

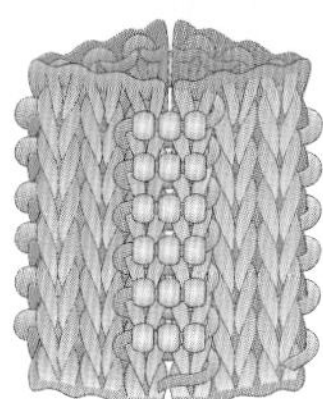

Ladder 72

Few people will look at this bracelet and think — Oh! It's I-cord! — but it is. I discovered the technique for the next 2 designs while experimenting with using a larger number of I-cord stitches and different stitch combinations. The cords became wider and flatter with the additional stitches, and the distance the yarn had to travel from the end of one round to the beginning of the next created a ladder of yarn that just screamed out to be beaded. Fill each rung of the ladder with an extra long bugle bead and you get the Ladder 72 bracelet. Fill the rungs with multiple beads of different colors, stitch the now flat cords together, and the result is the dramatic Chiaroscuro belt that follows.

ANCHOR 8 Perle Cotton
40 yds in 310 Topaz V. Dk

30mm Czech glass straight bugle beads
72 in Brown Satin

TOHO Size 8º glass seed beads
144 in 557 Galvanized Gold

Prepare

With beading needle, string 72 bugle beads.

Knit

With double-pointed needles (dpn), using a knit cast-on (see Notes), and leaving a 1½-yd tail, cast on 16.
Knit 1 row. Purl 1 row; do not turn work.
Begin I-cord: All rounds SB, k1, p14, k1.
Work until 1 bead remains (approximately 6¾"). Bind off in pattern, placing bead at beginning of row, leaving a 1½-yd tail.

Finish

Beaded edge, side 1

With fabric side of cuff facing, and beading needle, string 72 seed beads onto bind-off tail. Use stop bead to hold beads on tail.With smaller needle and tail, pick up and knit (PUK) along side of cuff as follows: SB, PUK in first edge stitch, **[SB, PUK in next edge stitch, bind off]** to end. Secure; do not cut tail.

Beaded edge, side 2

With beading needle, string 72 seed beads onto cast-on tail; PUK and bind off stitches along other side of cuff as for Side 1.

With tapestry needle and remaining tails, stitch 2 magnetic clasps to both knitted fabric AND first bugle bead. Weave in tails.

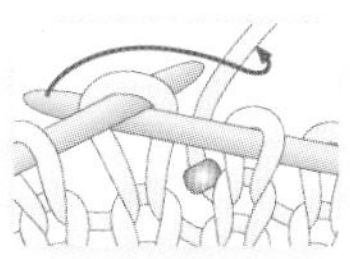

SB Slide bead close to last stitch worked.

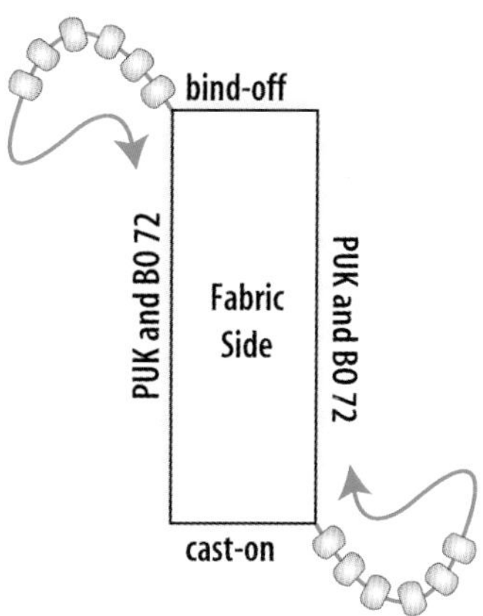

gauge

12 stitches and 10½ rounds to 1"
finished length 7½", including clasp

yarn

super fine weight
40 yds size 8 pearl cotton

beads

80 30mm Czech glass straight bugle beads
155 size 8° Japanese glass seed beads

needles

2 2.25mm/US1

1.75mm/US00

and …

beading needle
tapestry needle
2 Vermeil, gold-plated or gold-tone magnetic clasps

WHAT IF…

Magnetic clasps work well as a closure for this bracelet, but here are a couple of wonderful alternatives.

Stitch 2 of your favorite buttons to one end of the bracelet and beaded loops to the other.

String beads onto a few short lengths of stretchy elastic and sew the lengths to both ends of the bracelet. This will provide enough flexibility to slide the bracelet on like a bangle.

NOTES: intermediate

See page 160 for knitting abbreviations and techniques, and page 2 for beading basics.

This bracelet is worked as I-cord, sliding one 30mm bugle bead into place before the start of each new row. Tight tension is important to hold the bugle bead in place.

Using a knit cast-on is VERY important, as the long tail needs to be left at the beginning of the cast-on row for use in working one of the beaded edges later.

Chiaroscuro

Chiaroscuro

Shortly after college, I moved to New York City to pursue a career as an actress. It's clear how well that went.... But shopping in the city was always so much fun, even with no money. A girl can dream can't she? I'll never forget wandering into a store in Greenwich Village called Chiaroscuro, wondering at the time what the word meant. One step inside the store and it was obvious—every single thing in the store was black and white! I've never forgotten the word—in Italian, literally, light-dark—or the powerful impression the colors made.

JUDI & CO Groovy II
100 yds in Black
50 yds in White

MATTRESS STITCH

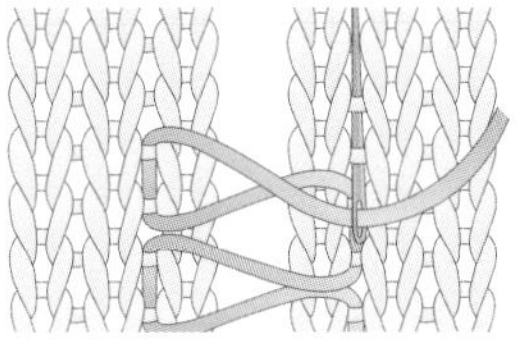

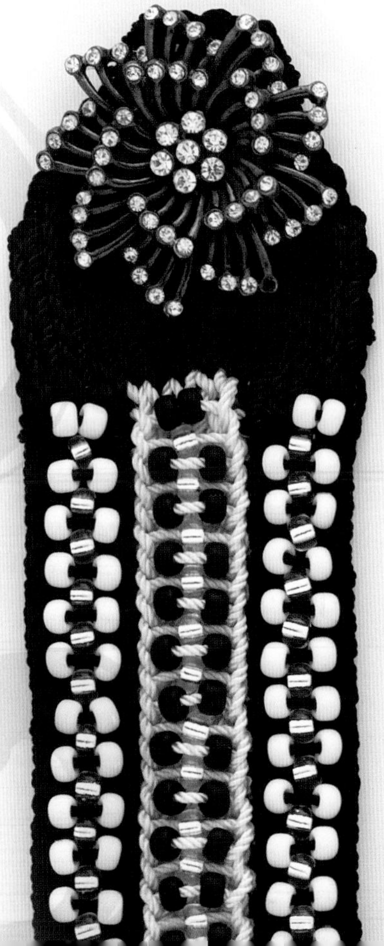

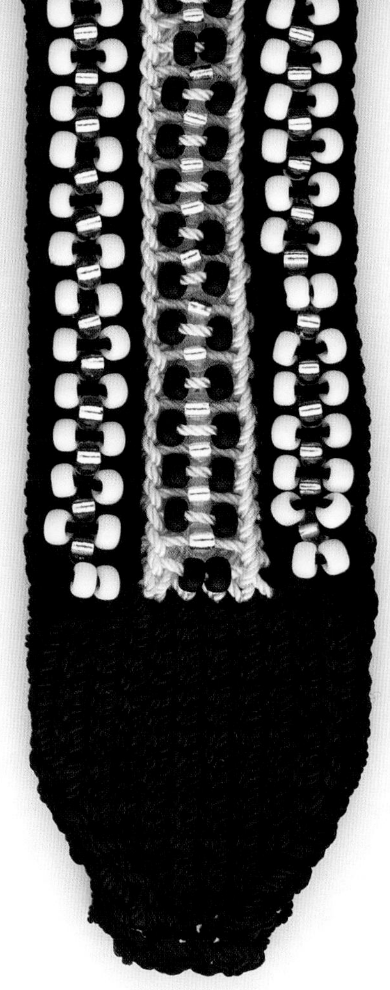

Prepare

Black cord

With beading needle, string **[2C, 1A]** 100 times, string 2C.

White cord

With beading needle, string **[2B, 1A]** 100 times, string 2B.

Knit

MAKE 2 BLACK CORDS AND 1 WHITE CORD

With waste yarn, crochet hook, double-pointed needles (dpn), and using a temporary crochet cast-on, cast on 6.

Row 1 (RS) With yarn, knit.

Row 2 K1, p3, k2tog—5 stitches. Turn work.

Begin I-cord: Round 3 S2B, k1, p3, k1.

Round 4 SB, k1, p3, k1.

Repeat Rounds 3 and 4 to 28" or desired length. Do not bind off. Cut yarn, leaving an 8" tail. Place stitches on hold.

Finish

Remove waste yarn from cast-ons, placing 15 stitches on 1 dpn. With WS facing, tapestry needle and nylon thread, and using mattress stitch, join I-cords.

Tab closures

Join yarn and work over 15 stitches at cast-on end as follows:

Rows 1, 3, 5, 7 (RS) Knit.

All WS rows Purl.

Row 9 K1, SSK, k9, k2tog, k1.

Row 11 K1, SSK, k7, k2tog, k1.

Row 13 K1, SSK, k5, k2tog, k1.

Row 15 K1, SSK, k3, k2tog, k1.

Bind off purlwise.

Repeat at other end of cords, transferring stitches from holders to needle. Weave in tails.

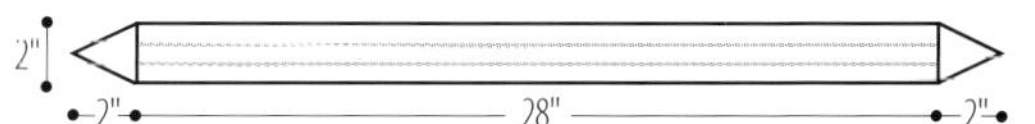

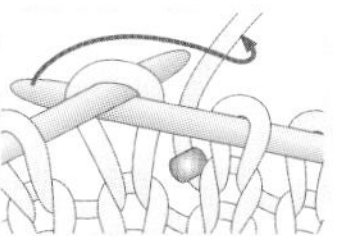

SB Slide ***1*** bead close to last stitch worked.
S2B Slide ***2*** beads.

gauge

over I-cord, 7 repeats of beading pattern = 2"
finished length 30" closed

yarn

medium weight
100 yds black, **50 yds** white

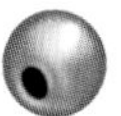

beads

960 size 5º Japanese glass seed beads, shown in 3 colors

needles

2 3.75mm/US5

and...

tapestry needle
beading needle
waste yarn
crochet hook
heavy-duty nylon thread in black

NOTES: easy

See page 160 for knitting abbreviations and techniques, and page 2 for beading basics.

This belt is constructed from 3 separate beaded I-cords which are then stitched together.

The length can be adjusted by working longer or shorter cords. For every 2" added, you will need an additional 21A, 14B, and 28C (7 more repeats of the bead-stringing pattern per I-cord).

MIYUKI Size 5º glass seed beads
300 in 131S Silver-lined Crystal (A)
202 in 401F Matte Black (B)
404 in 402FR Matte White AB (C)

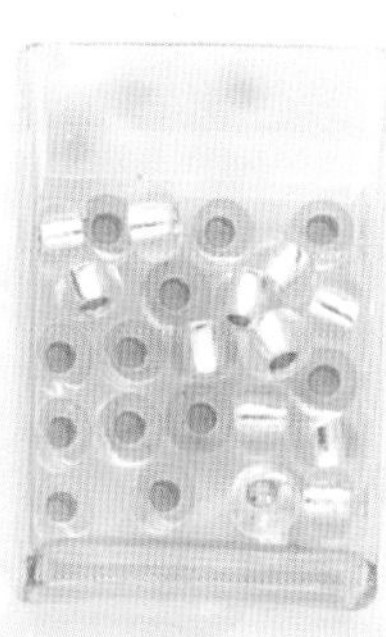

WHAT IF...

I used a wonderful old piece of costume jewelry to pin the Chiaroscuro belt closed, but you could also sew heavy-duty snaps onto the belt tabs, or close the belt with a shawl pin.

"What if. . ." creativity

So if it's true that inspiration rarely comes via the lightening strike of the next great idea, where DO the ideas come from? I'm sure it works slightly differently for each individual, but if we can't just sit around waiting for ideas, what CAN we do to bring them on, to kick-start a project or two? Here are a few things that have worked for me.

Start to build a personal profile of things to which you have a strong visual reaction. How many times a day does something catch your eye? (As an aside, what a great idiom—to "catch your eye.") Think about it for a moment. You know what I mean. You see something—an ad in a magazine, a great piece of fashion, or even just an everyday object—and you have a reaction to it. Usually we are in such a hurry that we limit our response to one of two extremes: either "I like it" or "I don't like it." But what if you were to take just an extra minute or two to try and figure out WHAT it is you like or don't like? Is it the color, the shape, the texture? Maybe it's where and how it's displayed or how it feels. The next step is to try and recognize any patterns in those likes and dislikes. You may be surprised to learn how narrow—or how broad—your range is. Why is this an important exercise? Because you need to start somewhere, and if you have some idea of the colors, shapes, and textures that appeal to you on a consistent basis, why not start there?

Understand that there is nothing new under the sun. This may be a cliché, but that doesn't mean it's without value. Other people's work is a great place to start. I've had so many students tell me they are excellent knitters but can't imagine ever creating their "own" design. They then proceed to show me a wonderful project that is "based on" the design of another knitter. Yes, they confess, they have tweaked a few things—the color, stitch pattern, length, collar, or sleeve styling—but still don't think of this creation as their own. My response is invariably, "If it's not yours, whose is it?" Many new ideas are actually variations on existing ideas. There is much to learn and to borrow from what has come before. If you let yourself believe this, the creative process will lose much of its mystery.

"What if. . .?" For me, this question is the evolutionary (revolutionary?) DNA of every new design. Just two little words, have transformed the challenge of design creation from an intimidating abstraction into a manageable, concrete process. No need to attempt big scary leaps when small baby steps will do the trick. Here's how it works. Once you recognize the visual and physical elements that please or interest you, and lose your inhibitions about using others' work as a starting point, you are free to begin tweaking what has come before with the techniques, colors or materials that get your own creative juices flowing. I think of "What if...?" as the secret ingredient to successful tweaking. For example: "What if, instead of using merino yarn, I use that shiny rayon ribbon I have?" Or: "What if, instead of stockinette, I use that stitch pattern I liked in my friend's sweater?" Or one of my favorites: "What if I add beads?" You can test each tweak with a small swatch to see if the choices come together as you had imagined. Sometimes they do, and it's thrilling! And sometimes... Well, let's just recognize that learning what you don't like can be as important as recognizing what you do. In either case, no major investment is required. And how wonderful, when your new combination of ingredients yields something totally unexpected, and you discover you like it even better than what you were hoping to find. And best of all, it's all yours!

Give it a try. It's really fun! And it's okay to start small and move at your own speed. Happily, there's an endless number of What ifs? to ask, and only yourself to please. So take your time. There is always more to learn along the way.

River Rocks *bracelet (2009)*
Glass beads, fiber, moss agate/sterling silver clasp
The design for this bracelet had one clear objective: Finding a way to showcase this very special closure.
Technique link: Intermittent beaded tube

Tubes

TECH TRIALS

NOTES
See page 160 for knitting abbreviations and techniques, and page 2 for beading basics.

I love tubes! There are so many wonderful ways to make and use them. (For the sake of full disclosure, I also love tubes because the space inside them is perfect for burying tails and fibers from attaching closures or embellishing the outside of the tube.) I-cord is the simplest form of knitted tube, but for a true tubular form, the I-cord technique only works over a relatively small number of stitches. If you want to create a larger tube without using bulkier yarns, other techniques are necessary. It is useful to note that the fact that plain stockinette knitting wants to curl in at the sides — often thought to be a disadvantage of the stitch — can actually be an advantage to be exploited in a positive way when tube-making is your goal.

WHAT YOU NEED

Any size 6° beads

Smooth sock- to DK-weight wool or wool-blend yarn in a solid, light color

Knitting needles in a size you would normally use for the yarn (usually 3.25–3.75mm/US3–5)

AND set of 4 double-pointed needles

Beading needle

Tapestry needle

Waste yarn

Crochet hook

Plain tube, horizontal construction

These tubes are worked as flat pieces of fabric, starting with waste yarn and a temporary crochet cast-on. After working the desired number of rows, do not bind off. Remove the waste yarn and form the tube by grafting the live stitches on the needle together with the live stitches from the cast-on.

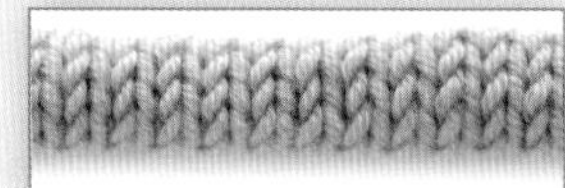
Stockinette: knit side out

Knit side out

With waste yarn and a temporary crochet cast-on,
cast on 25.
Row 1 (RS) With yarn, knit.
Row 2 P23, p2tog — 24 stitches.
Rows 3–9 Work even in stockinette.
Do not bind off; leave stitches on needle. Cut yarn,
leaving a 36" tail.
Remove waste yarn from cast-on, placing 24 stitches
on a second needle.
With RS facing, tapestry needle, and tail, use stockinette graft to join stitches on both needles.

If you'd like to see the purl side out, just turn the tube inside out after grafting.

BEAD-KNIT CHARTS

Purl side out

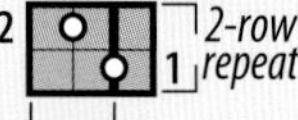

Stitch key
- *Purl on RS, knit on WS*
- *SB, p1 on RS*
- *SB, k1 on WS*

Knit side out

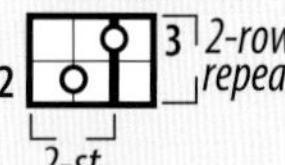

Stitch key
- *Knit on RS, purl on WS*
- *SB, p1 on WS*
- *SB, k1 on RS*

All-over bead-knit tube, horizontal construction

These tubes are worked as flat pieces of fabric with an all-over pattern of beads knit on the reverse-stockinette side of the fabric. Each tube is formed using a different combination of cast-on and finishing techniques.

Purl side out with Zipper Graft

With beading needle, string 80 beads. With long-tail cast-on, cast on 21.
Row 1 (RS) P1, **[SB, p2]** to end — 10 beads.
Row 2 K1, **[SB, k2]** to end.

Purl side out with Zipper Graft

Repeat Rows 1–2 for a total of 7 rows, end with Row 1.
Bind off in pattern, placing beads as in Row 2. Cut yarn, leaving a 24" tail.
With beads on the outside of the tube, tapestry needle, bind-off tail, and using Zipper Graft, join cast-on and bound-off edges.

Knit side out with graft over finished edges

With beading needle, string 60 beads.
Cast on 22.
Row 1 (WS) P1, **[SB, p2]** to end — 10 beads placed.
Row 2 K1, **[SB, k2]** to end.
Repeat Rows 1–2 for a total of 5 rows, end with Row 1.
Bind off in pattern, placing beads as in Row 2.
Cut yarn, leaving a 24" tail.
With beads on the inside of the tube, tapestry needle, and bind-off tail, graft the cast-on and bound-off edges together.

Knit side out with graft over finished edges

Align stitches as shown. Graft over cast-on and bound-off edges. Adjust tension.

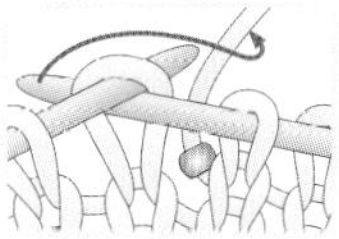

SB Slide bead close to last stitch worked.

TEMPORARY CROCHET CAST-ON

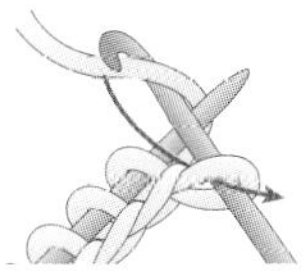

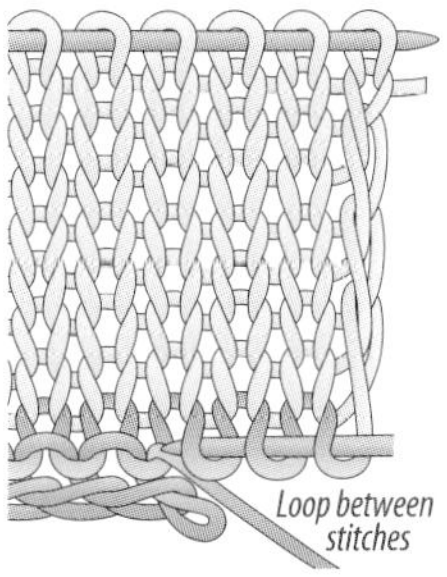

PICKING UP LOOPS FROM A TEMPORARY CAST-ON

Temporary cast-ons use waste yarn to hold the loops that form *between* stitches under the needle. When this waste yarn is removed, these loops can be placed on a needle. There will be 1 fewer loops than cast- on stitches. Casting on 1 extra stitch and decreasing 1 on Row 2 of the pattern results in the same number of stitches and loops for the graft.

Intermittent bead-knit tube, horizontal construction

On this tube, rather than using an all-over beading pattern, beads have been knit at intervals. This technique allows more of the yarn to show and creates spaces that may be wrapped with yarn or other beads if desired. The tube is formed using a Zipper Graft.

Purl side out with Zipper Graft

With beading needle, string 48 beads. With long-tail cast-on, cast on 21.
Row 1 (RS) P1, **[SB, p2, SB, p6]** 2 times, **[SB, p2]** 2 times.
Row 2 K1, **[SB, k2, SB, k6]** 2 times, **[SB, k2]** 2 times.
Repeat Rows 1–2 for a total of 7 rows, end with Row 1.
Bind off in pattern, placing beads as on Row 2. Cut yarn, leaving a 24" tail.
With beads on the outside of the tube, tapestry needle, bind-off tail, and using Zipper Graft, join cast-on and bound-off edges.

Chart

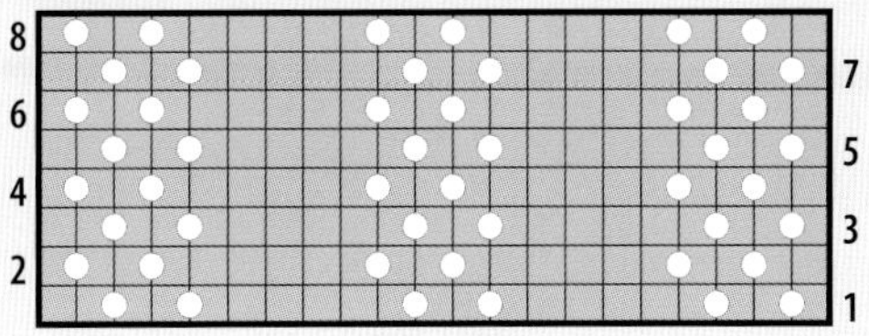

21 stitches

Stitch key

- *Purl on RS, knit on WS*
- *SB, p1 on RS*
- *SB, k1 on WS*

ZIPPER GRAFT

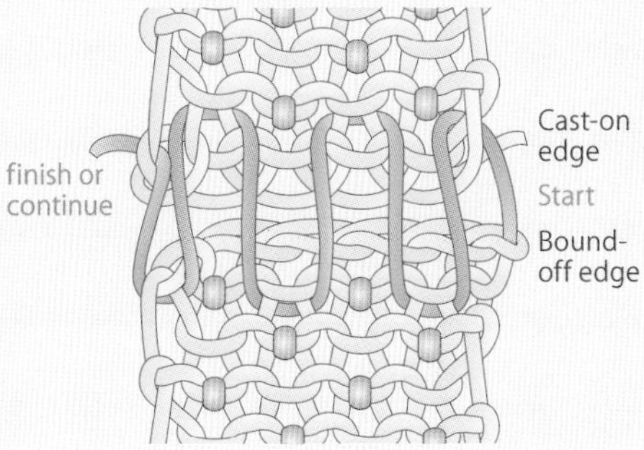

Cast on with long-tail cast-on whenever a Zipper Graft will be used.

Zipper Graft

Having worked out a pattern to create an all-over bead-knit fabric that still allowed the yarn to show through, I invented the Zipper Graft as a way of seamlessly grafting cast-on and bound-off edges together. I had tried all of the other seaming and grafting techniques I knew, but none pulled the beads close to each other while maintaining their staggered pattern. It is this pattern, always worked as a 2-row repeat, that suggested the name. The beads from the cast-on and bound-off rows are pulled together by the grafting stitches, much like the teeth of a zipper. This grafting technique requires working deeper into the fabric than other seaming or grafting methods, but that's what makes it look seamless. When the Zipper Graft will be used, make sure to use a long-tail cast-on (as in our drawing).

Straps

TECH TRIALS

When you define a strap as any flat, narrow piece of knitted fabric, there are lots of applications for them in knitting projects of all kinds. There's the obvious—handles for bags or purses—but straps can also decorate your wrists, warm your ears, and hold up your pants or a tube top. They can be constructed either horizontally or vertically as flat, single pieces of fabric. Join 2 flat straps with some beaded finishing techniques and they become stronger and more durable, not to mention more decorative. You can also make them doubly strong by constructing them in the round. Knitting in beads adds fun and increases the versatility of these wonderfully simple yet versatile straps.

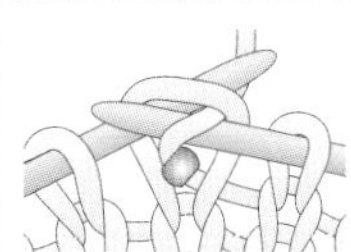

KBL Knit bead through stitch with standard wrap. On next round, knit stitch through back loop.

Single strap, horizontal construction

This single strap in garter stitch is knit horizontally with a beaded cast-on and bind-off. It is simple to make and will function quite differently depending upon the stretch of the fiber and the firmness of the gauge. This sample has beads on every other cast-on and bound-off stitch, but using beads on every stitch (or every third, fourth, etc.) works just as well.

Garter strap with beaded cast-on and beaded bind-off (every other stitch)

BEADED CAST-ON

Slide bead between every other cast-on stitch.

BEADED BIND-OFF

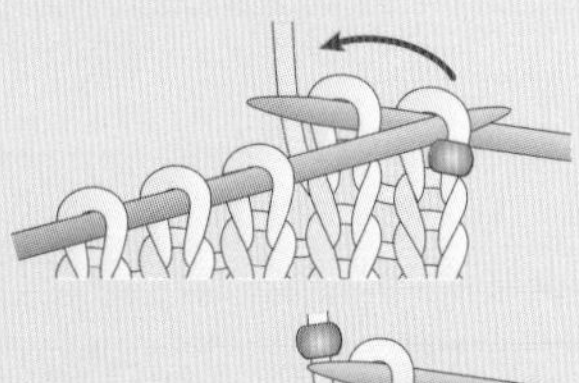

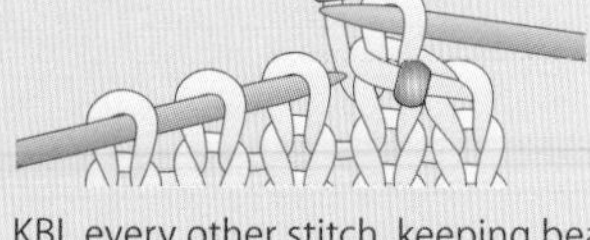

KBL every other stitch, keeping beads to the front of the work and making sure bound-off stitch passes over both the stitch ahead of it AND the bead on that stitch.

To review both beaded cast-on and bind-off, see page 9.

With beaded cast-on and bind-off

With beading needle, string 40 beads.

Beaded long-tail cast-on Place slip knot on needle, cast on 1, **[SB, cast on 2]** 20 times—42 stitches and 20 beads.

Knit 6 rows.

Beaded bind-off K1, **[KBL, bind off, k1, bind off]** 20 times, k1, bind off. Cut yarn.

Double strap, horizontal construction

This is just one way to create a double-thick strap that is beaded on one side and plain on the other. You could also work the 2 sides separately and then join them together, with or without additional beads in the join (next page, top photo).

With beaded reverse stockinette on one side and plain stockinette on the other, with Zipper Graft

With beading needle, string 64 beads.

With long-tail cast-on, cast on 17.

Row1 (RS) P1, **[SB, p2]** 8 times.

Row 2 K1, **[SB, k2]** 8 times.

Rows 3–4 Repeat Rows 1 and 2.

Rows 5–11 Work in stockinette, starting with a knit row.

Row 12 (WS) Knit.

Rows 13–15 Repeat Rows 1–3.

Bind off in pattern, placing beads as in Row 2.

Before finishing

Cut yarn, leaving a 24" tail.

With beads on the outside of the tube, tapestry needle, bind-off tail, and using Zipper Graft, join cast-on and bound-off edges, then flatten so beads are all on one side.

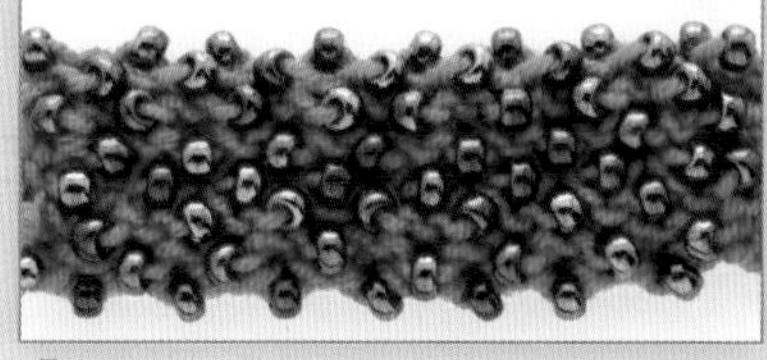

Front

Back

Double strap in stockinette, finished with Alternating Beaded Join

Knit in the round, with beaded edges

Knit flat, with Single-side Beaded Join

Double strap, vertical construction

Knit flat, with alternating beaded join

For a sturdier strap, 2 pieces of knit fabric can be placed WS together, then joined along both side edges by picking up stitches and working a 3-needle bind-off with beads. If you are placing beads on every bound-off stitch, alternating the placement of the beads (front-back, front-back) creates a wonderfully balanced and decorative edge that shows equally well on both sides of the strap. You can work the straps in any stitch you like.

Make 2 stockinette straps as follows:
Cast on 8. Work 21 rows stockinette. Bind off.
With 2 knitting needles, pick up and knit an equal number of stitches along *left edge of 1 strap and along right edge of the other strap*. With beading needle, string yarn with one fewer bead than the number of stitches picked up on one strap. With WS together, and using a 3-needle bind-off with beads, join the 2 pieces, alternating the placement of the beads (to the front of one stitch, then to the back of the next stitch, etc.), and knitting a bead through every stitch except the last one. Repeat along opposite edge.

Knit in the round, with beaded edges

This double strap is actually a tube that is knit in the round, then flattened into a strap when taken off the needles. The beads are placed so they lie along the edges of the flattened strap. The strap can be worked in any stitch desired—even with different stitches on each side.

With beading needle, string 40 beads.
With double-pointed needle (dpn), cast on 18 and divide evenly onto 3 dpn, join without twisting, and place marker to work in the round.
Round 1 K4, KBL, k8, KBL, k4.
Round 2 K4; with bead to front of work, k1tbl; k8; with bead to front of work; k1tbl, k4.
Round 3 Knit.
Repeat Rounds 1–3 until 20 beads have been placed on each edge.
Bind off.

Knit flat, with single-side beaded join

If you want a sturdy strap but only need to see beads on one side, picking up and then binding off stitches, each with a bead placed on it, will join the edges and show the beads on the surface of one side of the fabric.

Make 2 stockinette straps as follows:
Cast on 8. Work 21 rows stockinette. Bind off.
String 10 beads.
Step 1 With WS together, insert a knitting needle or crochet hook through the first edge stitch of both pieces.
Step 2 SB; pick up and knit a stitch.
Step 3 Leave bead on far side of strap and pull picked-up stitch through to near side.
Step 4 Insert needle through the next edge stitch of both pieces; repeat Steps 2 and 3.
Step 5 There are now 2 stitches on the needle. Pass the first stitch over the second stitch.
Repeat Steps 4 and 5 along length of strap.
Repeat along opposite edge to complete the strap.

3-NEEDLE BIND-OFF WITH BEADS IN ALTERNATING PLACEMENT

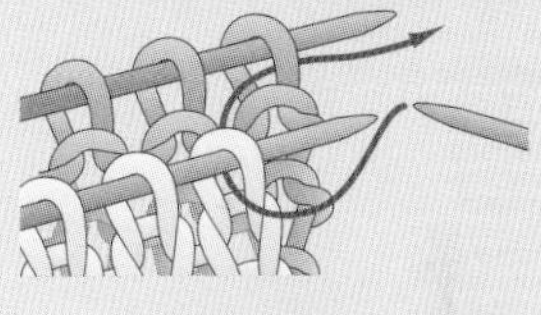

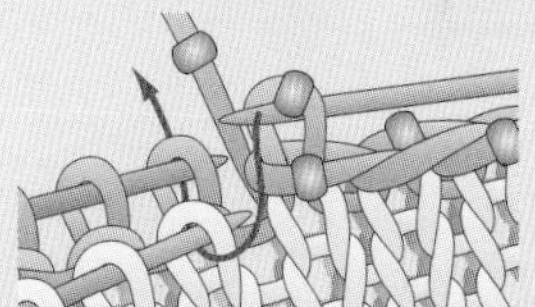

To review 3-needle bind-off, see page 162.

Twilight

Twilight

At first look, people assume that the technique used to create this bead-knit tube is anything BUT what it actually is. The guesses include I-cord, bead crochet, even Kumihimo, the Japanese braiding technique. Nope! None of the above. It is simply a wide, rectangular piece of bead-knit stockinette fabric with all of the beads placed on the purl side. And what does stockinette fabric want to do? Curl! All I had to do was exploit this natural tendency and then find a way to join the cast-on and bound-off edges together seamlessly. I lost count of my attempts to figure that out, but I can be pretty stubborn and finally worked out what I now call a Zipper Graft. This seamless, bead-knit tube is one of my favorite components and surely one of the most versatile.

FIESTA YARNS Gelato
100 yds in Onyx

MIYUKI Size 6º glass seed beads
407 in 152FR Matte Transparent Gray AB (A)
33 in 131S Silver-Lined Crystal (B)

Prepare

With beading needle, string 440 beads: primarily A beads, with B beads strung at random intervals.

Knit

Leaving an 8" tail and using a long-tail cast-on, cast on 89.

Begin chart: Row 1 (RS) P1, **[SB, p2]** to end—44 beads.
Row 2 K1, **[SB, k2]** to end.
Rows 3–8 Repeat Rows 1 and 2.
Row 9 Repeat Row 1.
Bind off in pattern, placing beads as in Row 2.
Cut yarn, leaving a 30" tail.

Finish

With RS facing, tapestry needle, bind-off tail, and using Zipper Graft, join cast-on and bound-off edges. Use cast-on and bind-off tails to sew on clasp. Weave tails inside the tube and trim.

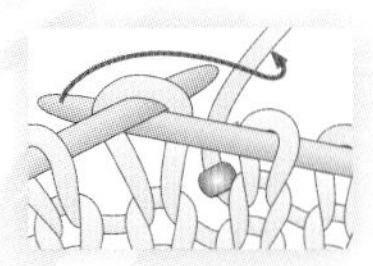

SB Slide bead close to last stitch worked.

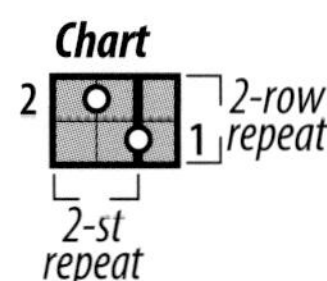

Stitch key

Purl on RS, knit on WS
SB, p1 on RS
SB, k1 on WS

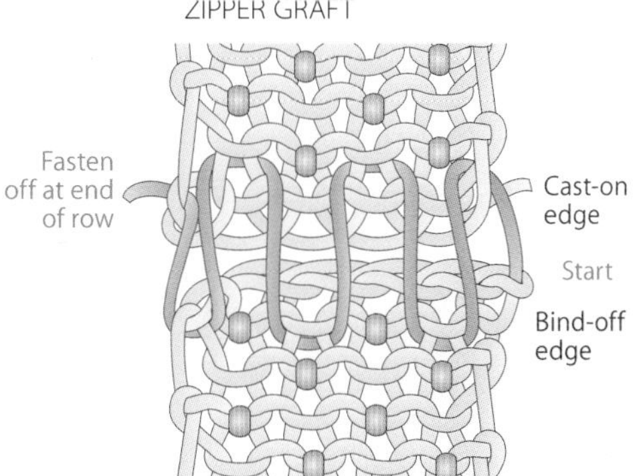

gauge

6 stitches = 1" over pattern
finished length 15¼" closed, including clasp; knitted piece measures 14½"

yarn

medium weight
100 yds ribbon tape

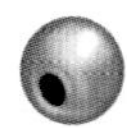

beads

465 size 6° Japanese seed beads, shown In 2 colors

needles

2.75mm/US2, 60cm (24") long

and...

beading needle
tapestry needle
single-strand clasp

NOTES: easy

See page 160 for knitting abbreviations and techniques, and page 2 for beading basics.

Crystal beads are added at random as the beads are strung. How many to use is knitter's choice. The sample used about 33 crystal beads out of 440 total beads.

To lengthen or shorten circumference of necklace: for every 2 additional stitches per row, string 10 more beads.

WHAT IF...

The design possibilities for bead-color combinations and placement on this kind of bead-knit tube are truly endless. The entire tube does not have to be beaded—you can leave sections where the yarn shows through. When considering beading patterns for a tube like this, make sure to remember the continuity required—you'll want the pattern to continue seamlessly when cast-on and bound-off edges are grafted together.

Think of using this kind of tube as a decorative handle for a purse, as a belt, or even as an applied trim or embellishment.

Wineberry

Wineberry

This lariat takes the all-over bead-knit tube technique used to create the Twilight necklace on page 46 and bumps it up another level, asking the knitter to leave defined spaces without beads AND requiring a specific bead-stringing order to create alternating patterns with beads. Welcome to the world of following a bead-knitting chart. Challenging? For sure. Worth the effort? I think so!

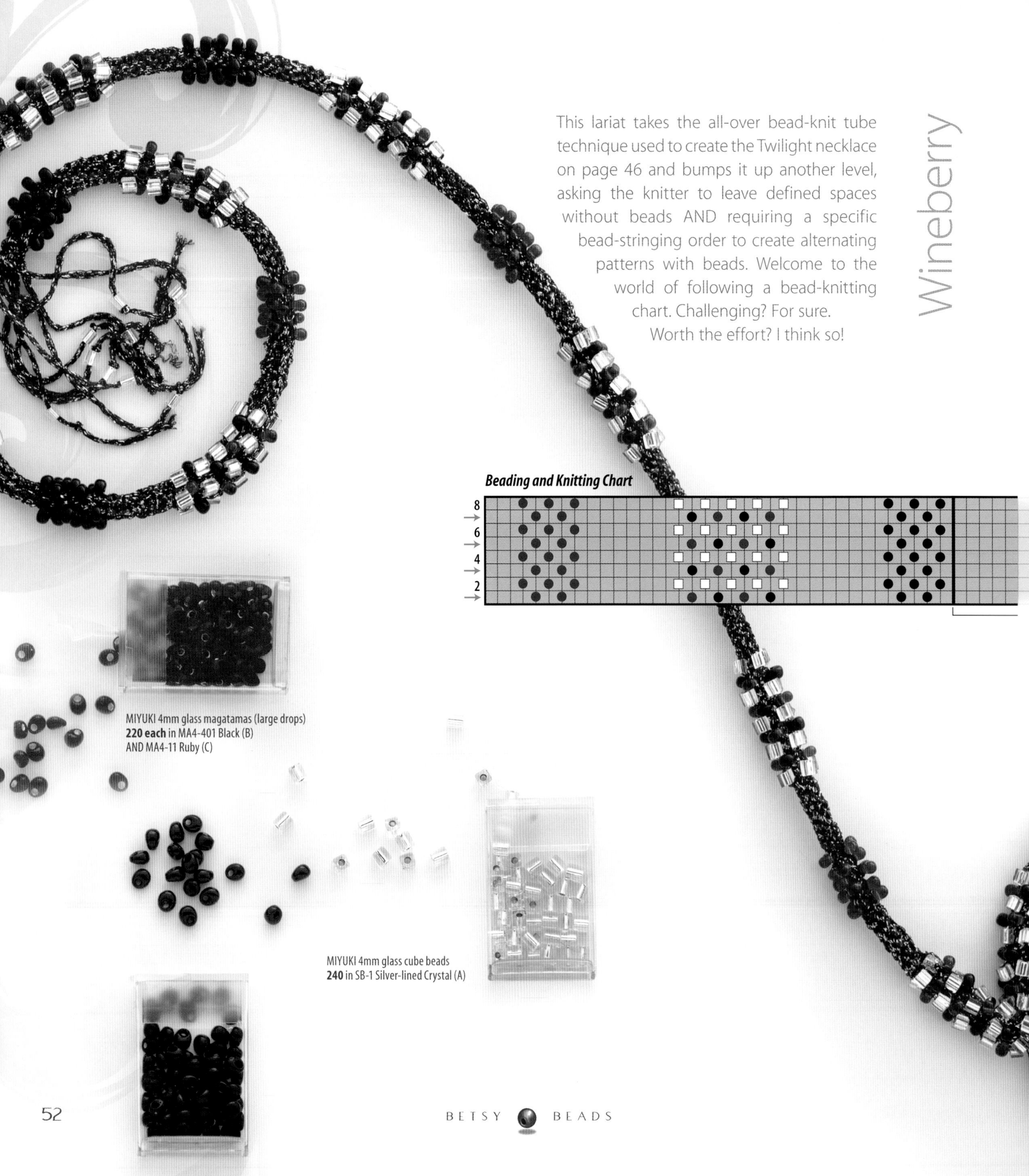

Beading and Knitting Chart

MIYUKI 4mm glass magatamas (large drops)
220 each in MA4-401 Black (B)
AND MA4-11 Ruby (C)

MIYUKI 4mm glass cube beads
240 in SB-1 Silver-lined Crystal (A)

NOTE: Each row of knitting uses a new length of yarn onto which beads are strung before the row is worked. Leave a 10" tail at the beginning of the row; at the end of the row, cut yarn, leaving a 10" tail.

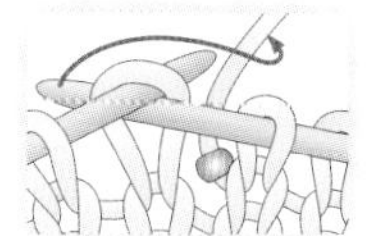

SB Slide bead close to last stitch worked.

Stitch key

- Purl on RS, knit on WS
- SB, p1 on RS
- SB, k1 on WS
- → Direction of bead stringing

Bead key

- □ A
- ● B
- ● C

Prepare and knit

Leaving a 10" tail, cast on 318. Cut yarn, leaving a 10" tail.

Row 1 (RS) With beading needle, string **[3C, 1B, 1C, 3B, 1C, 1B, 1C, 1B]** 5 times, 3C, 1B, 1C, 3B—68 beads. Work Row 1 of Chart: p4, **[(SB, p2) twice, p8, (SB, p2) 4 times, p8]** 11 times, **[SB, p2]** twice, p2. Cut yarn.

Row 2 With beading needle, string **[3B, 5A, 3C, 5A]** 5 times, 3B, 5A, 3C—91 beads.

K3, **[(SB, k2) 3 times, k6, (SB, k2) 5 times, k6]** 11 times, **[SB, k2]** 3 times, k1. Cut yarn.

Row 3 With beading needle, string **[2C, 1B, 1C, 1B, 1C, 3B, 1C, 1B, 1C]** 5 times, 2C, 1B, 1C, 1B, 1C, 2B—68 beads. Work as for Row 1.

Row 4 Repeat Row 2.

Rows 5–7 Repeat Rows 1–3.

Row 8 With beading needle, string as for Row 2. Bind off in pattern, placing beads as for Row 2.

gauge

7 stitches = 1"

finished length 45", excluding fringe

yarn

fine weight

100 yds tubular chainette ribbon

beads

255 4mm Japanese glass cube beads

445 4mm Japanese glass magatamas, shown in 2 colors

needles

3mm/US2, 80cm (32") long

and...

beading needle

tapestry needle

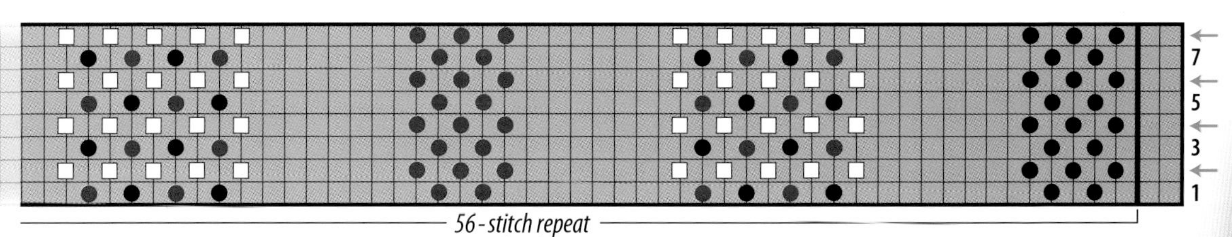

NOTES: advanced

See page 160 for knitting abbreviations and techniques, and page 2 for beading basics.

Bead stringing may be done from the chart or from written directions. Begin stringing with the last bead in the row, ending with the first bead that will be knit.

Finish

With tapestry needle and yarn, and using Zipper Graft, join cast-on and bound-off edges. Knot cube beads along tails to create lightly beaded fringe of desired length.

WHAT IF...

If stringing a large number of beads in a specific order AND following a bead-knitting chart feels like too much to tackle all at once, just choose a single color and use it for ALL the beads on the lariat.

PRISM YARNS Elise
100 yds in Cabernet

Precious hoops

Precious hoops

You can buy hoop-earring findings or an inexpensive pair of hoop earrings to use with this pattern, but think about using a pair that you already have. It doesn't matter if they are pierced or clip-on — this pattern will make them new again. Gorgeous beads can turn a $6 pair of silver hoops into an eye-catching pair of special occasion earrings. Isn't that worth getting over any fears you may have of working with small needles, beads, and thread? This pattern has you knitting the same tube that creates the Twilight necklace, and at this scale you don't even have to graft the edges to secure the tube around the metal earring — a simple overcast stitch does the trick. Give it a try!

KREINIK Cable
2 spools in 002P Gold

MIYUKI Size 8° glass hex-cut beads
96 in 02 My Precious Cut Mix

Prepare

With beading needle, string 96 beads in random order.

Knit

Leaving a 6" tail, cast on 33.

Row 1 (RS) P1, **[SB, p2]** to end—16 beads.

Row 2 K1, **[SB, k2]** to end.

Rows 3–4 Repeat Rows 1–2.

Row 5 Repeat Row 1.

Bind off in pattern, placing beads as in Row 2.

Cut thread, leaving a 12" tail.

Chart

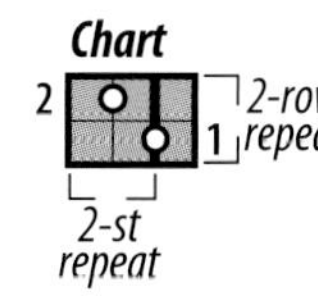

Stitch key

Purl on RS, knit on WS

SB, p1 on RS

SB, k1 on WS

Finish

Wrap the bead-knit tube around the hoop earring. With darning needle and bind-off tail, and using an overcast stitch, join the cast-on and bound-off edges. Weave in tails.

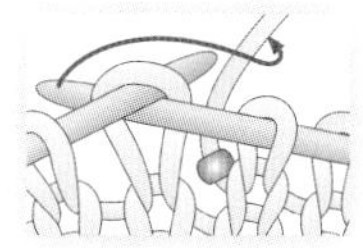

SB Slide bead close to last stitch worked.

OVERCAST STITCH

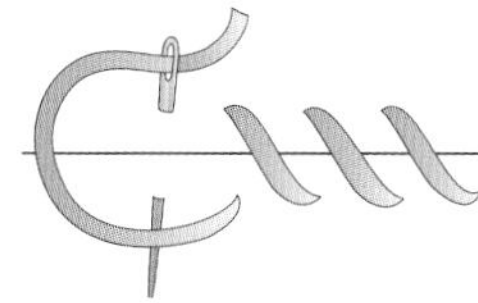

Earrings aren't the only rings you can wrap this way. Here, 1" book rings (yes, the kind you find at the office supply store) provide elegant closures for the Infinity necklaces. For Infinity I (page 84), string 108 beads on CC and cast on 37; for Infinity II (page 88), string 90 and cast on 31. Then work as above. Start sewing the tube at the opening of the ring, so center of wrapper is at hinge. Tube is long enough to cover ring opening when closed.

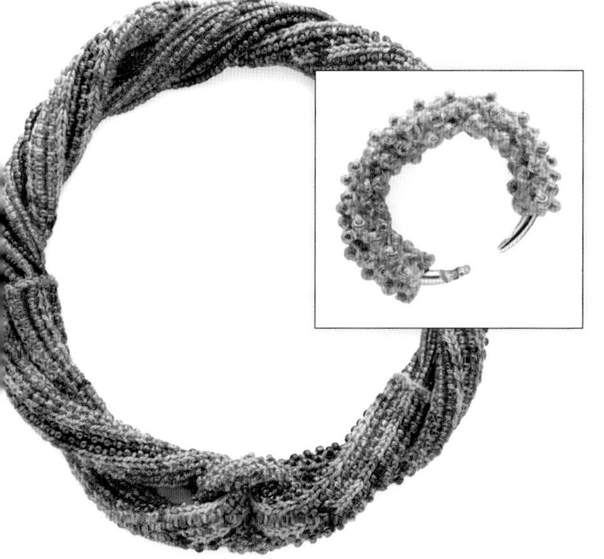

gauge

12 stitches to 1", over pattern

yarn

super fine weight
20 yds cable thread

beads

96 size 8° Japanese glass hex-cut beads

needles

1.75mm/US00

and…

beading needle
darning needle
1 pair silver-plated endless hoop earrings, approximately 1" diameter

NOTES: intermediate

See page 160 for knitting abbreviations and techniques, and page 2 for beading basics.

Try not to be intimidated by the small size of the fiber and needles—it's still just knitting! You are creating a small piece of bead-knit fabric, which will be wrapped around the hoop earring and stitched together along the cast-on and bound-off edges to form a tube.

The cable thread is uniquely appropriate for working with hex beads, which tend to have very sharp edges and can eventually tear weaker fibers. Cable thread has the strength and look of wire but with greater flexibility, so it will not hurt your fingers.

WHAT IF…

If bling isn't your thing, use any size 8° seed or hex beads that tickle your fancy. You can string these beads onto a lovely silk thread or even a #8 pearl cotton. The choice is always yours.

These earrings work up quickly, so make several pairs and give them as gifts!

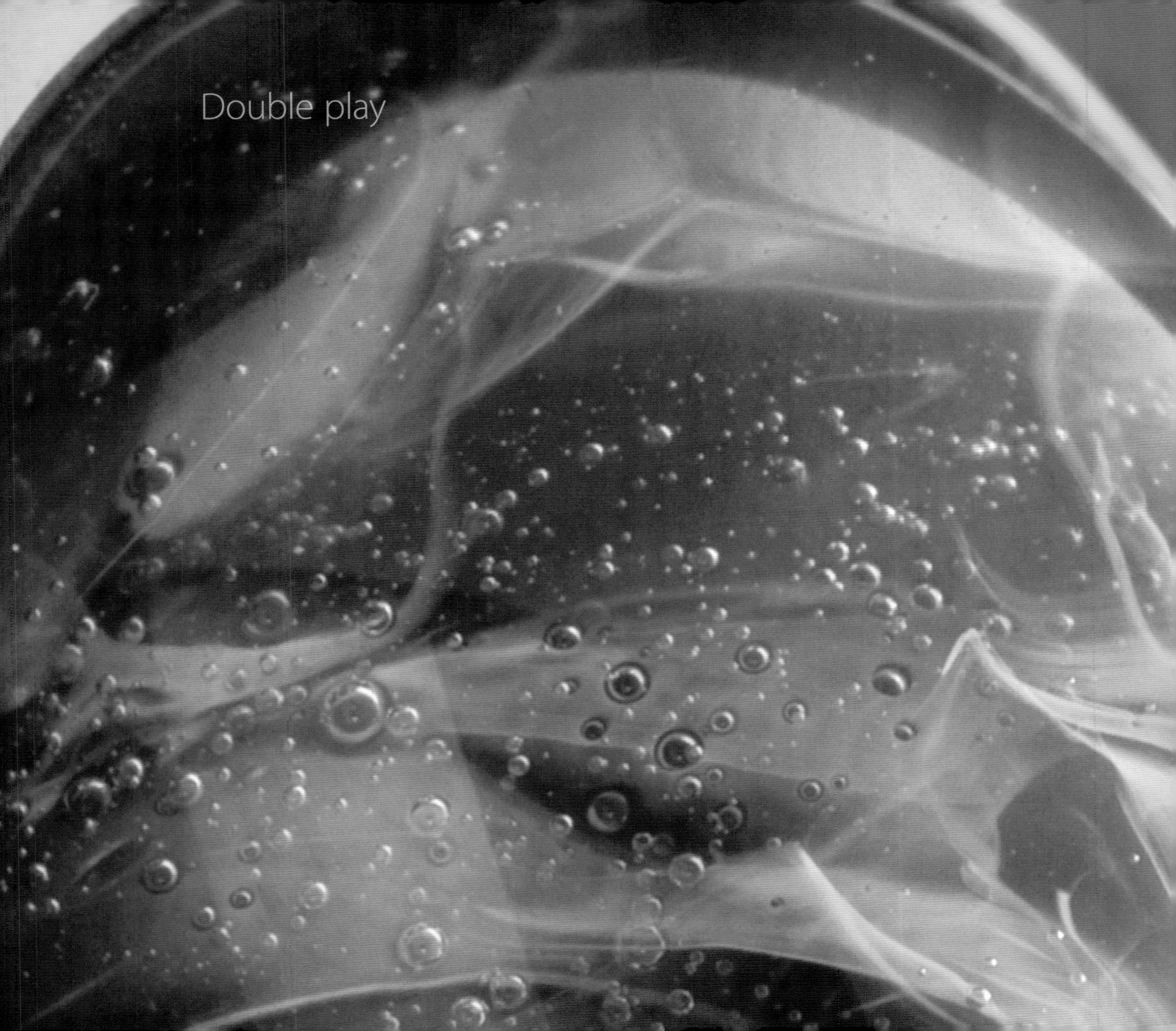
Double play

Double play

I am often inspired to create a piece to show off a special yarn, bead or, in this case, a one-of-a-kind clasp. Incredibly, I already had the beautiful rayon ribbon yarn in colors that coordinated perfectly with the art glass in the clasp — a great example of why the only rationale we need to justify buying yarn is because we love it (as if we really need one). Hail to the stash! But even with a different clasp, this bracelet can hold its own. This project was truly an evolution. I originally thought it would be fun to use clear crystal beads with this intensely colored ribbon, with the idea that it would be interesting to see that glorious color filtered through the beads. Once the beaded tube was done, however, I missed the intensity of the ribbon's colors and decided to use an unbeaded length of ribbon to make I-cord. Which one to use for a bracelet? Why not both of them, twisted and stitched together? That actually makes this bracelet a *double* double play — beaded and unbeaded ribbon yarn, AND tubes created with two different techniques. Double the fun. Double the impact.

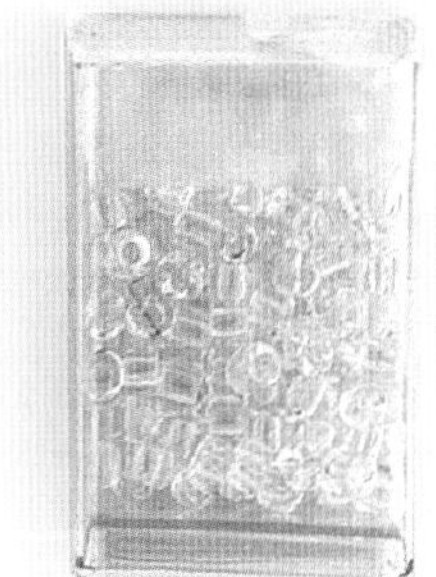

MATSUNO Size 6° glass seed beads
230 in 004 Transparent Crystal

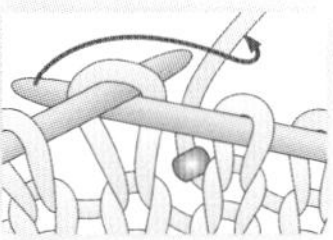

SB Slide bead close to last stitch worked.

PRISM YARNS Quicksilver
30 yds in Woodlands

Prepare

With beading needle, string 230 beads.

Knit

Beaded tube

Leaving a 12" tail, cast on 47.

Row 1 (RS) P1, **[SB, p2]** to end—23 beads.

Row 2 K1, **[SB, k2]** to end.

Repeat Rows 1–2 for a total of 9 rows, end with Row 1.

Bind off in pattern, placing beads as in Row 2.

Cut yarn, leaving an 18" tail. With tapestry needle and bind-off tail, and using Zipper Graft, join cast-on and bound-off edges.

I-cord

With double-pointed needles and leaving a 24" tail, cast on 5.

Begin I-cord: All rounds Knit. Work to a length at least twice as long as the beaded tube. Do not bind off. Place stitches on hold.

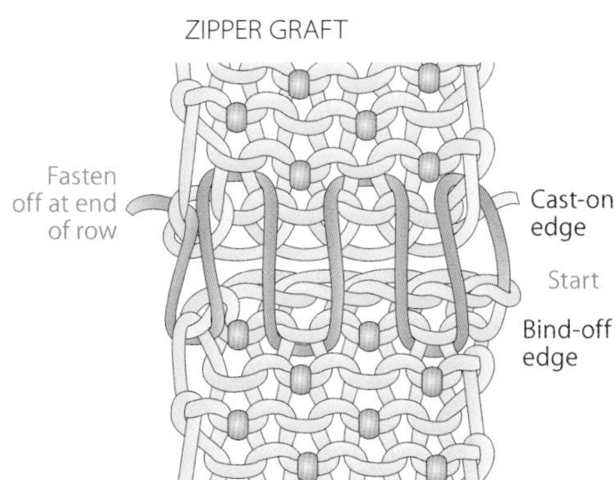

Finish

Wrap I-cord around beaded tube and, with tapestry needle and cast-on tail, secure I-cord in several places. If necessary, adjust length of I-cord by adding or removing rounds. Cut yarn. With tapestry needle, thread yarn through stitches on hold, gather, and secure. Use cast-on and bind-off tails to sew on clasp. Weave tails inside cord and trim.

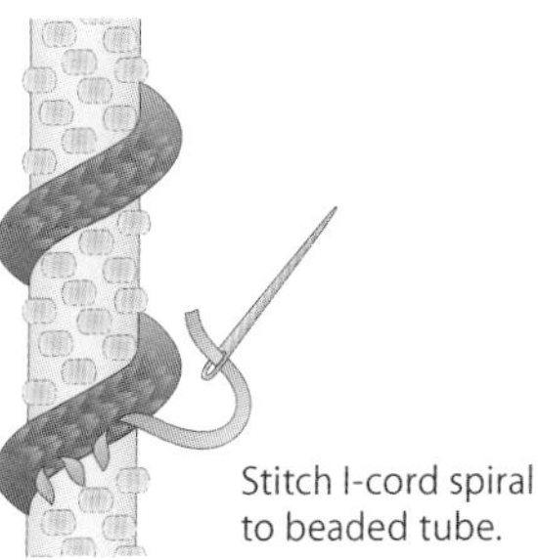
Stitch I-cord spiral to beaded tube.

gauge
7 stitches = 1", over pattern
finished length 8", including clasp; knitted piece measures 6¾"

yarn
light weight
40 yds tubular chainette ribbon

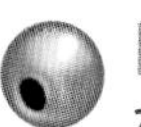
beads
250 size 6° Japanese glass seed beads

needles
2.75mm/US2

2 2.75mm/US2

and...
beading needle
tapestry needle
clasp

WHAT IF...

For a simpler project, the tubes don't have to be twisted. Just work them to equal lengths and attach each to a single clasp. Or work 3 tubes, partially beading the third. Any combination of beaded and unbeaded tubes will make a great-looking bracelet.

NOTES: easy

See page 160 for knitting abbreviations and techniques, and page 2 for beading basics.

The bracelet is comprised of two separate pieces—a beaded tube and a plain piece of I-cord—twisted into a spiral and sewn together.

Bunch bands

Bunch bands

I like to say that inspiration is everywhere and often where least expected. These bracelets came to mind after seeing a great-looking raincoat in a fashion magazine. It wasn't the raincoat, however, that intrigued me — it was the raincoat's belt! What I noticed and loved was the fact that it was ruched. A ruche is defined as "a frill or pleat of fabric as decoration on a garment or home furnishing." I like to think of it simply as a ripple. But how to use it in knitting? I tried to think of where else I had seen rippled fabric before, and then I remembered trying to replace the elastic in a pair of sweatpants and saw in my mind how the fabric scrunched together as I worked the elastic into its cloth tunnel. Another "Eureka!" moment: Elastic could be drawn through a bead-knit tube! Making the tube considerably longer than the elastic would allow me to bunch it up before seaming the elastic and provide the length necessary for the elastic to stretch as I slipped a bracelet over my hand. The same technique could allow a belt to stretch to varying lengths for a comfortable fit at the waist. The yarn and bead choices used here are just the tip of the iceberg of possibilities for this kind of design.

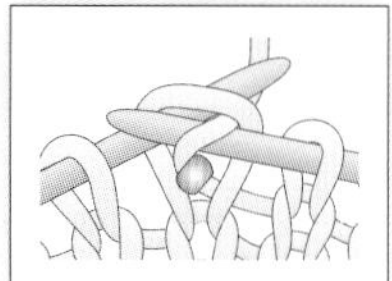

KBL Knit bead through stitch. On next round, knit stitch through back loop.

BLUE HERON YARN Egyptian Mercerized Cotton
50 yds in 711 Mossy Place for ½" OR 1" Bands

½" (1") BAND

Prepare

The number of beads to string depends on your gauge and the finished length for your bracelet (see Note 2). This design requires 2 beads for every other round plus approximately 45–60 more for finishing.

With beading needle, string approximately 200 beads onto yarn.

Knit

With a double-pointed needle (dpn) and leaving an 18" tail, cast on 12 (18) and divide evenly onto 3 dpn, join without twisting and place marker to work in the round.

Round 1 K2 (4), KBL, k5 (8), KBL, k3 (4) — 2 beads.

Round 2 K2 (4); with bead to front of work, k1 tbl; k5 (8); with bead to front of work, k1 tbl; k3 (4).

Repeat Rounds 1–2 to desired length. Bind off. Cut yarn, leaving a 12" tail.

MIYUKI Size 8º glass seed beads
200 in 408 Opaque Red for 1" Band

MATSUNO 8º glass seed beads
200 in 222M Matte Clear Sea Foam for ½" Band

Possible tools for pulling elastic through tube

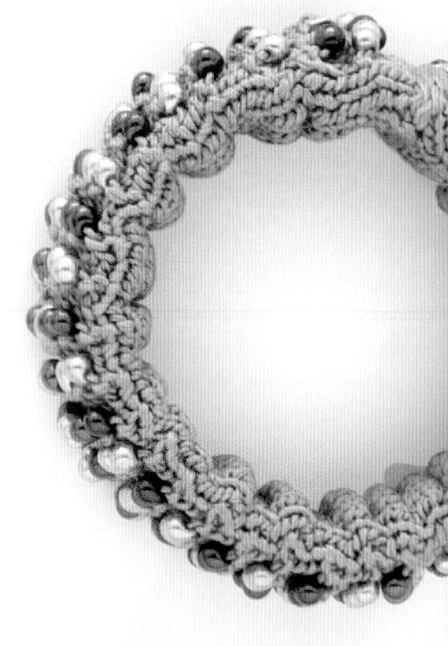

¾" SILKEN BAND

Prepare

The number of beads strung depends on your gauge and the finished length for your bracelet (see Note 2). This design requires 6 beads for every 6 rounds.

With beading needle, string 192 beads onto yarn, alternating 2A and 2B.

Knit

With a double-pointed needle (dpn) and leaving an 8" tail, cast on 16 and divide evenly onto 3 dpn, join without twisting and place marker to work in the round.

Rounds 1–5 Knit.

Round 6 K6, **[p1, SB]** 6 times, p1, k3 — 6 beads.

Repeat Rounds 1–6 until all beads have been used.

Bind off. Cut yarn, leaving a 12" tail.

Finish

Cut elastic 4" longer than finished length of bracelet. Mark elastic ½" from one end (mark X) and again at finished length from X (mark Y). Using a short length of yarn, attach stole needle (or crochet hook or circular needle) to Y end of the elastic. Draw the elastic through the tube to X and pin at X to secure. Flatten the tube so the knit-in beads align with the edges of the elastic. Gather the band up the elastic until Y shows and pin to secure. Trim elastic to ½" beyond mark. Overlap the ends of the elastic so each cut edge touches a mark, and stitch together with strong nylon thread or monofilament. Remove pins.

For the ½" and 1" Bands

With big-eye beading needle and 18" tail, overcast the ends of the tube together, stringing 4–5 beads on each stitch on the outside of the bracelet. Secure and weave in ends.

For the Silken Band

With a tapestry needle and 12" tail, stitch the edges of the tubes together. Secure and weave in ends.

gauge

10 stitches and 15 rounds = 1"
finished length shown 6½"
in general, knit tube twice your desired finished length

yarn

fine weight
50 yds per Band

beads

220 size 8° glass seed beads per Band
220 2.8mm glass drop beads, shown in 2 colors for Silken Band

needles

2.25mm/US1

and...

big-eye beading needle
8" stole needle OR crochet hook OR circular needle
sewing needle
½", ¾", OR 1" non-roll elastic
strong nylon thread or monofilament
pins
fine waterproof marker

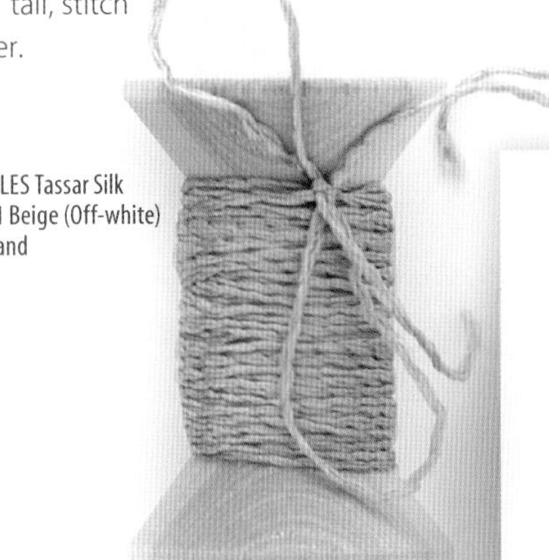

HABU TEXTILES Tassar Silk
50 yds in 41 Beige (Off-white) for Silken Band

NOTES: easy

See page 160 for knitting abbreviations and techniques, and page 2 for beading basics.

Before beginning, measure your wrist, decide how you want the bracelet to fit, and add any ease required for your bracelet's finished length. The fit can be snug (as shown here) or loose (and worn as a bangle).

To allow for the gathering of the knit tube over the elastic, knit the tube at least twice the desired length of the finished bracelet.

The number of beads strung for each bracelet will depend on the finished length of the bracelet and the knitter's gauge.

WHAT IF...

Think about using the idea of the Stash Buster belt (next page) as a bracelet. What a great way to use up really small bits of leftover yarn! Or what about using one of these bracelet designs for a belt? The heavily beaded silk bracelet would make an incredible belt for a special-event dress. No other jewelry necessary!

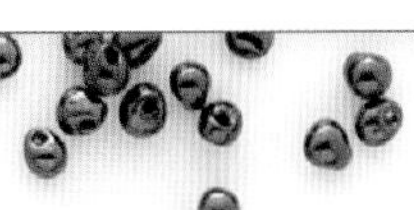

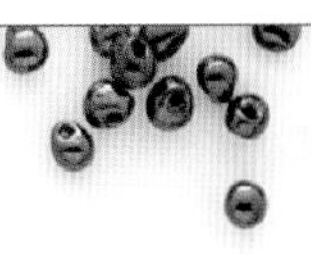

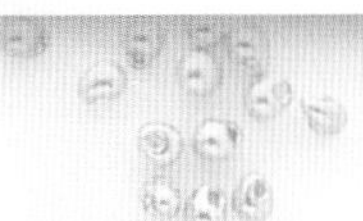

MIYUKI 2.8mm glass drop beads
96 each in 451 Gunmetal (A) AND 181 Galvanized Silver (B) for Silken Band

Stash buster

WHAT IF. . .

you really want a belt, not a bracelet. Here's an expanded version of the Bunch Bands, knit in the round with beads on one side of the finished, flattened tube. It's designed as a great way to use up lots of small amounts of yarns and beads — a stash buster. (Yes, soon you too will have a bead stash!) In the real world of stash knitting, each knitter chooses which yarns and beads to use, when to change yarns, and where to place beads along the way. Now it's your turn. Head to your stash, choose your favorites, and mix and match! Ready, set, go!

Shown in assorted colors of KOIGU Premium Merino

NOTES: easy

For a 2" wide belt at a gauge of 7 to 7½ stitches to the inch, cast on 32 and use 2" elastic.

Most of the belt is worked in stockinette stitch (knit every round), changing yarn color and working Beading Charts as desired.

PREPARE AS YOU GO When changing to a new yarn, decide if you want to use beads with it. If so, string beads before joining yarn.

Knit 1½ times the finished length (a little less ruching than the bracelet) to show the variety of beading patterns.

Slide and gather the tube over the elastic (see Finishing, page 65). Sew the elastic onto a buckle, and close the ends of the knit tube with an overcast stitch.

The yarn and bead specifics for the belt shown here are available online at **knittinguniverse.com/Beads**.

Beading Charts

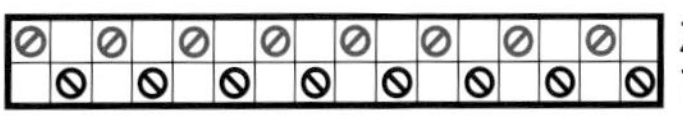

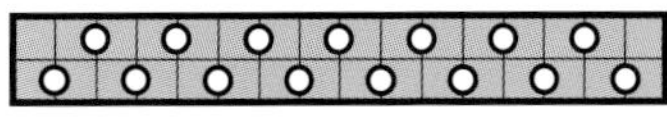

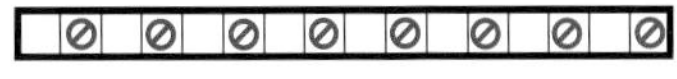

16 sts

Chart notes

Place these beading patterns anywhere in a section of knitting that pleases your eye. Work Beading Chart over first 16 stitches of round; knit to end.

Stitch key

- *Knit*
- *Purl*
- *SB, p1*
- *KBL with standard wrap. On next round, knit stitch tbl with bead to RS of work.*
- *KBR with reverse wrap. On next round, knit stitch with bead to RS of work; stitch twists because of reverse wrap.*

Coloring inside the lines

I know so many people who would love to be able to sing. I'm not talking about singing on Broadway or being a soloist in a choir. They would just like to feel comfortable singing Happy Birthday at a child's party, or feel proud to join the crowd singing the National Anthem at a baseball game. Several of these people have told me about a single day, way back in elementary school, when a well-meaning but insensitive teacher told them they COULDN'T sing. The teacher asked them to please just "mouth the words" alongside their classmates who had been judged worthy to sing out loud. For them, from that day forward, any and all desire to sing—or to even think about learning to sing—was quashed by the fear of further embarrassment. How sad that a single judgment has the power to shape a child's self image, and to limit their potential.

I've often been reminded of these non-singing friends as I write about this creative process I've been discovering for myself. I was never told I couldn't sing, thank goodness, as it has always been one of my greatest pleasures. But I vividly remember being told in elementary school (never at home) to make sure that I colored inside the lines. And I liked it. The biggest choice—which picture to color—was still mine, and I never thought of those lines as boundaries that limited me. They were there to help me, to show me where to begin to draw. They never dictated any of the other choices about my coloring: which colors to use, how heavily to color in the defined space, etc. I still had lots of other choices I could make within the confines of those lines. I found the lines comforting and reassuring.

A little later on, I often heard the parents of friends talking about how they had always known that their children were destined to be artistic. How did they know? Well in those elementary-school years, their children had always colored OUTSIDE the lines. Others listening to this description would invariably nod their heads in agreement. Of course! It seemed obvious to them that the willingness to venture outside the lines was the definitive characteristic of an artistic sensibility. With no other meaningful input available to challenge these judgments, I accepted my place in the creative universe. Coloring outside the lines = Artistic. Coloring inside the lines = Not So Much. And so it seemed. But still I wondered, "Why?"

Scientists describe the human brain as having two distinct lobes, left and right, each of which controls distinctly different functions of human behavior. When I first discovered this theory, it clarified some of the lingering questions I had about my own creative potential. It turns out that while people process information using both sides of the brain, most people are either left- or right-brain dominant. Simply stated, left-brained people are more skilled at tasks that require logic, language, and analytical thinking, while right-brained people tend to be more intuitive and creative. With a few minor exceptions, it turns out that I am clearly left-brain dominant, or, as my sister describes me, "concrete, linear, sequential." No wonder I like to color inside the lines!

But here's the critical, unexpected piece of information I discovered while exploring my newfound passion for bead knitting. It turns out that left brained folks like me are not necessarily lacking in creativity. Given our love of logic and order and the propensity for right-brained folks to find their way into artistic fields, we are just more likely to THINK of ourselves as not being creative. But being right-brained doesn't mean you are effortlessly über-talented at playing an instrument, writing poetry, or painting like the great Masters. Everyone has to find their own way to express their unique creativity. Left- and right-brained folks often just go about it in different ways. The creative process I use when I'm designing is just that—a PROCESS that works for me. It's a set of logical, repeatable steps that moves me forward, comfortably inside the lines, along a path from something familiar to something new and exciting.

So it turns out that there's a lot to discover, both inside and outside those lines. You just have to believe that there is always more than one way to accomplish any goal, and then find and trust in the way that works for you—YOUR way.

Thunderbird *necklace (2009)*
Glass beads, fiber
A little creative fabric manipulation curls flat, bead-knit fabric into these T-shaped, soft beads.
Technique link: Soft bead-knit beads

Stitch pattern embellishment

TECH TRIALS

NOTE
See page 160 for knitting abbreviations and techniques, and page 2 for beading basics.

WHAT YOU NEED

Any size 6° beads

Smooth sock- to DK-weight wool or wool-blend yarn in a solid, light color

Knitting needles in a size you would normally use for the yarn (usually 3.25–3.75mm/US3–5)

Beading needle

Tapestry needle

Cable needle

Surface embellishment is all the rage these days, but what if you could embellish your knitting at the same time you knit it? In this book I have focused on 2 of my favorite ways to knit with beads: sliding beads between stitches and knitting beads through stitches, primarily in stockinette, the most commonly used stitch pattern. But I also love to pick up a stitch dictionary and look through the

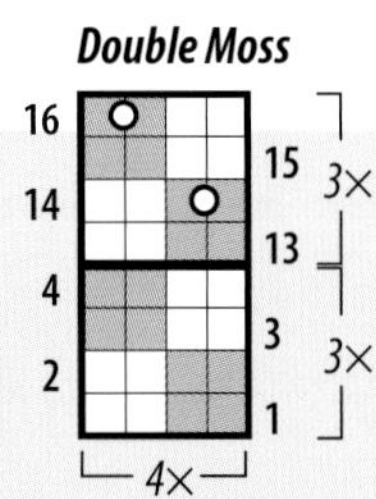

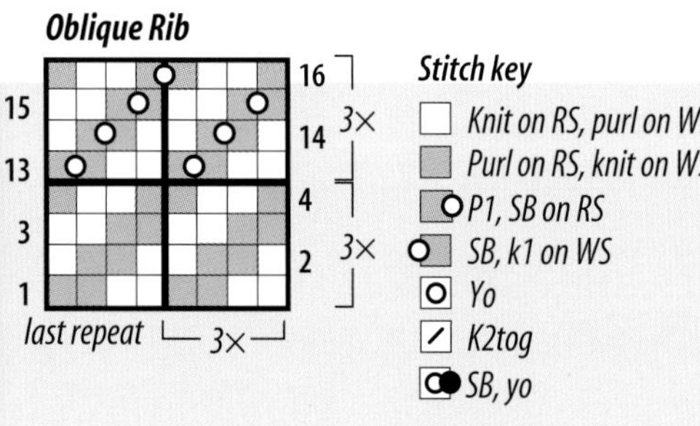

Double Moss *MULTIPLE OF 4*

Look at this pattern.The double purl stitches cry out to have a bead between them! I think beads enhance the textural effect of this simple but effective stitch pattern.

With beading needle, string 24 beads. Cast on 16.

Without beads

Rows 1–2 **[P2, k2]** 4 times.
Rows 3–4 **[K2, p2]** 4 times.
Rows 5–12 Repeat Rows 1–4.

With beads

Row 13 (RS) **[P2, k2]** 4 times.
Row 14 **[P2, k1, SB, k1]** 4 times.
Row 15 **[K2, p2]** 4 times.
Row 16 **[K1, SB, k1, p2]** 4 times.
Rows 17–24 Repeat Rows 13–16.

Oblique Rib *MULTIPLE OF 4*

A slight alteration in Double Moss produces a stitch pattern that appears to have been knit on the bias. The strategic placement of beads, once again between 2 purl stitches, really shows off the slant of this great stitch pattern.

With beading needle, string 45 beads. Cast on 16.

Without beads

Row 1 (WS) **[K2, p2]** 4 times.
Row 2 **[K1, p2, k1]** 4 times.
Row 3 **[P2, k2]** 4 times.
Row 4 **[P1, k2, p1]** 4 times.
Rows 5–12 Repeat Rows 1–4.

With beads

Row 13 (WS) **[K1, SB, k1, p2]** 4 times.
Row 14 **[K1, p1, SB, p1, k1]** 4 times.
Row 15 **[P2, k1, SB, k1]** 4 times.
Row 16 **[P1, k2, p1, SB]** 3 times, end last repeat without SB.
Rows 17–24 Repeat Rows 13–16.

available stitch patterns for opportunities to add beads. My favorites are patterns in which the addition of beads will help highlight what is already unique about the pattern. Each sample here first introduces a stitch pattern without beads, and then includes one way that beads might be added. There are almost always alternative ways to add beads to any single stitch pattern. These samples are simply a place to start. I hope they will inspire you to come up with ways to use beads to enhance your favorite stitches!

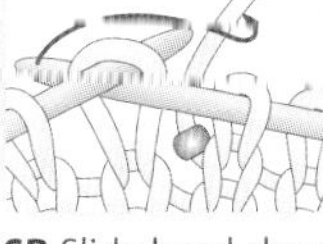

SB Slide bead close to last stitch worked.

Trellis

Last row

last repeat 3×

1/2 LC *Sl 2 to cn, hold to back, k1; p2 from cn*

1/2 RC *Sl 1 to cn, hold to front, p2; k1 from cn*

SB, 1/2 LC

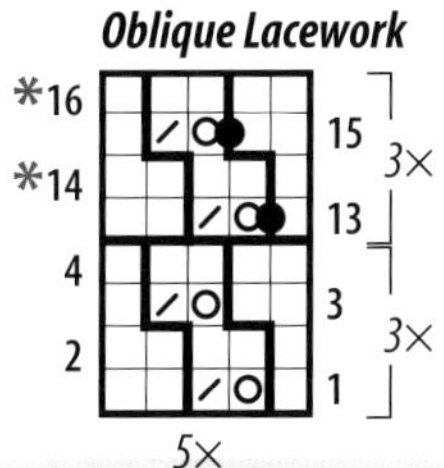

* On Rows 14 and 16, place point of right needle ABOVE bead (if present) when purling the stitch.

Oblique Lacework *MULTIPLE OF 2 + 1*

Here's another stitch pattern that reads as knitting on the bias, but this pattern is more open. Sliding a bead up before a yarn-over is a great technique for lace knitting, where yarn-overs abound. On occasion a bead may get stuck in a higher position than the others, but is easily moved down with a little help from the knitter.

Although this stitch pattern is ordinarily a multiple of 2, an additional stitch makes for neater edges when beads are added.

With beading needle, string 30 beads. Cast on 13.

Without beads

Row 1 (RS) K1, **[yo, k2tog]** 5 times, k2.

Row 2 Purl.

Row 3 K2, **[yo, k2tog]** 5 times, k1.

Row 4 Purl.

Rows 5–12 Repeat Rows 1–4.

With beads

Row 13 (RS) K1, **[SB, yo, k2tog]** 5 times, k2.

Row 14 With all beads facing you, and placing point of right needle ABOVE the bead, purl all stitches.

Row 15 K2, **[SB, yo, k2tog]** 5 times, k1.

Row 16 Repeat Row 14.

Rows 17–24 Repeat Rows 13–16.

Trellis *MULTIPLE OF 6*

It seems to me that this stitch was created with bead knitting in mind. Tucking a bead between the purl stitches inside the honeycomb of the knit-stitch trellis makes this pattern come alive. The instructions make it appear more complex than it is. It's actually easy and lots of fun to knit.

With beading needle, string 49 beads. Cast on 24.

Without beads

Rows 1, 3 (RS) **[P2, k2, p2]** 4 times.

Rows 2, 4 **[K2, p2, k2]** 4 times.

Row 5 **[1/2 RC, 1/2 LC]** 4 times.

Rows 6, 8, 10 **[P1, k4, p1]** 4 times.

Rows 7, 9 **[K1, p4, k1]** 4 times.

Row 11 **[1/2 LC, 1/2 RC]** 4 times.

Row 12 Repeat Row 2.

Rows 13–16 Repeat Rows 1–4.

With beads

Row 17 **[1/2 RC, SB, 1/2 LC]** 4 times.

Row 18 **[P1, k1, SB, k2, SB, k1, p1]** 4 times.

Row 19 **[K1, p2, SB, p2, k1]** 4 times.

Rows 20–21 Repeat Rows 18–19.

Row 22 **[P1, k4, p1]** 4 times.

Row 23 **[1/2 LC, 1/2 RC, SB]** 4 times, end last repeat without SB.

Row 24 K2, p1, **[p1, k1, SB, k2, SB, k1, p1]** 3 times, p1, k2.

Row 25 P2, k1, **[k1, p2, SB, p2, k1]** 3 times, k1, p2.

Rows 26–27 Repeat Rows 24–25.

Row 28 **[K2, p2, k2]** 4 times.

Last row Repeat Row 5.

Stitch pattern embellishment

TECH TRIALS

Seeded Rib with Bead Weaving

MULTIPLE OF 4 + 1

I recognize that bead knitting with pre-strung beads is not for everyone. And not everyone has the patience to apply beads with a crochet hook along the way. So here is a way to create a bead-knit look with no bead knitting whatsoever. This Seeded Rib pattern creates alternate rows of knit and purl stitches on either side of a column of knits, a perfect little pathway to weave beads into a knit fabric. This is not the only pattern that can be woven in this way, but it sure is a great one! Check out 4 possible ways to weave added interest into this pattern with a high-contrast metallic yarn and beads.

Although this stitch pattern is a multiple of 4, an additional stitch makes for neater edges when beads are added.

Cast on 17.

Row 1 (RS) K2, **[p1, k3]** 3 times, p1, k2.

Row 2 **[P1, k3]** 4 times, p1.

Rows 3–26 Repeat Rows 1–2.

Seeded Rib

2 · 1 · 13× · 4X

With this pattern stitch, there are columns of knit stitches (the peaks) and columns of purl stitches (the troughs), with columns of seed stitch on either side of them. It is these vertical columns of alternate purl stitches through which fiber and/or beads are woven using a tapestry or beading needle. The Bead Weaving chart shows the 4 examples.

Bead weaving

top of photo, right to left

With metallic thread (A)

With metallic thread, with beads in every other space (B)

With yarn, with beads in every other space, alternately on left and right seed-stitch column (C)

With yarn and beads in every space on seed-stitch columns (D)

Bead Weaving

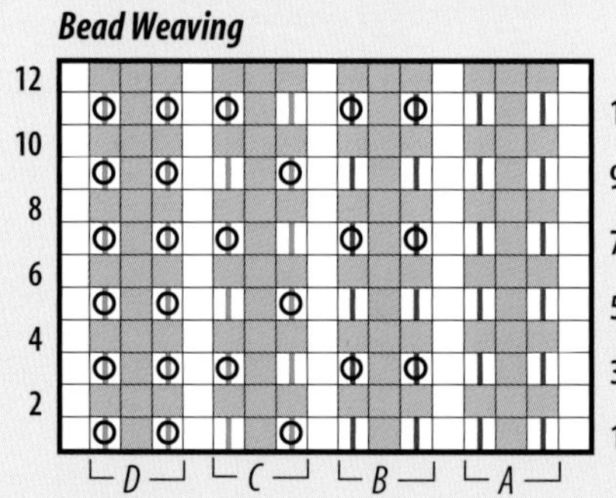

Stitch key

- *Knit on RS, purl on WS*
- *Purl on RS, knit on WS*

Weaving key

- *Bead woven over RS of knit stitch*
- *Metallic thread woven on RS of knit stitch*
- *Yarn woven on RS of knit stitch*

After knitting, weave yarn or metallic thread along a column of stitches: over the knits and under the purls, weaving through beads where shown

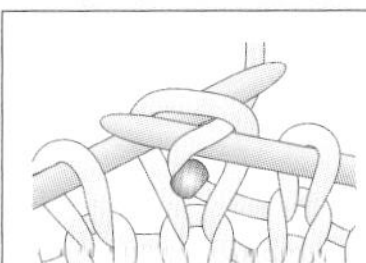

KBL Knit bead through stitch with standard wrap. On next row, purl stitch through back loop.

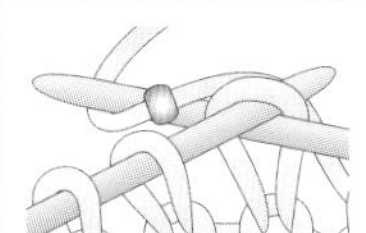

KBR Knit bead through stitch with reverse wrap. On next row, purl stitch in front loop — stitch twists because of reverse wrap.

Garter Ridge *MULTIPLE OF 2 + 1*

Beads could easily be placed between the purl stitches on the garter ridges of this pattern, but in this sample I've chosen to knit beads through the knit stitches between the ridges. If you look carefully, you'll notice that in alternate beaded rows the beads slant on the diagonal in opposite directions. This may not always be easily noticeable on a finished garment, but there are definitely places where the ability to alter the slant of a knit-in bead can highlight a stitch pattern or shaping technique. This sample provides an opportunity to practice the techniques that force the beads onto one or the other of the 2 arms of the V-shaped knit stitch.

With beading needle, string 24 beads. Cast on 17.

Without beads

Rows 1–5 Work stockinette, beginning with a knit row.
Row 6 (WS) Knit.
Rows 7–18 Repeat Rows 1–6.

With beads

Row 19 Knit.
Row 20 Purl.
Row 21 K1, **[KBL, k1]** 8 times.
Row 22 Purl (purling stitches with beads on them through back loop (tbl), with beads to the RS of work, and the point of the right needle entering the stitch ABOVE the bead). Beads will rest on the LEFT arm of the knit stitch.
Rows 23–25 Knit.
Row 26 Purl.
Row 27 K1, **[KBR, k1]** 8 times.
Row 28 Purl (purling stitches with beads to the RS of work; stitch twists because of reverse wrap). Beads will rest on the RIGHT arm of the knit stitch.
Rows 29–30 Knit.
Rows 31–36 Repeat Rows 19–24.

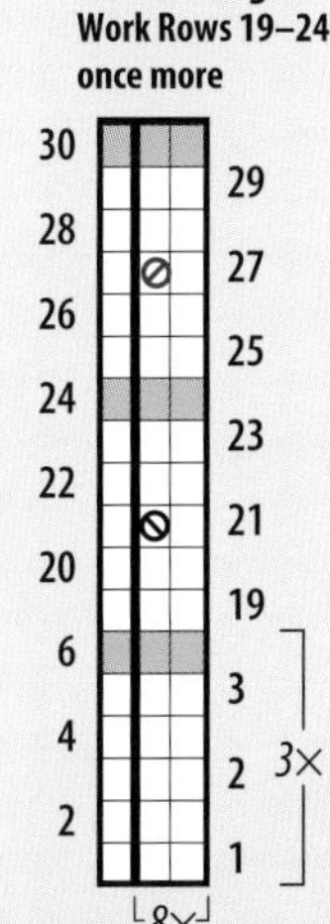

KBL with standard wrap. On next row, purl stitch tbl with bead to RS of work.

KBR with reverse wrap. On next row, purl stitch with bead to RS of work; stitch twists because of reverse wrap.

K3, P3 Rib *MULTIPLE OF 6 + 3*

Once again, the more obvious choice might be to place beads between the purl stitches of a rib, but in this sample beads are worked through the knit stitches of the rib, creating a slightly zig-zagged pattern that contrasts interestingly with the otherwise straight lines of the ribbing.

With beading needle, string 18 beads. Cast on 21.

Without beads

Row 1 (RS) P3, **[k3, p3]** 3 times.
Row 2 **[K3, p3]** 3 times, k3.
Rows 2–12 Repeat Rows 1–2.

With beads

Row 13 P3, **[k1, KBL, k1, p3]** 3 times.
Row 14 **[K3, p3]** 3 times, k3 (purling stitches with beads on them tbl, with beads to the RS of work, and the point of the right needle entering the stitch ABOVE the bead). Beads will rest on the LEFT arm of the knit stitch.
Row 15 P3, **[k1, KBR, k1, p3]** 3 times.
Row 16 **[K3, p3]** 3 times, k3 (purling stitches with beads to the RS of work; stitch twists because of reverse wrap). Beads will rest on the RIGHT arm of the knit stitch.
Rows 17–24 Repeat Rows 13–16.

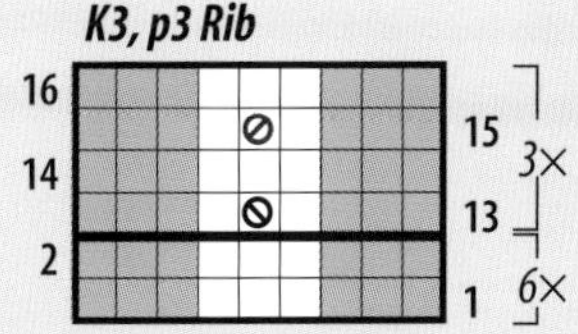

Color it yours

Color it yours

When you start to explore the inclusion of beads in stitch patterns other than stockinette, a whole world of possibilities opens up. I really like this easy stitch pattern and how the beads peek out of the spaces created by the yarn-overs. This lovely, smooth cotton yarn from Isager is great for bead knitting and comes in many wonderful colors. The color-blocked design allows you to combine your personal favorites. After a quick look, you might assume that the scarf was worked on the bias. Not so. The stitch pattern skews the knitted fabric. I didn't anticipate this effect when I started, but I love the result!

OBLIQUE LACE

Row 1 (RS) K2, **[SB, yo, k2tog]** 6 times, k1.
Row 2 With all beads facing you and placing point of right needle ABOVE the bead, purl all stitches.
Row 3 K3, **[SB, yo, k2tog]** 5 times, k2.
Row 4 Repeat Row 2.

TRANSITION ROWS

Rows 1–3 With current color and next color held together, knit.
Row 4 Cut current color; with next color, purl.

Oblique Lace

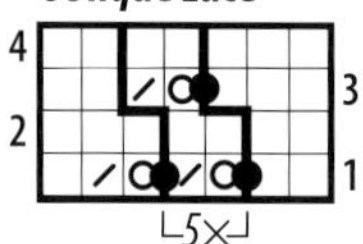

Stitch key

☐ *Knit on RS, purl on WS (placing point of right needle ABOVE bead, if present)*
☐ *K2tog*
☐ *SB, yo*

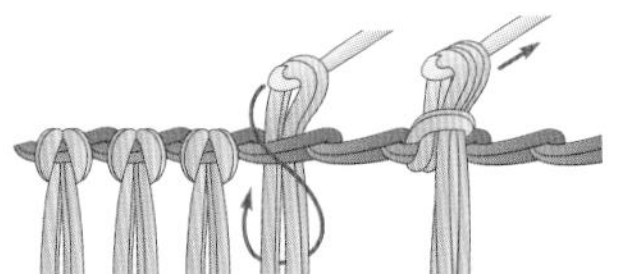

ATTACHING FRINGE

1 Insert crochet hook from wrong side of work through a stitch at edge. Draw center of strands through, forming a loop.

2 Draw ends through loop.

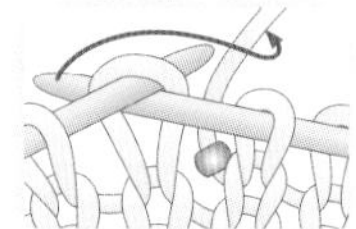

SB Slide bead close to last stitch worked.

Prepare

With beading needle, string each color of yarn with approximately 150 beads. Assign each color a number from 1–5.

Knit

With Color 1, cast on 15.
Work 2 rows in stockinette. Work Oblique Lace to desired length of color block, end with Row 4.
Work Transition Rows with Colors 1 and 2:
With Color 2, work Oblique Lace to desired length.
Work Transition Rows with Colors 2 and 3.
Continue as established until all 5 colors have been used, then repeat color sequence. Work 2 rows in stockinette. Bind off.

Finish

Fringe Using a variety of colors, cut sixteen 12" lengths. Attach 8 strands to each end of scarf.
Stop-bead fringe With beading needle, string a bead onto a piece of fringe; secure by threading needle through bead a second time. Add as many beads as desired onto each piece of fringe.

Stop Bead

gauge

7 stitches and 8 rows = 1" over Oblique Lace
finished size 2" by 67"

yarn

fine weight
40 yds each 2 ply Egyptian cotton, shown in 5 colors

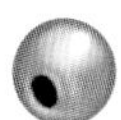

beads

1075 size 6º Japanese glass seed beads

needles

3.5mm/US4

and...

beading needle
3.5mm/E crochet hook

NOTES: easy +

See page 160 for knitting abbreviations and techniques, and page 2 for beading basics.

In this color-blocked design, the number of colors, the order of the colors, and the length of each block are up to the individual knitter.

Alter block lengths as desired. Before starting each new color, make sure sufficient beads to work the color block remain on the yarn and, if not, string additional beads.

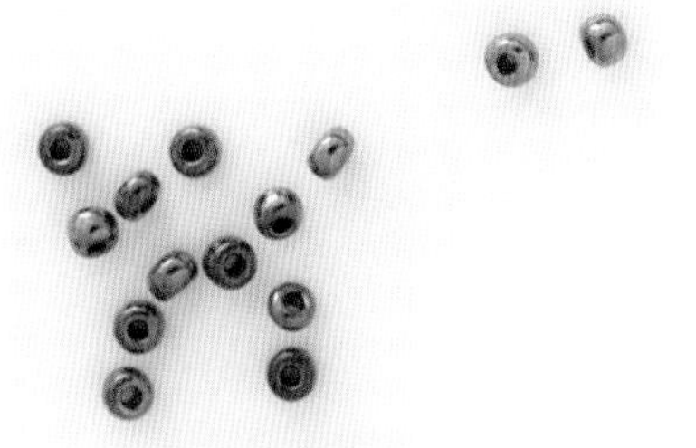

MIYUKI Size 6º glass seed beads
1006 in 462 Metallic Gold Iris

ISAGER Bomuld
40 yds each in 1 Orange, 2 Bright Green, 5 Golden Yellow, 9 Light Turquoise, AND 13 Gray Green

WHAT IF...

Consider wearing this lightweight scarf in place of a necklace or as a belt.

You don't have to place beads in every yarn-over space. Try a different pattern placement, perhaps working them into every other row. Or place a bead whenever the spirit moves you and see what emerges.

It's elementary

It's elementary

These 2 projects are about as far from serious as you can get and are designed for anyone with a sense of humor about accessories. I wanted to demonstrate a few ways to add beads and some great sequins to two popular stitch patterns that are uniquely suited to the task at hand. The space between 2 purl stitches is the perfect place for a bead, and Double Moss stitch alternates 2 purls with 2 knits on every row. It's a bead knitter's paradise! Double Seed stitch staggers knit stitches every other row, a perfect place to add sequins while knitting — no pre-stringing.

The child's version is worked with primary colors, just right for an elementary-school-aged wearer. And the length is adjustable, so all the work done to create these suspenders isn't quickly outgrown. Note that the beads are worked only into the front of the suspenders, so on the rare occasion you can get a child of this age to sit in a chair, there are no beads on the back to be an annoyance.

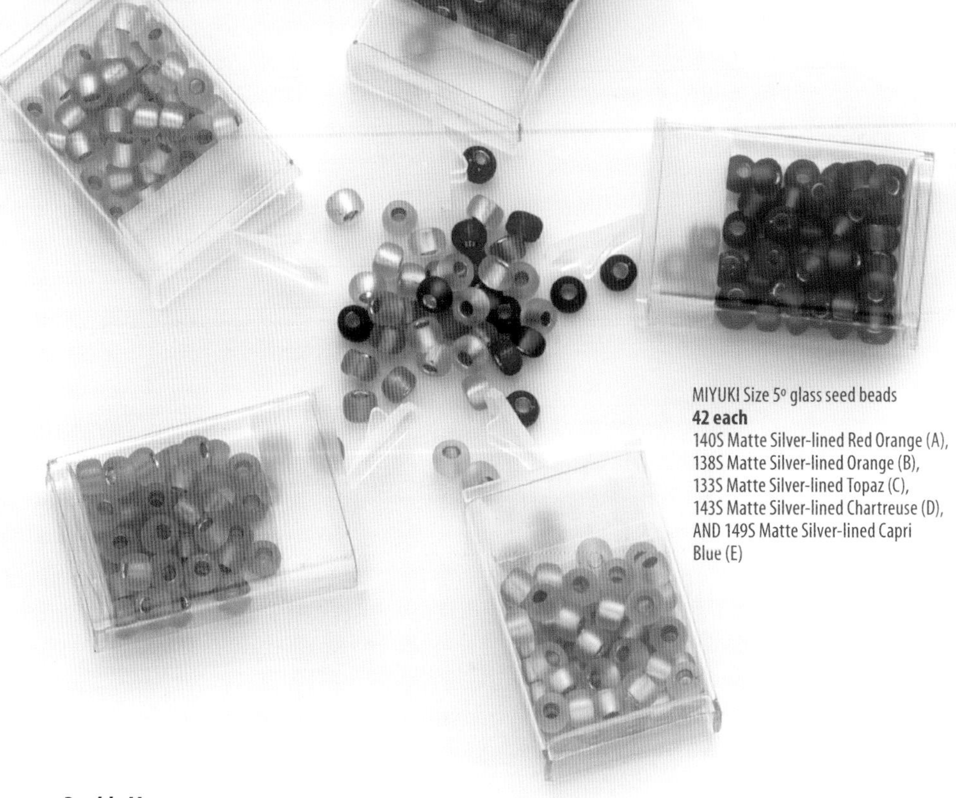

MIYUKI Size 5° glass seed beads
42 each
140S Matte Silver-lined Red Orange (A), 138S Matte Silver-lined Orange (B), 133S Matte Silver-lined Topaz (C), 143S Matte Silver-lined Chartreuse (D), AND 149S Matte Silver-lined Capri Blue (E)

Double Moss

4 3 2 1

6 stitches

DOUBLE MOSS

Row 1 (RS) P1, SB, p1, k2, p1, SB, p1.
Row 2 K2, p2, k2.
Row 3 K2, p1, SB, p1, k2.
Row 4 P2, k2, p2.

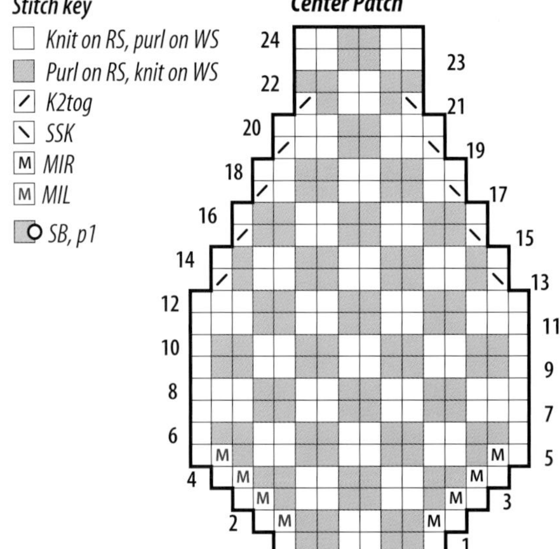

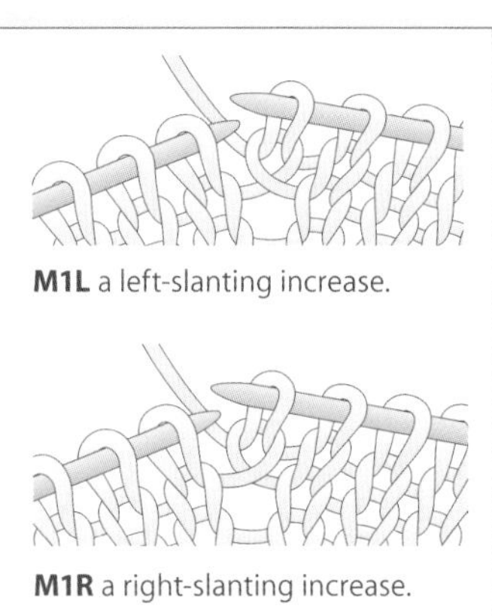

M1L a left-slanting increase.

M1R a right-slanting increase.

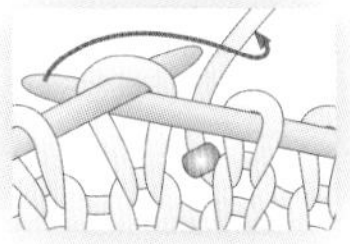

SB Slide bead close to last stitch worked.

LION BRAND YARNS Incredible
75 yds in 203 City Lights

Prepare

Front straps

String beads for Right Strap, complete Right Strap, then string beads for Left Strap.

Right Strap With beading needle, string **[3A, 3B, 3C, 3D, 3E]** 7 times.

Left Strap With beading needle, string **[3E, 3D, 3C, 3B, 3A]** 7 times.

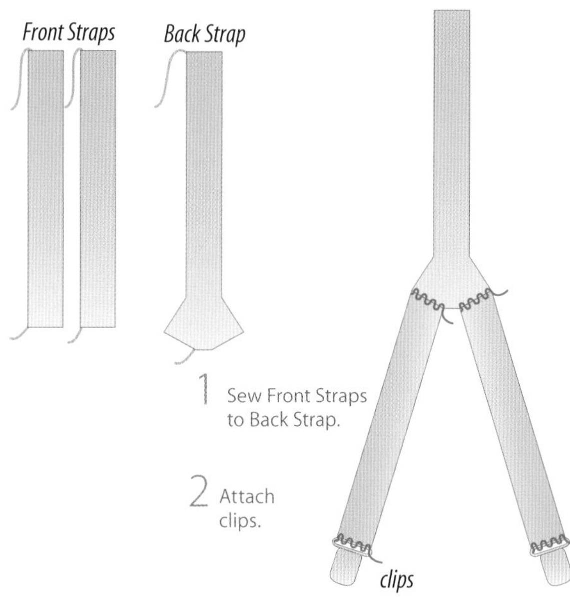

Front Straps
Back Strap
1 Sew Front Straps to Back Strap.
2 Attach clips.
clips

Knit

Front Straps *MAKE 2*

Leaving a 12" tail, cast on 6. Work Double Moss chart until all beads are placed — 140 rows. Continue working in Double Moss chart, without beads, for 56 more rows. Bind off.

Center Patch and Back Strap

Cast on 8. Work Center Patch chart. Continue in Double Moss over 6 stitches for approximately 11". Bind off, leaving a 12" tail.

Finish

1 Using bind-off tails, stitch bound-off edges of Front Straps to diagonal tops of Center Patch.

2 Using cast-on tails, stitch cast-on edges of Front Straps to suspender clips.

3 Using strong sewing thread and sewing needle, stitch 5½" of fuzzy Velcro strip to WS of Back Strap, below Center Patch. Stitch ½" of loopy Velcro strip to bottom of WS of Back Strap.

4 Thread Back Strap through suspender clip, then connect the Velcro strips. The Velcro allows the length of the suspenders to be adjusted.

gauge

8 stitches and 10 rows = 1"
finished size 1" wide, adjustable length

yarn

medium weight
75 yds ribbon yarn

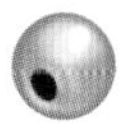

beads

250 size 5º Japanese glass seed beads, shown in 5 colors

needles

3.75mm/US5

and…

beading needle
tapestry needle
strong sewing thread
sewing needle
8" length of tape Velcro, 1" wide
3 suspender clips

NOTES: easy +

See page 160 for knitting abbreviations and techniques, and page 2 for beading basics.

These suspenders are sized for an elementary-school-aged child. They should not be made for a baby or toddler, or for any child for whom a beaded accessory would be a choking hazard.

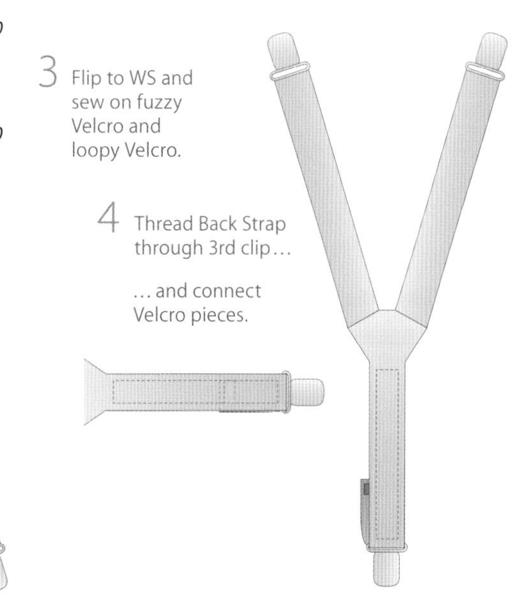

loopy Velcro ½"
fuzzy Velcro 5½"
3 Flip to WS and sew on fuzzy Velcro and loopy Velcro.
4 Thread Back Strap through 3rd clip…
… and connect Velcro pieces.

WHAT IF…

While I chose to pattern the beads on the child's suspenders and to randomly distribute the colors of the spangles on the grown-up version, consider doing the reverse. Sprinkle the primary-color beads on the multicolor ribbon yarn, and place the spangles in a pattern of your choosing.

Disco 'spenders

I named the more grown-up version of these suspenders after the reflective spangles that cover them. I know I'm dating myself, but aren't they just a bit reminiscent of a disco ball? One day, I would love to see a fashion-forward 20-something wearing these suspenders over a great T-shirt and clipped to a fabulous pair of black designer jeans! Party!!

210 20mm (¾") Paillettes in Red, Silver, AND Black

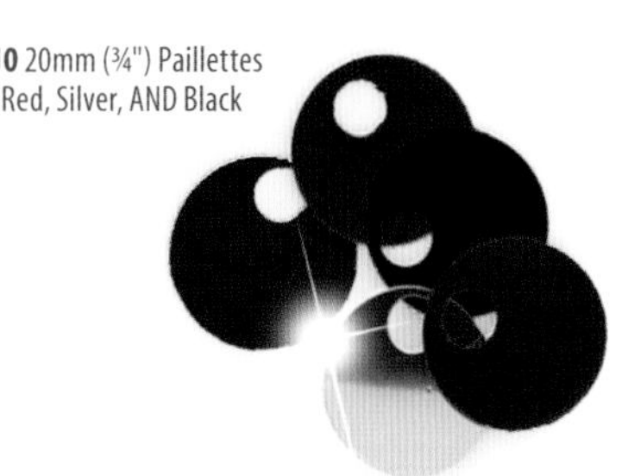

KNIT PAILLETTE

Place the paillette on right needle and knit next stitch, making sure to draw new stitch through paillette (see drawings, below).

Note While Double Seed with Paillettes shows all possible places to knit-in a paillette, you can also work as in the sample shown, placing as many or as few as you want.

DOUBLE SEED

Row 1 (RS) **[K1, p1]** 3 times, k1.
Rows 2–3 **[P1, k1]** 3 times, p1.
Row 4 **[K1, p1]** 3 times, k1.

DOUBLE SEED WITH PAILLETTES

Row 1 (RS) **[P1, k1 OR knit paillette]** 3 times, p1.
Row 2 **[K1, p1]** 3 times, k1.
Row 3 K1, **[p1, k1 OR knit paillette]** twice, p1, k1.
Row 4 **[P1, k1]** 3 times, p1.

Stitch key
- *Knit on RS, purl on WS*
- *Purl on RS, knit on WS*
- *Knit OR knit paillette*

Double Seed
2-st repeat

Double Seed with Paillettes
7 stitches

SCHULANA Damasco
100 yds in 10 Black

Straps *MAKE 2*

Leaving a 12" tail, cast on 7.
Work Double Seed for 10 rows, end with Row 2 of pattern.
Placing paillettes as desired (see third note), work Double Seed with Paillettes for 78 rows, end with Row 2 of pattern.
Work Double Seed for 112 rows or to desired length. Bind off, leaving a 12" tail.

Finish

With tapestry needle and cast-on tail, and using an overcast stitch, attach cast-on edge to a suspender clip. Using strong sewing thread and sewing needle, stitch 5½" of fuzzy Velcro strip to WS of strap, starting 12" above bound-off edge. Stitch ½" of loopy Velcro strip to WS of strap just above bound-off edge (see page 81, drawings 3 and 4). Thread strap through clip, then connect the Velcro strips. The Velcro allows the length of the suspenders to be adjusted. Weave in ends.
Repeat for other strap.

WHAT IF...

If your disco days have passed you by (or were never there at all), but these suspenders still seem like fun, here are a few alternatives.

Use a matte sequin or knit in your favorite Size 5º beads using the Double Moss pattern from It's Elementary.

Make a plain knit pair for the fashion forward, suit-wearing man in your life or, using a lighter weight yarn with beads or smaller sequins, make the suspenders shorter and attach them to a tube top for your favorite young girl.

gauge
7 stitches and 10 rows = 1"
finished size 1" wide, adjustable length

yarn
light weight
100 yds tightly twisted cotton

beads
210 20mm (¾") paillettes, shown in 3 colors

needles
2.75mm/US2

and ...
tapestry needle
strong sewing thread
sewing needle
11" length of tape Velcro, 1" wide
4 suspender clips

NOTES: easy

See page 160 for knitting abbreviations and techniques, and page 2 for beading basics.

These suspenders are worked as 2 separate straps that can either be worn in either a parallel fashion or crisscrossed in the back.

Paillettes are applied while knitting (not strung in advance) in random placement and color order to the front straps, from the waist to the middle of the shoulder. Some paillettes overlap, others don't. The back straps are worked in the pattern stitch without paillettes.

Infinity I

Infinity I

These 2 closely related projects illustrate a great way to achieve a bead-knit look without actually knitting beads into the fabric. Yet another interesting stitch pattern, Seeded Rib, makes this possible. I first used this idea in a pattern for a small purse and have loved it ever since. After the knitting is completed, the weaving fiber is passed underneath the alternate-row purl bumps of the stitch pattern, trapping a bead between each set of purl stitches. Fully beaded and knotted-bead strands complete the look. When the strands are connected—completing the round—a single twist turns each necklace into a Moebius strip long enough to fit over the head, so no clasp is required. To my eye, the rougher, unfinished edges of the flat version appear almost tribal, while the tubular version, completely surrounded by smooth, fully beaded strings, offers a more contemporary look. Different strokes….

Stitch key

- ☐ *Knit on RS, purl on WS*
- ▒ *Purl on RS, knit on WS*

Weaving key

— *Weave CC and filament along a column of stitches: over the knit stitch, through a bead, and under a purl stitch*

Bead Color key

- *A*
- *B*
- *C*
- *D*
- *E*
- *F*

1 WEAVING BEADS
Weave colored beads, CC, and filament through Seeded Rib, leaving 24" tail at cast-on and 8" tail at bind-off. See Weaving key.

2 FILAMENT TAILS
String 24" filament tails with beads and attach to base of 8" tails as shown.

3 CC TAILS
String 24" CC tails with groups of 1, 2, 3, or 4 beads and attach to base of 8" tails as shown.

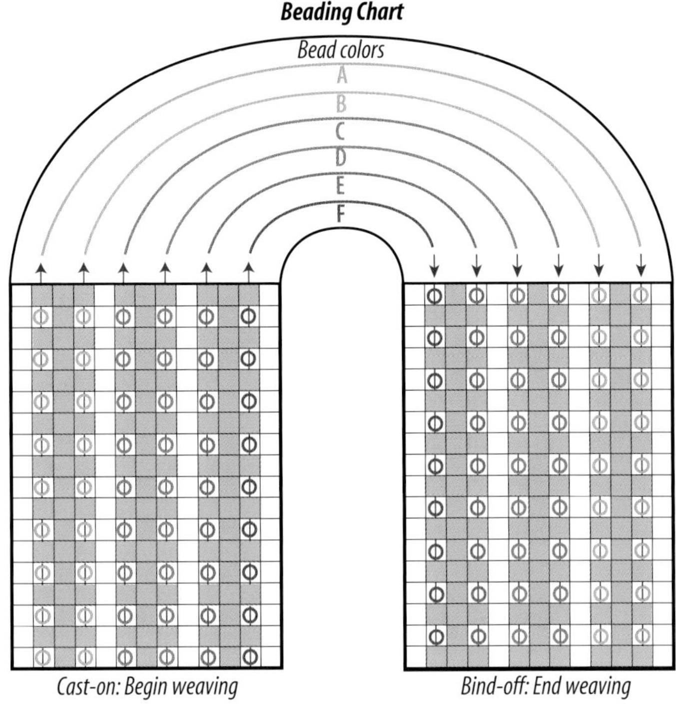

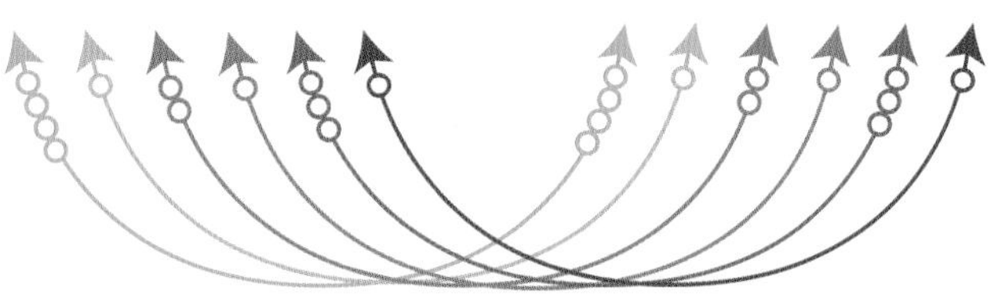

MIYUKI Size 8º glass seed beads
362 each in 459 Metallic Olive (A) AND 187 Copper Plated (D)

TOHO Size 8º glass seed beads
362 each in 559 Galvanized Light Gold (B), 223 Dark Gold Bronze Metallic (C), 552 PF Light Dusty Rose (E), AND 222 Dark Copper (F)

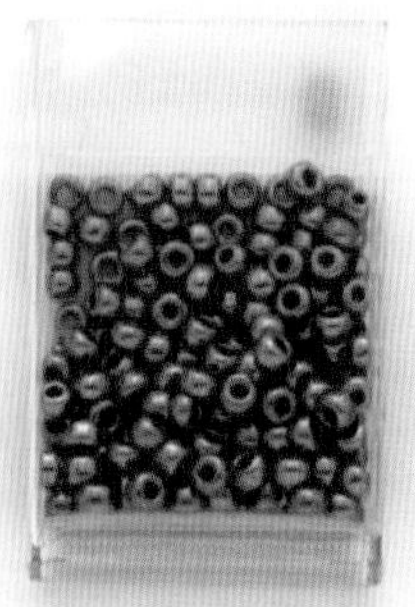

JUST OUR YARN Aziza
75 yds (MC)

INFINITY I

SEEDED RIB
Row 1 (RS) K2, **[p1, k3]** twice, p1.
Row 2 **[P1, k3]** 3 times, p1.
Repeat Rows 1–2.

A bead-wrapped ring provides a completely different way to wear this necklace; see how on page 57.

gauge

woven strap 1" × 20"
finished length 36"

yarn

super fine weight
75 yds tencel yarn
10 yds metallic yarn

beads

2280 size 8º Japanese glass seed beads, shown in 6 colors

needles

2mm/US0

and…

big-eye beading needle
tapestry needle
WildFire beading filament, green

Knit

With MC, cast on 13. Work in Seeded Rib for 24" or desired length. Bind off in pattern. Cut yarn and weave in tails.

Weave beads

1 Changing color as shown in Beading chart, weave beads through each seed-stitch column as follows: Working directly from the spool or ball, thread weaving needle with CC and monofilament. With RS facing, bring needle from WS between purl bumps at left side of cast-on edge, **[thread 1 bead on needle, weave under purl bump]** along seed-stitch column, ending at bound-off edge. For ease in working, pull 8–12" of threads through first bead; when you need additional length, lay the piece flat and gently pull 8–12" more. When finished, adjust tension of weaving threads. Cut yarns and secure, leaving 24" tails at cast-on edge and 8" tails at bound-off edge.

String beads and finish

2 With beading needle, string each 24" filament tail with 14" of beads to match the corresponding bead-woven row. Use a Stop Bead to temporarily hold beads on each tail.

When all the filament tails have been strung, remove Stop Beads one at a time and knot the filament strand to the 8" filament tail at the opposite side of the fabric (from a column of different-colored beads) as shown, thus creating a Moebius strip. Weave remaining length into fabric and trim.

3 With beading needle, string each 24" CC tail with 1, 2, 3, or 4 beads, varying the color of the beads along each strand, and placing each bead as a Stop Bead. Knot each knotted-bead CC strand to the 8" CC tail at the opposite side of the fabric as for the fully beaded filament strands. Weave remaining length into fabric and trim.

Stop Bead

NOTES: intermediate

See page 160 for knitting abbreviations and techniques, and page 2 for beading basics.

The beads are woven into the fabric, creating a bead-knit look without having to pre-string all those beads!

WHAT IF…

Don't skip these projects because of the number of bead colors that I used. I think a single-color alternative could be very dramatic!

TRENDSETTER YARNS
Toreador
10 yds in 157 Copper (CC)

Infinity II

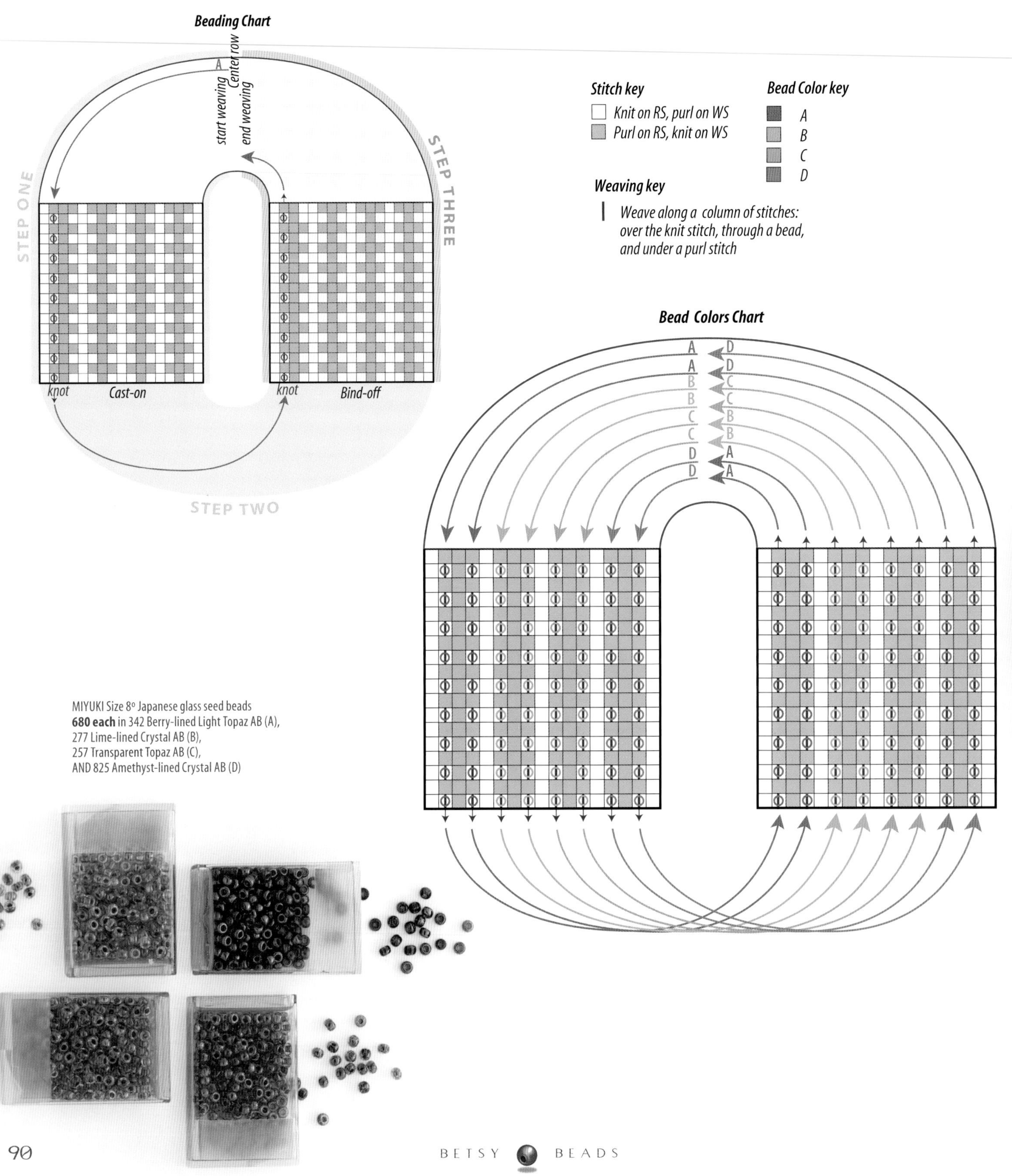

MIYUKI Size 8º Japanese glass seed beads
680 each in 342 Berry-lined Light Topaz AB (A),
277 Lime-lined Crystal AB (B),
257 Transparent Topaz AB (C),
AND 825 Amethyst-lined Crystal AB (D)

SEEDED RIB

Row 1 (RS) K2, **[p1, k3]** 3 times, p1, k2.

Row 2 **[P1, k3]** 4 times, p1.

Repeat Rows 1–2.

Knit

Cast on 17. Work in Seeded Rib for 27" or desired length. Bind off in pattern. Cut yarn and weave in tails.

Weave beads

1 Fold knitted fabric in half and mark the center row. Thread a 3-yd length of yarn in beading needle. With RS facing, leaving a 12" tail, and beginning at center row, **[weave under purl bump, thread 1 bead on needle]** along seed-stitch column to cast-on edge, as shown in Beading Chart. For ease in working, pull 8–12" of yarn through first bead; when you need additional length, lay the piece flat and gently pull 8–12" more.

String beads

2 Adjust tension of weaving yarn; secure by knotting to the WS of the fabric. String remaining length with 12" of beads to match the bead-woven row. Use a Stop Bead to temporarily hold beads on tail. Repeat Steps 1 and 2 for each seed-stitch column, changing bead colors as shown.

Weave beads

3 When all the yarn lengths have been strung, remove Stop Beads one at a time, adjust tension, and secure to the WS of the bound-off edge as shown in Bead Colors chart. Bring yarn through to the RS and continue bead weaving back to the center row. When all columns have been bead woven, adjust tension and knot each length to the adjacent 12" tail at the center row. Weave in tails.

Finish

With tapestry needle, yarn, and using mattress stitch, join side edges of bead-woven fabric, creating a tube. Secure and weave in tails.

The bead-wrapped ring shown on page 57 provides a completely different way to wear this necklace.

gauge

Beaded tube ½" × 28"
finished length 40"

yarn

super fine weight
75 yds tencel yarn

beads

2860 size 8° Japanese glass seed beads, shown in 4 colors

needles

2mm/US0

and...

big-eye beading needle
tapestry needle
locking stitch marker

NOTES: intermediate

See page 160 for knitting abbreviations and techniques, and page 2 for beading basics.

The Infinity II is knit as a long, narrow, flat piece that is then bead woven, joined at the ends with beaded strands, and seamed into a tube.

JUST OUR YARN Aziza
75 yds

Faux Louboutin

Faux Louboutin

I am not what anyone would call a fashionista. I like looking through fashion magazines, often for inspiration, but I usually depend on my daughter for personal fashion advice. It was she who first told me about Christian Louboutin shoes, the insanely expensive women's shoes easily recognizable by their signature bright red soles. I LOVE red. It's my power color. It makes me feel energized and happy. The big leather chair I work in is red. If I could have a personal signature color it would be red. So while I originally designed this dressy little bag to show how you can use an all-over bead-knit pattern to paint a design, I couldn't resist making the 'sole' of this little bag red in tribute — to the shoes and to a designer who clearly shares my love of a particularly wonderful color.

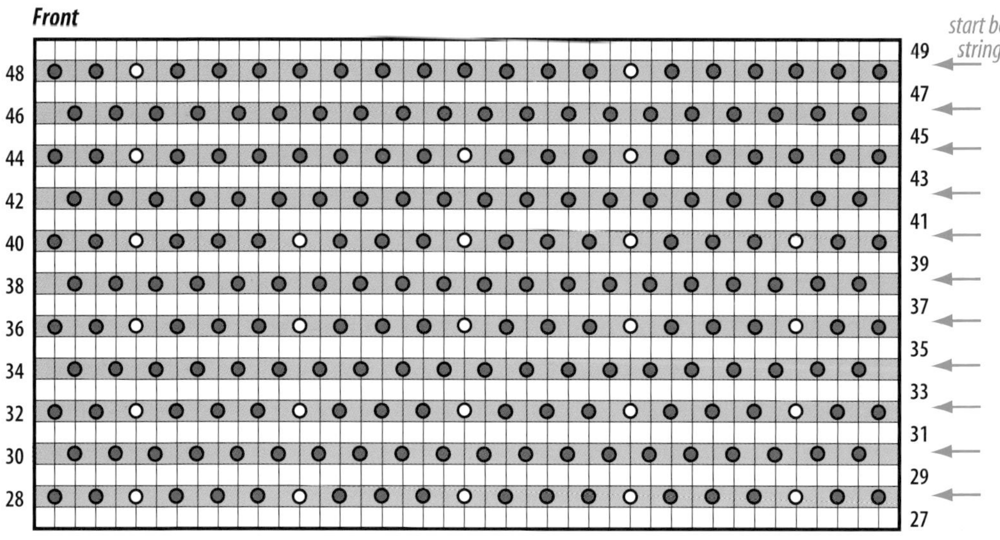

FRONT stringing sequence

start → 6BB, 1AA, 11BB, 1AA, 28BB, 1AA, 3BB, 1AA, 7BB, 1AA, **[24BB, 1AA, (3BB, 1AA) 4×]** 4×, 2BB *end*

FLAP stringing sequence

start → 21AA, 143BB, **[1AA, 1BB]** 10×, **[2AA, 2BB]** 5×, **[1AA, 1BB]** 11×, 1BB, **[2AA, 2BB]** 5×, 1BB, **[1AA, 3BB]** 4×, 1AA, 2BB *end*

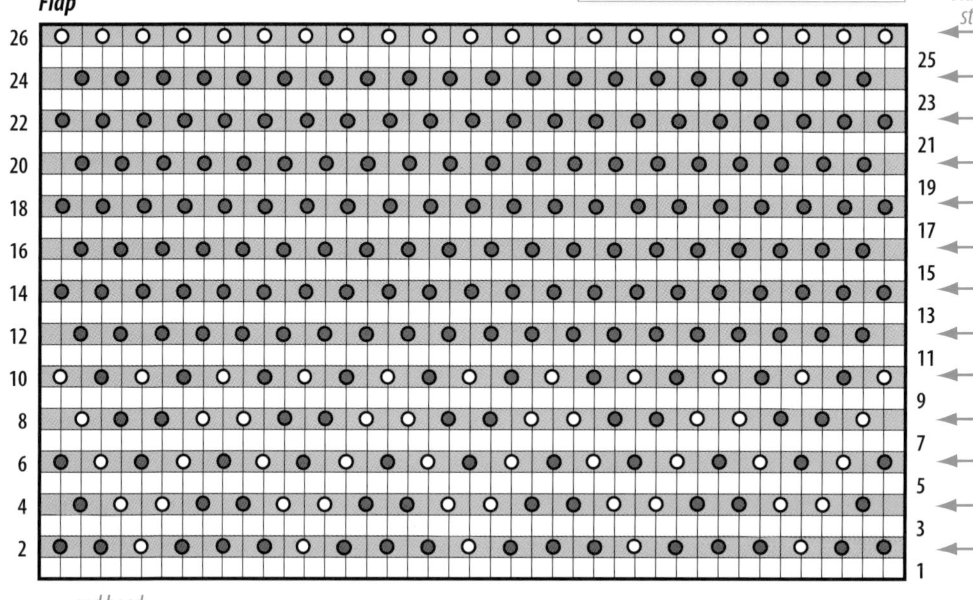

SB Slide bead close to last stitch worked.

Stitch key

- *Knit on RS, purl on WS*
- *Purl on RS, knit on WS*
- *SB, k1*
- *Direction of bead stringing*

Bead key

- ○ *AA*
- ● *BB*

SCHULANA Damasco
150 yds in 10 Black (B)
50 yds in 20 Red (A)

MIYUKI Size 5º glass seed beads
247 in 131S Silver-lined Crystal (AA)
401 in 401F Matte Black (BB)

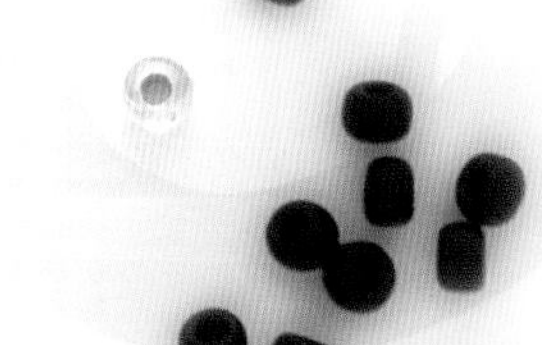

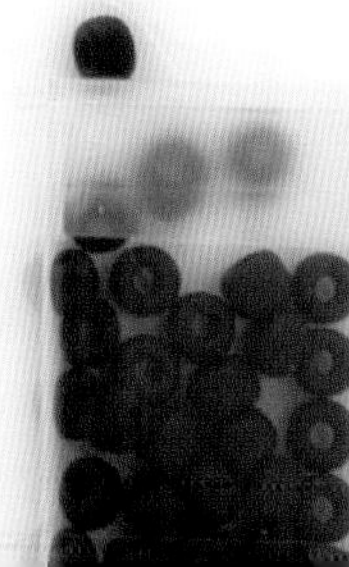

Back and Flap

Prepare With beading needle, string beads on B according to Stringing Sequence or Flap chart.

Knit With B, cast on 42.

Rows 1–26 Work Flap chart.

Rows 27–75 Knit.

Bind off. Cut yarn.

Front

Prepare With beading needle, string beads on B according to Stringing Sequence or Front chart.

Knit With B, cast on 42.

Rows 1–26 Knit.

Rows 27–49 Work Front chart.

Bind off. Cut yarn.

Gusset

1 With B, cast on 6.

Rows 1–39 Work in stockinette, starting with a knit row.

Row 40: Turning ridge Knit.

Rows 41–98 With A, work in stockinette.

Row 99 With B, knit.

Row 100: Turning ridge Knit.

Rows 101–138 Work in stockinette.

Bind off. Cut yarn.

Finish

2a, 2b With tapestry needle and B, and using an overcast stitch, sew Gusset to Front and Back as shown. Work 3 overcast stitches into every other knit stitch along the edge of the gusset.

Strap

3a Thread a 1½-yd length of B in beading needle and secure to top back of one end of gusset. String 145 AA beads, secure to top back of opposite end of gusset, and skim needle through edge to front of gusset.

3b String 5 AA beads, skip 5 beads of strap and thread needle back through center 135 beads of strap, string 5 AA beads, attach to front of opposite end of gusset, and skim through edge to back of gusset.

Adjust tension so no yarn shows between beads. Secure and weave in tails.

Line if desired.

1

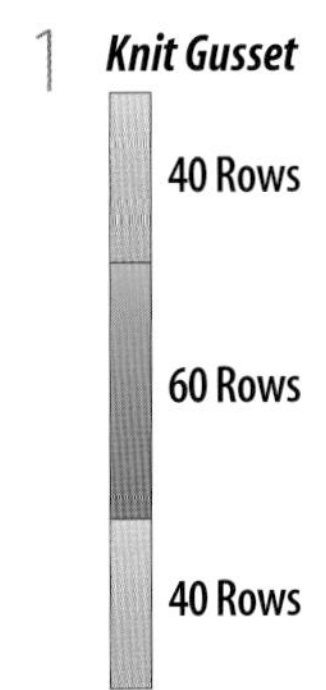

2a

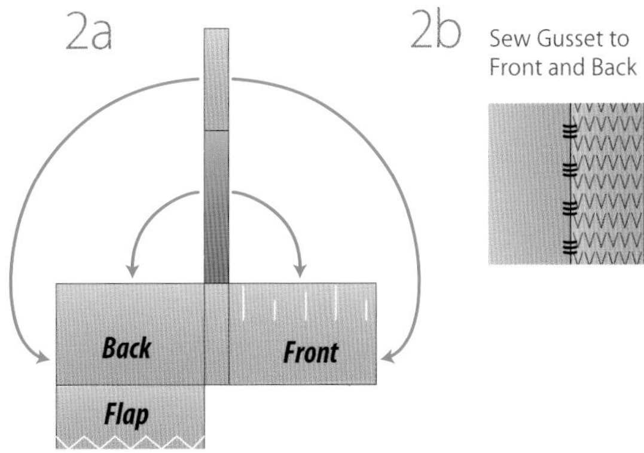

2b Sew Gusset to Front and Back

3a

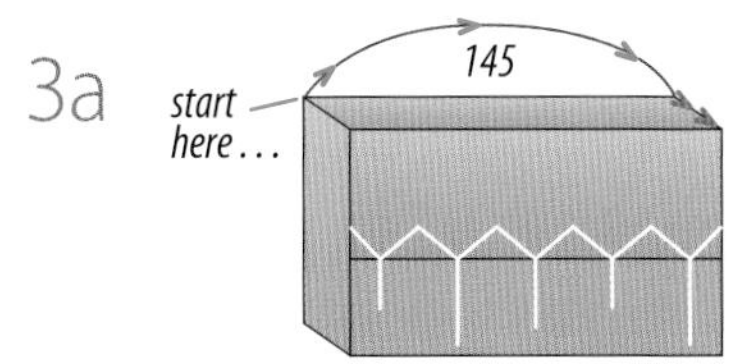

3b

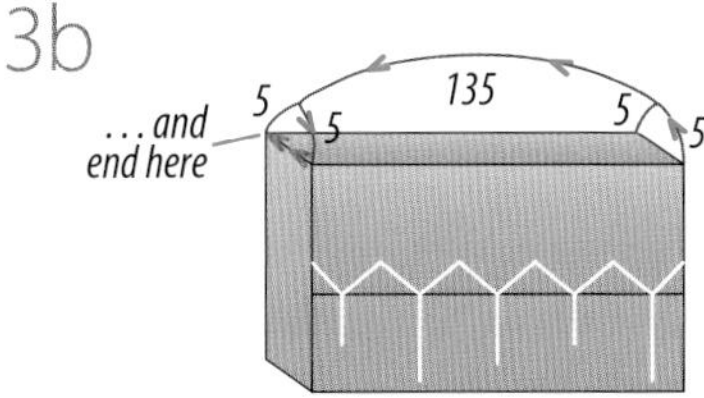

> *Direction of stringing beads on fiber for strap*

> *No beads (skim yarn through top edges of gusset)*

5, 135, 145 *Number of beads*

gauge

5½ stitches and 12 rows (6 ridges) = 1", over garter stitch

finished size 1½" wide, 1" high, and 1" deep

yarn

light weight

200 yds tightly twisted cotton, shown in 2 colors

beads

680 size 5º Japanese glass seed beads, shown in 2 colors

needles

3.5mm/US4

and . . .

beading needle
tapestry needle
optional lining fabric

NOTES: advanced

See page 160 for knitting abbreviations and techniques, and page 2 for beading basics.

Use cable cast-on throughout.

This bag is worked in 3 pieces. The back, with beaded front flap, and the half-beaded front, both in black, are worked entirely in garter. The black and red gusset is worked in garter and stockinette. The pieces are knit separately and then sewn together using an overcast stitch.

WHAT IF...

Of course it is your choice, but this is one project that I would love for you to make exactly as it's shown — at least the first time you make it.

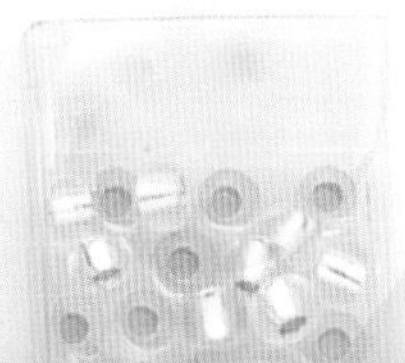

Marge's yarmulke

Marge's yarmulke

This bead-knit yarmulke is a great way to practice the technique of knitting beads through stitches. This project is filled with meaning for me, although not in the way you might expect. Many years ago I took a part-time job in a local knitting store, working for the most versatile craftswoman I've ever known. She saw something in me, and my love for knitting, and invited me to work with her on a project she had been contemplating for years. The idea floating around in her mind was to put together a small book with patterns for knit yarmulkes, the small skull caps worn by Jews all over the world, and she asked me if I could come up with a design or two. (She recognized that I was capable of creative design before I even had a clue.) We were both intrigued because, while we had seen lots of crocheted yarmulkes, we'd never seen an interesting knit one. Sadly, she became ill and passed away before we were able to really get going on this project. Marge, this one's for you.

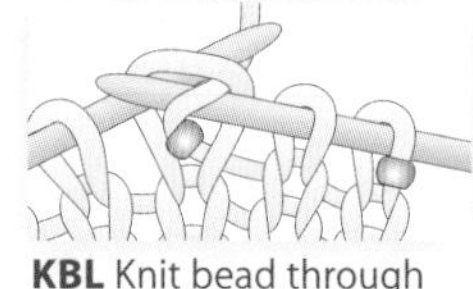

KBL Knit bead through stitch. On next round, knit stitch through back loop.

FONTY Serpentine
100 yds in 932 Royal Blue

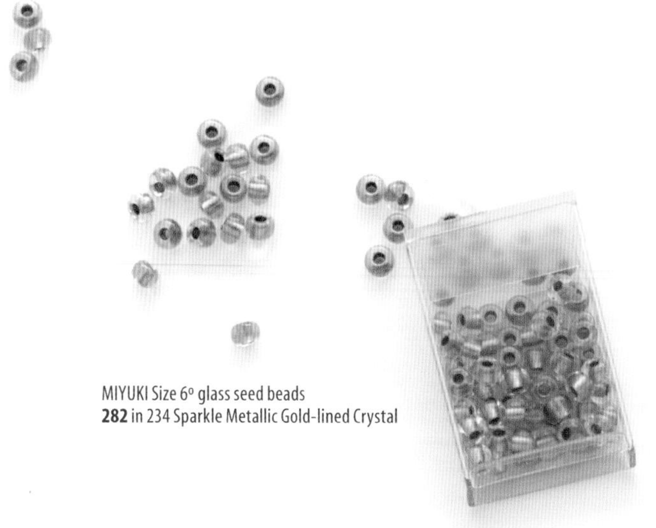

MIYUKI Size 6º glass seed beads
282 in 234 Sparkle Metallic Gold-lined Crystal

Prepare

With beading needle, string 282 beads.

Knit

Cast on 6 and divide evenly onto 3 double-pointed needles, join without twisting, and place marker, to work in the round:

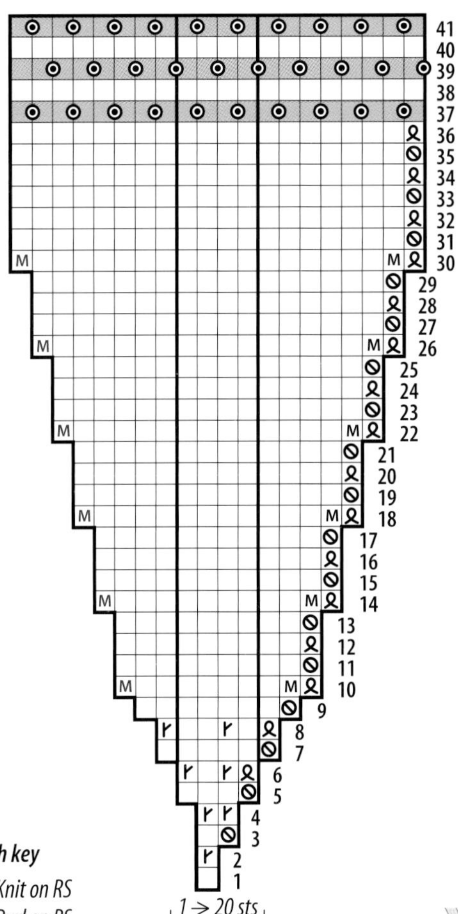

Stitch key

- Knit on RS
- Purl on RS
- SB, p1
- KBL with standard wrap
- Kf&b, knit in front and back of stitch
- MIR
- MIL
- Knit in back loop with bead to RS of work

Round 1 Knit.
Round 2 **[Kf&b]** 6 times — 12 stitches.
Round 3 **[KBL, k]** 6 times.
Round 4 **[Kf&b]** 12 times — 24 stitches.
Round 5 **[KBL, k3, place marker]** 5 times, KBL, k3.
Round 6 **[Ktbl, kf&b, k1, kf&b]** 6 times — 36 stitches.
Odd-numbered rounds 7–35 **[KBL, knit to marker]** 6 times.
Round 8 **[Ktbl, k1, kf&b, k2, kf&b]** 6 times — 48 stitches.
Round 10 **[Ktbl, M1R, k7, M1L]** 6 times — 60 stitches.
Round 12 **[Ktbl, k9]** 6 times.
Round 14 **[Ktbl, M1R, k9, M1L]** 6 times — 72 stitches.
Round 16 **[Ktbl, k11]** 6 times.
Round 18 **[Ktbl, M1R, k11, M1L]** 6 times — 84 stitches.
Round 20 **[Ktbl, k13]** 6 times.
Round 22 **[Ktbl, M1R, k13, M1L]** 6 times — 96 stitches.
Round 24 **[Ktbl, k15]** 6 times.
Round 26 **[Ktbl, M1R, k15, M1L]** 6 times — 108 stitches.
Round 28 **[Ktbl, k17]** 6 times.
Round 30 **[Ktbl, M1R, k17, M1L]** 6 times — 120 stitches.
Rounds 32, 34, 36 **[Ktbl, k19]** 6 times.
Round 37 P1, **[SB, p2]** 59 times, SB, p1.
Rounds 38, 40 Knit.
Round 39 **[SB, p2]** 60 times.
Round 41 Repeat Round 37.
Bind off purlwise.
Cut yarn; weave in tails.

Finish

Block in cool water and shape over an appropriate-sized bowl turned upside down.

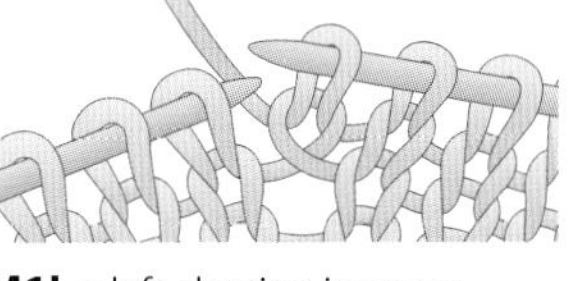

M1L a left-slanting increase.

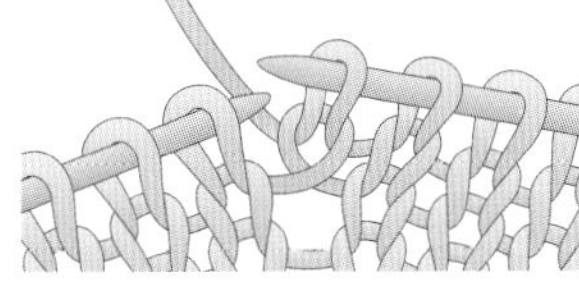

M1R a right-slanting increase.

gauge

8 stitches = 1"
finished circumference 15"

yarn

light weight
100 yds tubular chainette ribbon

beads

300 size 6° Japanese glass seed beads

needles

3.25mm/US3

and...

beading needle
tapestry needle
stitch marker

NOTES: advanced

See page 160 for knitting abbreviations and techniques, and page 2 for beading basics.

WHAT IF...

Because I used a shiny blue ribbon yarn for this project, the finished yarmulke looks a lot like the blue satin ones that are popular in many synagogues. It is also the color used in the Israeli flag. But yarmulkes come in all kinds of colors and materials, and you should feel free to use any color or fiber you like. You can use the pattern's shaping even if you choose not to include the beads. Unlike many flatter yarmulkes, this one should sit securely on your head.

Technically speaking. . .

I was fortunate to have my mother as my first knitting teacher, and not just because she's a very experienced knitter who was always available to fix my mistakes. Of course that was wonderful, but the more important gift was that she insisted I learn how to correct them myself, and taught me how to do it. The crucial part of that process was also the most basic: learning about what I like to call "stitch architecture."

Think about it. What makes a knit stitch a KNIT and a purl stitch a PURL? If you don't understand things as basic as this, how will you ever learn how to count the stitches and rows of all kinds of patterns—even those pesky first and last little knit stitches that disappear around the edges of stockinette fabric? I'll admit it. At first it felt a little like punishment: doing all of that counting, picking up dropped stitches and making sure to return them to the needles in the correct orientation (I can hear some of you thinking, correct orientation?), learning how to drop down several rows to correct a faulty stitch. My mother taught me all of these, and many more technical tricks of the trade that drive you crazy at first. Then the Ah-ha! moment comes when you realize that the understanding of all these nit-picky (knit-picky?) details has the power to set you free as a knitter and, should you choose, as a designer of your own work.

I believe that mastering technique is at the root of all creative endeavor. I have no concrete way of proving this, but I'm pretty sure that even the creators of the most avant-garde, abstract works of art—the ones who make left-brained, concrete-linear-sequential people like me scratch their heads in confusion—are technically well-trained. It really does help to learn the rules before you try and break them. Learning different techniques provides the tools of your trade, and increases the vocabulary you have available to express yourself. What you do with those tools and that vocabulary is your choice. The more techniques you know, the wider your range of choices, and the fewer trips you'll have to make to your local knitting guru to help you get back on track. Taking the time to learn HOW to do what you enjoy is the best investment you can make. The return on that investment can be as simple and rewarding as becoming a completely independent knitter, or as liberating as giving you the confidence to try new things, and the freedom to explore your own creativity.

Thanks Mom!

Bead balls *beads (limited edition)*
Fiber, glass beads, wooden beads
Very fine yarn, small needles, and tiny beads come together in these individually patterned bead balls. So many possibilities here. . .
Technique link: Hard beads

Knit beads

TECH TRIALS

NOTES
See page 160 for knitting abbreviations and techniques, and page 2 for beading basics.

These samples were worked at a gauge of approximately 7 stitches and 9 rows = 1" over stockinette. If your gauge is very different, adjust the stitch and row counts to fit the wooden bead, or use a bead of a different size.

Be warned! Knitting beads is a completely addictive activity. When I first decided to try knitting jewelry, the cords and straps were the easiest and most obvious components to develop—they already looked like the necklaces and bracelets I wanted to make. Beads, the other most common and easily identifiable component of jewelry, were another story. Most knitting is basically flat, constructed in two dimensions. Creating beads involved moving into a third dimension, and that was a challenge. The more I thought about it, the more I realized that creating a knit garment involved turning flat knitting into a form that covers a 3-dimensional shape—the human body. It then became clear that I could make a bead by knitting a small 2-dimensional shape and then wrapping it around an existing 3-dimensional one—a pre-made, lightweight wooden bead!

Hard beads

So that's how it started. Lots of "What ifs…?" and lots of trial and error followed as I found different shapes of wooden beads and experimented with ways to cover them that showed off the materials I wanted to use and allowed what I came to call **wrappers** to seamlessly cover the underlying forms. I've kept a few of those first samples — not a pretty sight. But before long I was able to create both plain-knit and bead-knit wrappers for many different sizes and shapes: round beads, oval beads, rice beads, flat rectangular beads. Once my basic techniques are learned, adapting them to different shapes and sizes is simply a matter of checking gauge and making sample swatches with the yarns and shapes you want to use. There are lots of different ways to accomplish this task. Try a few and see which you like the best.

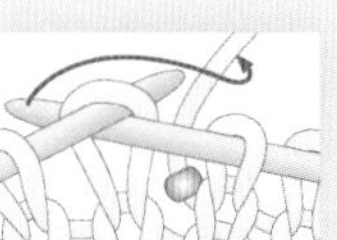

SB Slide bead close to last stitch worked.

WHAT YOU NEED

- Any size 6° beads
- Smooth sock- to DK-weight wool or wool-blend yarn in a solid, light color
- Knitting needles in a size you would normally use for the yarn (usually 3.25–3.75mm/US3–5)
- AND set of 4 double-pointed needles
- Beading needle
- Tapestry needle
- Waste yarn
- Wooden beads, assorted sizes and shapes
- Stitch marker

Plain tubular wrapper, vertical orientation

This stockinette wrapper is worked in the round on double-pointed needles. The completed wrapper is a tube that is slipped over the wooden bead with the hole in the bead running top to bottom in a vertical orientation. The open ends of the tube are gathered around the hole. The bead in the photo shows the knit side of the wrapper facing out, but the wrapper can also be turned inside out to show the purl side.

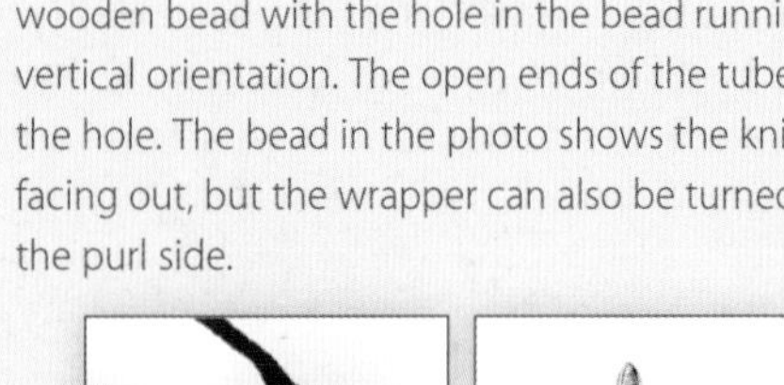

Tubular wrapper

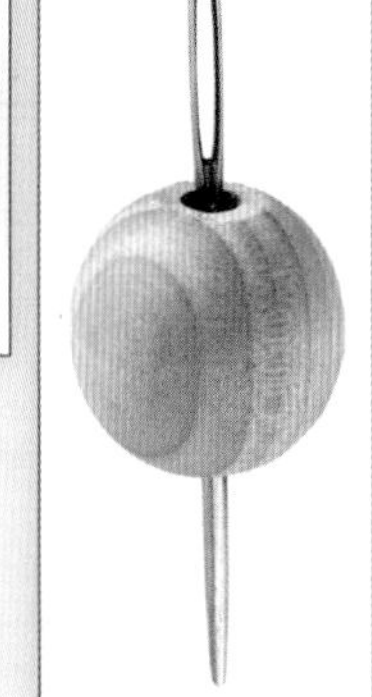

1" wooden bead

Wrapped bead

With double-pointed needle (dpn), and leaving a 12" tail, cast on 21 and divide evenly onto 3 dpn, join without twisting, and place marker to work in the round.
Knit 9 rounds.
Bind off. Cut yarn, leaving a 12" tail.
Finish tubular wrapper Slide a wooden bead into tube, aligning the hole in the bead with the cast-on and bound-off edges. With tapestry needle and cast-on and bind-off tails, cinch cast-on and bound-off edges around hole. Thread one tail through the hole so both tails are at the same side. Knot tails together, then weave between wrapper and wooden bead; trim.

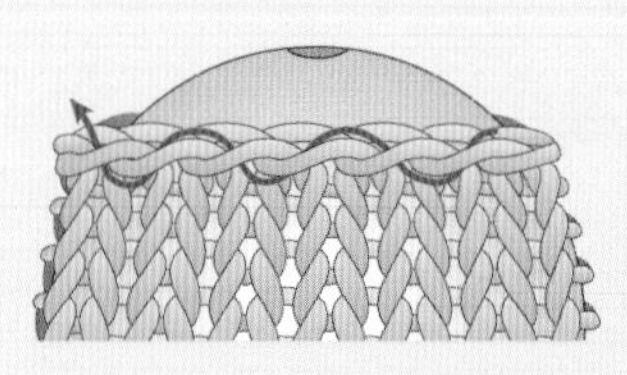

Cinch cast-on and bind-off of tubular wrapper around hole in wooden bead

Plain flat wrapper, horizontal orientation 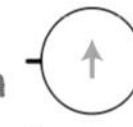

The plain piece of flat stockinette fabric is wrapped around the wooden bead with the holes in the bead running side to side in a horizontal orientation. A stockinette graft seamlessly joins the fabric around the bead. The edges of the fabric are then gathered around the hole. The wrapper can also be turned inside out after grafting to show the purl side.

Knit fabric with live stitches top and bottom

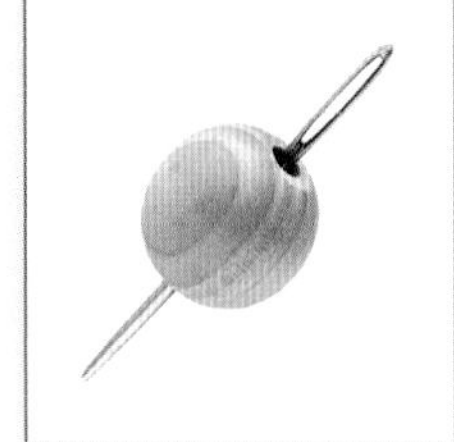

1" wooden bead

Wrapped bead with graft

With waste yarn and a temporary crochet cast-on, cast on 9.
Row 1 With yarn, knit.
Row 2 P7, p2tog 8 stitches.
Rows 3–23 Work in stockinette.
Do not bind off. Cut yarn, leaving a 12" tail.
Remove waste yarn from cast-on, placing 8 stitches on a second needle.
Finish flat wrapper With RS facing, tapestry needle, and 12" tail, use stockinette graft to join stitches on both needles. Slide a 1" wooden bead into the tube, aligning the hole in the bead with the opening of the tube. With tapestry needle and cast-on and bind-off tails, cinch edge stitches around hole. Thread one tail through the hole so both tails are at the same side. Knot tails together, then weave between wrapper and wooden bead; trim.

Bead-knit flat wrapper, horizontal orientation

Beads are knit into every row of this fabric, but are always placed on the purl side. The fabric is then wrapped around the wooden bead with the holes in the bead running side to side in a horizontal orientation. The fabric may be wrapped around the bead with either the beaded or plain side facing out. When the beaded side of the fabric faces inward, the firmness of the wooden bead presses the glass beads through the knit stitches so they peek through to the outside. The remaining edges of the fabric are then gathered around the holes.

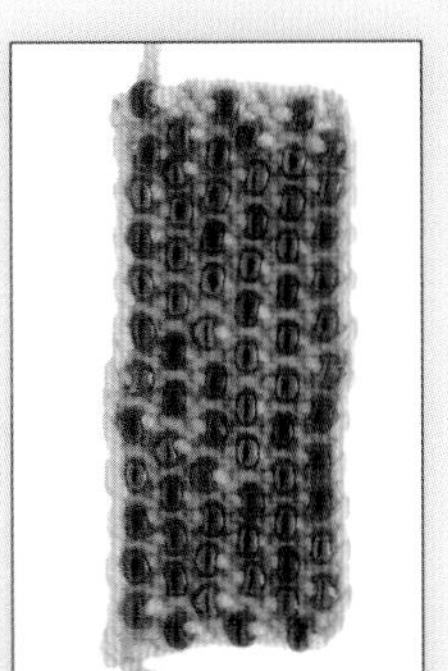

Bead-knit fabric, beads on reverse stockinette

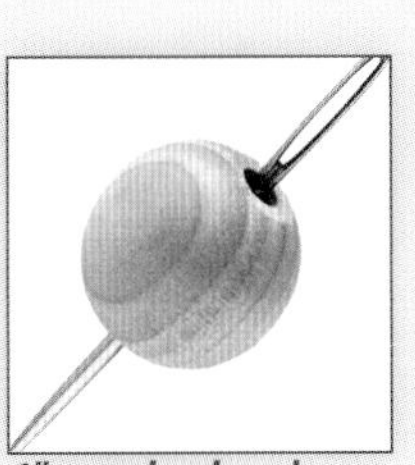

1" wooden bead

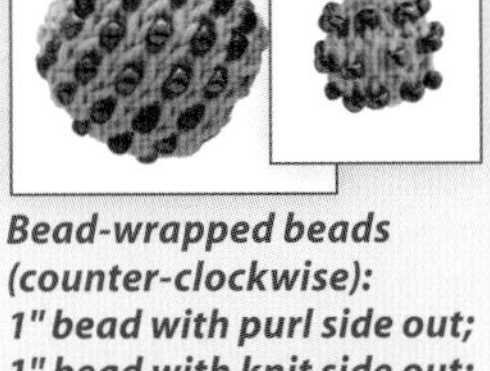

Bead-wrapped beads (counter-clockwise): 1" bead with purl side out; 1" bead with knit side out; 5/8" bead with purl side out

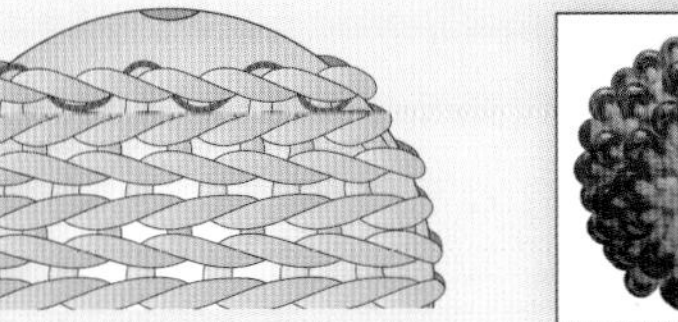

Cinch edge stitches of flat wrapper around hole in wooden bead

1" BEAD

With beading needle, string 72 beads. Using long-tail cast-on, cast on 7.
Row 1 P1, **[SB, p2]** 3 times.
Row 2 K1, **[SB, k2]** 3 times.
Rows 3–23 Repeat Rows 1–2, end with Row 1.
Bind off in pattern, placing beads as in Row 2. Cut yarn, leaving a 12" tail.

5/8" BEAD

With beading needle, string 24 beads. Using long-tail cast-on, cast on 4.
Row 1 P1, SB, p2, SB, p1.
Row 2 K2, SB, k2.
Rows 3–15 Repeat Rows 1–2, end with Row 1.
Bind off in pattern, placing beads as in Row 2. Cut yarn, leaving a 12" tail.

FINISH

Finish as for Plain Flat Wrapper EXCEPT: If the bead-knit fabric is wrapped with the purl side out, use a tapestry needle and Zipper Graft to join the cast-on and bound-off edges. If the bead-knit fabric is wrapped with the knit side out, use a tapestry needle and the bind-off tail to graft the cast-on and bound-off edges together (drawing below).

Align stitches as shown. Graft over finished edges. Adjust tension.

Knit beads

TECH TRIALS

Soft beads

Newer for me are what I call **soft beads**. The more I work on bead-knit jewelry, the more intrigued I become with the process of what in the sewing world is known as fabric manipulation. Here the idea is to take flat fabric and, with the application of different techniques, engineer the flat fabric into more highly textured or 3-dimensional forms. For my purposes, this translates into not using underlying forms for these beads, but instead manipulating a 2-dimensional piece of knit fabric in some way to create a small 3-dimensional shape that can be strung or applied as embellishment—just like a bead. I have come to think of this process as bead-knitting architecture. I've just begun to scratch the surface of the possibilities for these techniques, but I'm happy to offer a few samples of these new soft beads in hopes of piquing your interest and your own creativity.

Rolled bead, beads on the edge

Rolled, beaded-end soft bead

This fabric and the 3 that follow are worked horizontally—the fabric is wider than it is tall. The design of this soft bead gathers all of the glass beads in spirals at each end. The beads are knit as part of both the cast-on and bound-off edges. The bead is rolled, then the short, unbeaded edge is sewn to the body of the bead in a way that is almost invisible. Leaving the body unbeaded provides an opportunity to show off a beautiful yarn. Alternatively, the open space can be wrapped with yarn or with smaller beads.

With beading needle, string 38 beads.
Beaded long-tail cast-on Place slip knot on needle, **[SB, cast on 1]** 19 times—20 stitches and 19 beads.
Rows 1–10 Work in stockinette, starting with a knit row.
Beaded bind-off KBL, **[KBL, bind off]** 18 times, k1, bind-off.
Finish rolled bead as shown on page 105.

Knit fabric with beaded cast-on and bind-off

Rolled barrel bead, beads on the inside

Rolled, knit-side-out soft bead

Bead-knit fabric

For this bead, the fabric is rolled into a barrel shape, with the beads to the inside. Beading the entire piece of fabric and rolling the beads to the inside supports the shape of the soft bead and creates a more solid interior that forces the beads to peek through the columns of knit stitches on the outside. The shape is secured by sewing the short edge to the roll.

With beading needle, string 80 beads. Cast on 17.
Row 1 (WS) P1, **[SB, p2]** 8 times.
Row 2 K1, **[SB, k2]** 8 times.
Repeat Rows 1–2 for a total of 9 rows, end with Row 1.
Bind off in pattern, placing beads as in Row 2. Cut yarn, leaving a 12" tail.
Finish rolled bead as shown on page 105.

Rolled barrel bead, beads on the outside

Rolled, purl-side-out soft bead

Half-bead-knit fabric

Here only half of each row is knit with beads. This soft bead is rolled with the beads to the outside, starting with the plain end of the fabric and finishing with the bead-knit end. This bead is softer and lighter in weight (fewer beads!) than the knit-side-out soft bead, and the beads are more prominent.

With beading needle, string 50 beads. Cast on 22.
Row 1 P1, **[SB, p2]** 5 times, p11.
Row 2 K12, **[SB, k2]** 5 times.
Repeat Rows 1–2 for a total of 9 rows, end with Row 1.
Bind off in pattern, placing beads as in Row 2. Cut yarn, leaving 12" tail.
Finish rolled bead as shown on page 105 EXCEPT start at the unbeaded edge and roll fabric with purl side out AND use an overcast stitch.

FINISH ROLLED BEAD

1 With purl side facing, cast-on edge to your left, and bound-off edge to your right, roll the fabric from top to bottom. Knit side faces out.

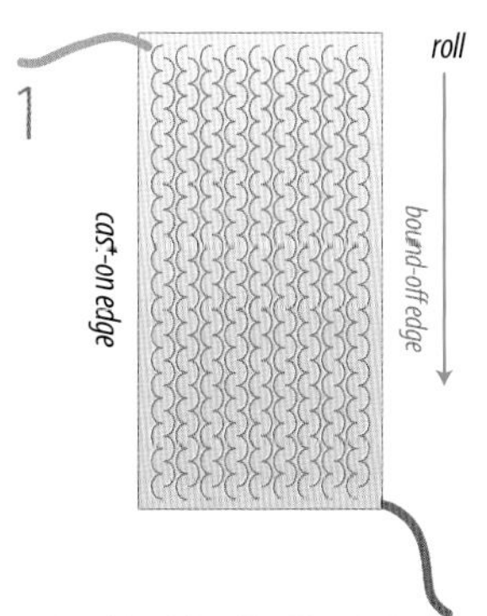

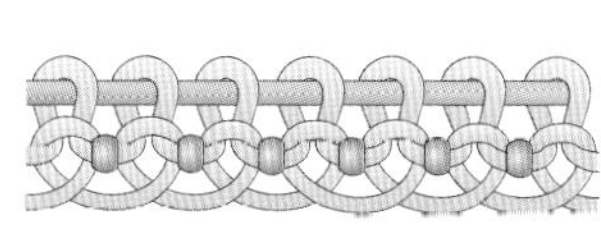

Beaded long-tail cast-on Slide bead close to last stitch before casting on next stitch.

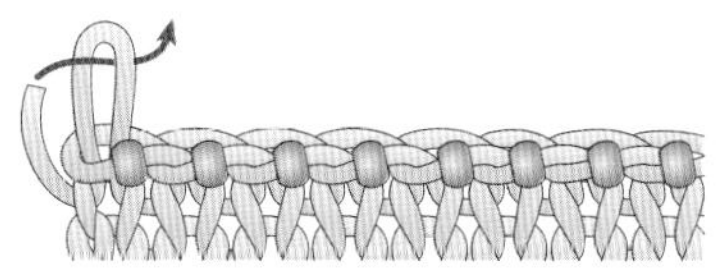

Beaded bind-off KBL every stitch EXCEPT the final stitch, keeping beads to the front of the work and making sure each bound-off stitch passes over both the stitch ahead of it AND the bead on that stitch.

To review both beaded cast-on and bind-off, see page 9.

2 Align the column of knit stitches on the edge of the fabric (the edge stitches) with a column of knit stitches in the roll (the roll stitches). Thread the bind-off tail in a tapestry needle. Insert the needle under the top layer of the roll, then back out next to the first roll stitch.

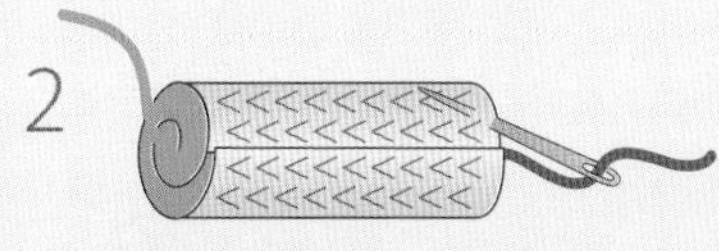

3 Working from right to left, insert the needle under the outer leg of the first roll stitch, then the outer leg of the first edge stitch as shown. The two half stitches come together to create the look of a full stitch. Working from left to right, repeat with the second edge and roll stitches. Continue as established, working back and forth until all stitches from both columns have been joined.

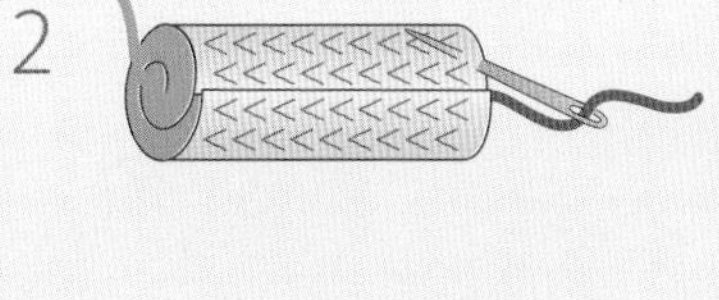

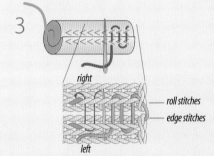

4 Insert the needle into the roll, then out next to the cast-on tail.

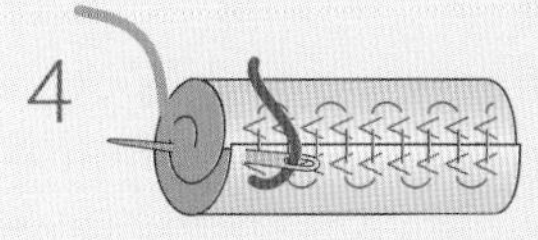

5 Knot the cast-on and bind-off tails together. Weave in ends.

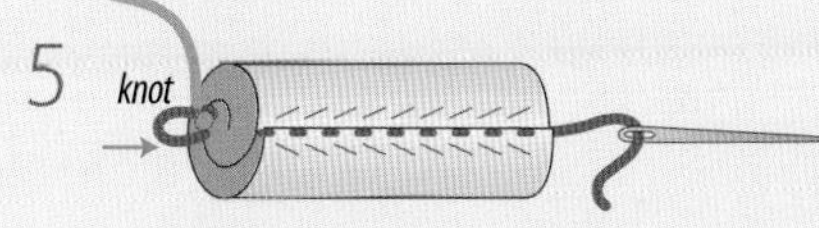

Plain knit soft link

Rolled link

This is a knit version of another common jewelry element — the link. This link is engineered from a short tube knit on double-pointed needles. Worked in stockinette, it naturally wants to roll into its final form, purl-side out. With purls on the outside, embellishing these links with beads is the natural next step (see Links and Loops, page 124).

Plain knit tube

With double-pointed needle (dpn), cast on 24 and divide evenly onto 3 dpn, join without twisting, and place marker to work in the round.
Knit 6 rounds.
Bind off. Cut yarn, leaving a 12" tail.
Fold tube in half with purl side facing out; shape into circle with fold along outer edge. With tapestry needle and cast-on tail, and using an overcast stitch, join cast-on and bound-off edges. Weave in tails.

OVERCAST STITCH

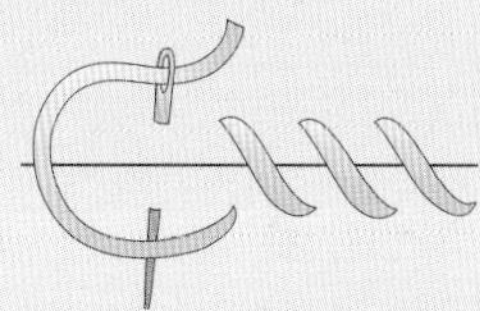

Four seasons

Four seasons

Winter

silk
4196 Dark Jade (4)
4093 Light Icy (5)
8055 Medium Dark Ash Grey (6)

beads
344 Lined Green AB (4)
2195 701 Silver-lined Crystal (5)
Taupe-lined Crystal AB (6)

The amazing range of materials available sets my knitter's brain spinning. This necklace is truly a labor born from love for the many different colors of glass beads, the different colors and types of fibers, and the different sizes and shapes of wooden beads to go underneath all of that bead knitting. This design was inspired by a few hanks of gorgeously hand-painted sock yarn from Ellen's Half Pint Farm. The 4 colorways were named for the 4 seasons. Super-short color repeats let each color in the colorway show on each bead ball. The missing link was the fiber choice for the solid-color bead balls. When I discovered Kreinik's Silk Serica (which comes in an incredible assortment of colors AND on conveniently small spools), I had everything I needed. I left the necklace without a clasp so you can rotate the colors around your neck, moving the colors of the current season to the front if you wish. Fun little earrings use the same techniques. Feel free to mix and match colors for the earrings.

Fall

silk
4096 Dark Icy (3)
1205 Dark Victorian Rose (2)
2067 Very Dark Pumpkin (1)

beads
4216 Duracoat Galvanized Dark Sea Foam (3)
4220 Duracoat Galvanized Eggplant (2)
4208 Duracoat Galvanized Berry (1)

VARIEGATED YARN
ELLEN'S HALF PINT FARM 100% Merino
Sock colors F, W, SP, S, shown here

SILK KREINIK Silk Serica
colors 1–12, shown here

BEADS MIYUKI Size 8º glass seed beads
colors 1–12, shown here

Spring

silk
1032 Lightest Pink (7)
4193 Light Jade (8)
6116 Dark Wisteria (9)

beads
275 Dk Peach-lined Crystal AB (7)
179 Transparent Green AB (8)
264 Raspberry-lined Crystal AB (9)

Summer

silk
6083 Light Grape (10)
1117 Very Dark Christmas Red (11)
3062 Lightest Henna (12)

beads
454 Metallic Dk Plum Iris (10)
254D Transparent Dk Red AB (11)
187 Copper Plated (12)

Prepare and knit

NECKLACE

Small Plain Bead 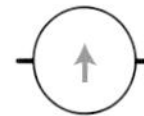

MAKE 8: 2 EACH IN VARIEGATED YARN COLORS SP, S, F, W

Flat wrapper With waste yarn and a temporary crochet cast-on, cast on 9.

Row 1 (RS) With variegated yarn, knit.

Row 2 P7, p2tog—8 stitches.

Rows 3–20 Work in stockinette.

Do not bind off; leave stitches on needle. Cut yarn, leaving a 12" tail.

Finish wrapper Using a ⅝" wooden bead, finish flat wrapper with stockinette graft (page 110).

Small Beaded Bead

MAKE 8: 1 EACH IN BEAD/SILK COLORS 1, 2, 4, 5, 7, 8, 10, 11

With beading needle, string each color of silk with 72 color-coordinated beads.

Flat wrapper Leaving an 12" tail, cast on 7.

Row 1 (RS) P1, **[SB, p2]** 3 times.

Row 2 K1, **[SB, k2]** 3 times.

Repeat Rows 1–2 for a total of 23 rows, end with Row 1.

Bind off in pattern, placing beads as in Row 2. Cut yarn, leaving a 12" tail.

Finish wrapper Using a ⅝" wooden bead, finish flat wrapper with Zipper Graft (page 110).

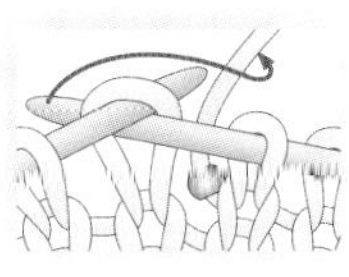

SB Slide bead close to last stitch worked.

Large Beaded Bead

MAKE 4: 1 EACH IN BEAD/SILK COLORS 3, 6, 9, 12

With beading needle, string each color of silk with 114 color-coordinated beads.

Flat wrapper Leaving a 12" tail, cast on 14.

Row 1 (RS) P1, **[SB, p2]** 6 times, SB, p1.

Row 2 K2, **[SB, k2]** 6 times.

Rows 3, 5, 7 Purl.

Rows 4, 6 Knit.

Row 8 K2, **[SB, k2]** 6 times.

Repeat Rows 1–8 for a total of 47 rows, end with Row 7.

Bind off in pattern, placing beads as in Row 8. Cut yarn, leaving a 12" tail.

Finish wrapper Using a 1" wooden bead, finish flat wrapper with Zipper Graft (page 110).

gauge

8 stitches = 1", using sock yarn

finished necklace length 32"

yarn

short-repeat variegated sock yarn,

10 yds each of 2 colors for earrings

20 yds each of 4 colors for necklace

yarn

silk thread

10 yds each of 2 colors for earrings

20 yds each of 12 colors for necklace

beads

size 8º Japanese glass seed beads

260 for earrings, shown in 2 colors

1500 for necklace, shown in 12 colors

Wooden beads for earrings

2 each ⅝" round, ¾" round

Wooden beads for necklace

16 ⅝" round

8 ¾" round

4 each 1" round, ⅞" × 2" oval rice

needles

1.75mm/US00

and…

beading needle
tapestry needle
waste yarn
crochet hook
stitch marker
beading monofilament, clear
Stretch Magic Cord
lever-back earring findings

NOTES: intermediate

See page 160 for knitting abbreviations and techniques, and page 2 for beading basics.

If you find it easier, work the Zipper Graft before inserting wooden bead in flat wrapper.

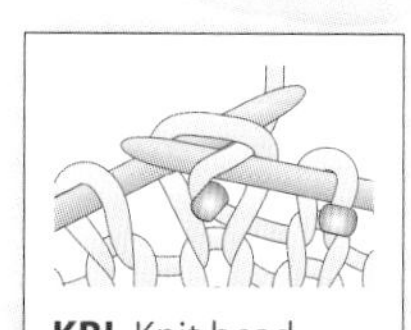

KBL Knit bead through stitch. On next row, knit stitch through back loop.

ZIPPER GRAFT

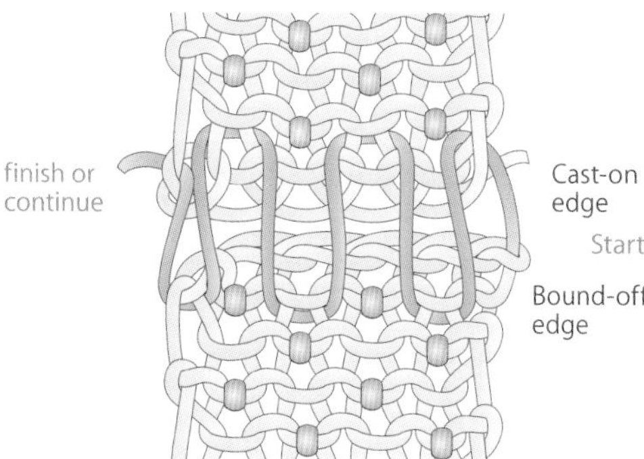

Medium Plain Silk Bead

MAKE 8: 1 EACH IN SILK COLORS 1, 2, 4, 5, 7, 8, 10, 11

Tubular wrapper Leaving a 12" tail, cast on 22 and divide evenly onto 3 double-pointed needles (dpn), join without twisting and place marker to work in the round. Knit 10 rounds. Bind off. Cut yarn, leaving a 12" tail.

Using a ¾" wooden bead, finish tubular wrapper.

Oval Bead

MAKE 4: 1 EACH IN BEAD/SILK AND VARIEGATED YARN COLORS 1, 2 AND F; 4, 5, AND W; 7, 8, AND SP; 10, 11, AND S.

With beading needle, string each color of silk with 22 color-coordinated beads.

Tubular wrapper With the first color of silk and leaving a 12" tail, cast on 22 and divide evenly onto 3 dpns, join without twisting and place marker to work in the round. Knit 8 rounds.

Bead round KBL to end. Cut silk and knot to variegated yarn.

Next round With yarn, and with beads on RS, knit all stitches through back loop (tbl).

Knit 12 rounds. Cut yarn and knot to second color of silk.

Bead round With second color of silk, KBL to end.

Next round With beads on RS, knit all stitches tbl.

Knit 8 rounds. Bind off. Cut yarn, leaving a 12" tail.

Finish wrapper Using an oval wooden bead, finish tubular wrapper.

EARRINGS

Small Plain Bead

MAKE 2: 1 EACH IN VARIEGATED YARN COLORS F, W

Tubular wrapper Leaving a 12" tail, cast on 16 and divide evenly onto 3 double-pointed needles (dpn), join without twisting and place marker to work in the round. Knit 10 rounds. Bind off. Cut yarn, leaving a 12" tail.

Finish wrapper Using a ⅝" wooden bead, finish tubular wrapper.

Medium Beaded Bead

MAKE 2: 1 EACH IN BEAD/SILK COLORS 3, 7

With beading needle, string each color of silk with 120 color-coordinated beads.

Flat wrapper Leaving a 12" tail, cast on 9.

Row 1 (RS) P1, **[SB, p2]** 4 times.

Row 2 K1, **[SB, k2]** 4 times.

Repeat Rows 1 and 2 for a total of 29 rows, end with Row 1. Bind off in pattern, placing beads as in Row 2. Cut yarn, leaving a 12" tail.

Finish wrapper Using a ¾" wooden bead, finish flat wrapper with Zipper Graft EXCEPT don't weave or trim tails.

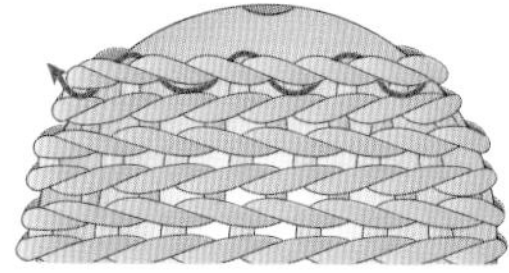

Cinch cast-on and bind-off of tubular wrapper OR edge stitches of flat wrapper around hole in wooden bead

Finish

FINISH TUBULAR WRAPPER

Slide a wooden bead into the tube, aligning hole in wooden bead with openings of tube. Using tails, cinch cast-on and bound-off edges around hole. Thread one tail through the hole so both tails are at the same side. Knot tails together, then weave between wrapper and wooden bead; trim.

FINISH FLAT WRAPPER

With Zipper Graft With RS facing, wrap knitting around a wooden bead. With tapestry needle, bind-off tail, and using Zipper Graft, join cast-on and bound-off edges.

With stockinette graft Remove waste yarn from cast-on, placing stitches on a second needle. With RS facing, wrap knitting around wooden bead. With tail, use stockinette graft to join stitches on both needles.

For both Align hole in wooden bead with openings of wrapper. Using tails, cinch edge stitches around hole. Thread one tail through the hole so both tails are at the same side. Knot tails together, then weave between wrapper and wooden bead; trim.

Finish necklace

With tapestry needle, string knit beads onto both monofilament and Stretch Magic cord in order shown. Knot thread and cord; thread tails through the nearest bead.

Finish earrings

For each earring, place the small bead above the medium bead, aligning the holes of both beads, with the knotted tails of the medium bead hanging from the bottom of the medium bead. Thread the tails back up through both beads and knot through the loop of the earring finding. Weave tails between wrapper and wooden bead; trim.

Winter
Fall
Spring
Summer
Necklace
3B
4
2
W
F
4B
2B
4
W
5
2
F
1
5B
1B
W
F
5
1
6B
12B
7
11
Sp
S
7B
11B
7
S
8
11
S
10
8B
10B
Sp
S
8
9B
10
Small bead
Medium bead
Large bead
Oval bead
1–12 Color of silk and bead
B Knit with beads
Sp, S, F, W Colorway of variegated yarn
Earrings
F
W
7B
3B

Silver orbits

Silver orbits

For many years I was asked if I made earrings and had to confess that I didn't. Then I discovered these endless-hoop earring findings and they got my mind spinning. Because of the way the hoop closes with a fine hinged wire inside of the tube, one end of the hoop is smooth enough and small enough to pass through the hole of a wooden bead. The Kreinik cable yarn only comes in silver and gold but is super strong and, when knit with very fine needles, really does look like sterling silver or yellow gold. You don't need a lot of fiber or beads or to do a lot of knitting to achieve a great look. They are named Silver Orbits because they look suspiciously like the planets in my 4th grade science project.

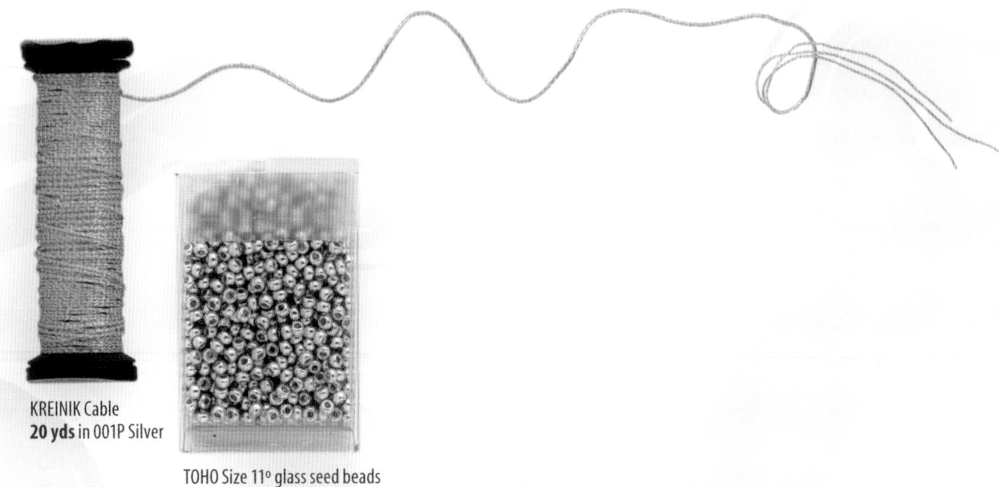

KREINIK Cable
20 yds in 001P Silver

TOHO Size 11° glass seed beads
76 in 558PF Galvanized PF Platinum Gold

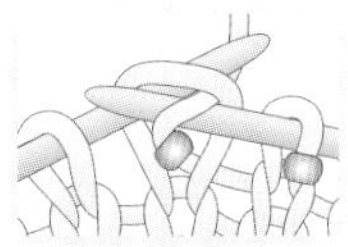

KBL Knit bead through stitch with standard wrap. On next round, knit stitch through back loop.

Cinch cast-on and bind-off of tubular wrapper around hole in wooden bead

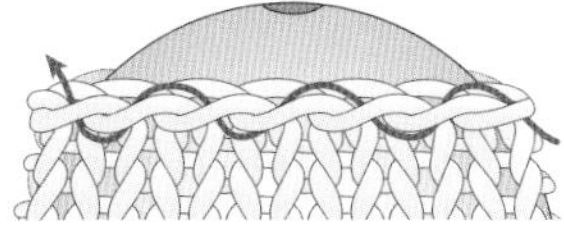

Earrings

Prepare

With beading needle, string 38 beads.

Knit

Leaving a 10" tail, cast on 19 and divide evenly onto 3 double-pointed needles, join without twisting, and place marker to work in the round.
Knit 6 rounds.
Bead round **[KBL]** to end.
Next round With beads to RS of work, knit all stitches through back loop.
Repeat last 2 rounds. Knit 5 rounds.
Bind off. Cut yarn, leaving a 10" tail.

Finish

Slide a wooden bead into the tube, aligning the hole in the bead with the cast-on and bound-off edges.
With darning needle and cast-on and bind-off tails, cinch cast-on and bound-off edges around hole. Thread one tail through the hole so both tails are at the same side. Knot tails together, then weave between wrapper and wooden bead; trim.
Thread bead onto endless hoop earring.

gauge
approximately 11 stitches = 1"

yarn
super fine weight
20 yds metallic cable

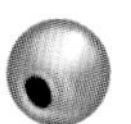

beads
90 size 11° Japanese glass seed beads

needles
1.75mm/US00

and...
beading needle
darning needle
stitch marker
2 9/16" round wooden beads
1 pair 1⅛" diameter endless hoop earrings

NOTES: intermediate

See page 160 for knitting abbreviations and techniques, and page 2 for beading basics.

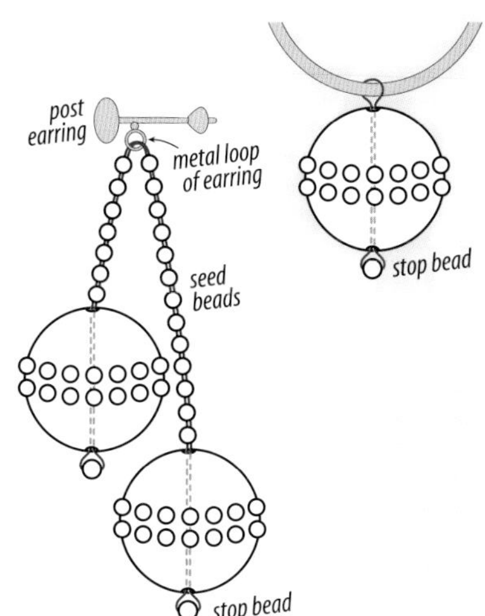

WHAT IF...

You could also attach these bead-knit balls to the bottom of the hoop by passing a fine thread through the hole, through a slightly larger Stop Bead, and then back through the bead hole a second time. The thread can then be knotted onto the hoop.

If you are not crazy about hoops, consider suspending one or more bead-knit balls on a beaded thread attached to other types of earring findings such as wires or posts.

Wrap and roll

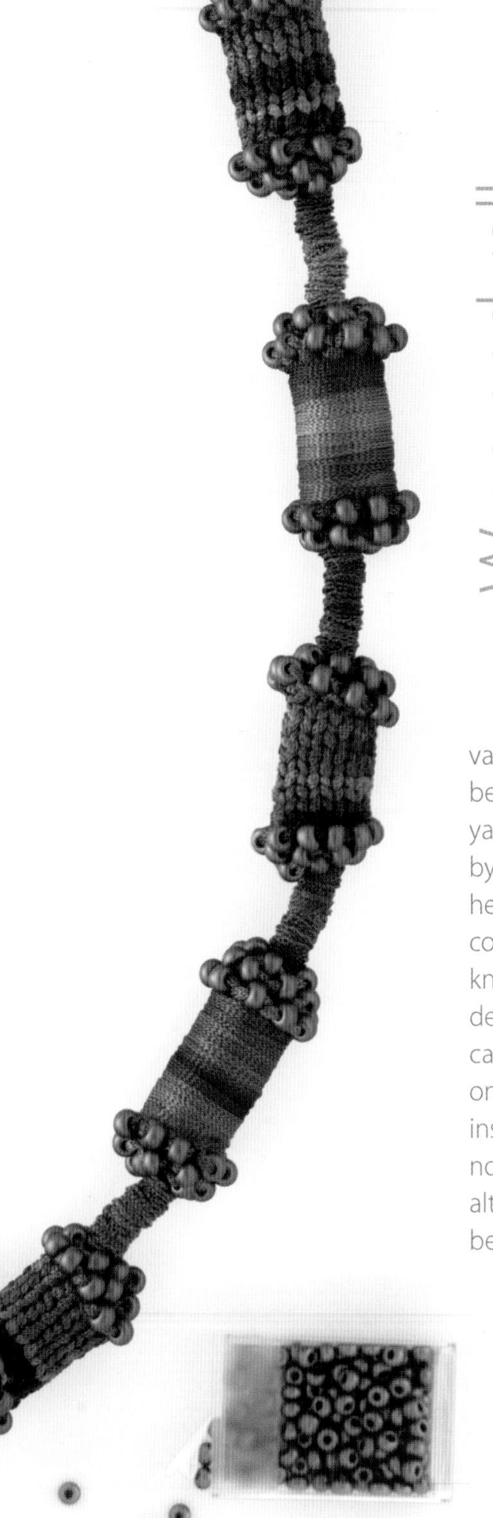

Wrap and roll

I spent years devising ways to knit plain and beaded wrappers for different sizes and shapes of wooden beads. A friend who is both a talented seamstress and a knitter shared a wonderful book about ways to manipulate cloth fabric, and I thought it might be fun to try similar techniques with knit fabric. My goal was to make knit beads that didn't require a solid structure to support the knitting—I call them "soft beads." These Wrap and Roll beads were among the first to result from my experimentation with these ideas. I love how they show off the gorgeous color changes in the variegated rayon ribbon. Notice the filler between the beads on the finished necklace? It's the same ribbon yarn I knit the beads with. I discovered this technique by playing with one of the tails from my knitting, and here's how it came about: When I explain the tubular construction of this fiber to my students, I slide a knitting needle inside the seemingly flat ribbon to demonstrate how it is actually a knit tube—I jokingly call it "knitting-needle panty hose." So while working on these beads, I happened to slip a knitting needle inside one of the tails, scrunched it up, and then noticed how cool it looked—turns out to be a great alternative to stringing glass beads in the spaces between the knit beads.

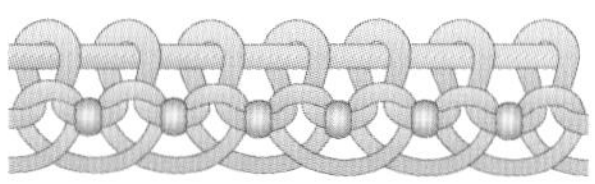

Beaded long-tail cast-on
Slide bead close to last stitch before casting on next stitch.

ROLLED BEAD

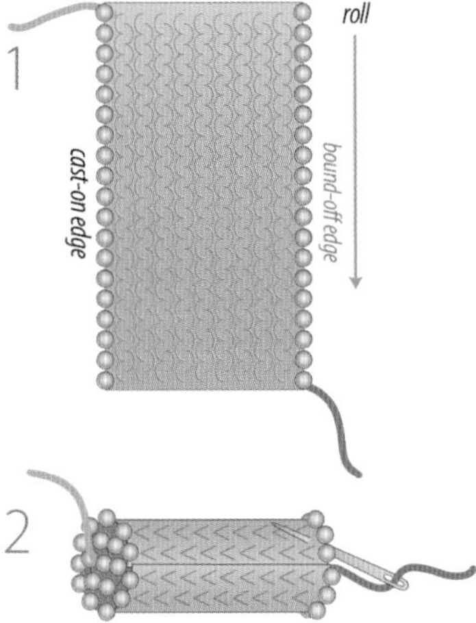

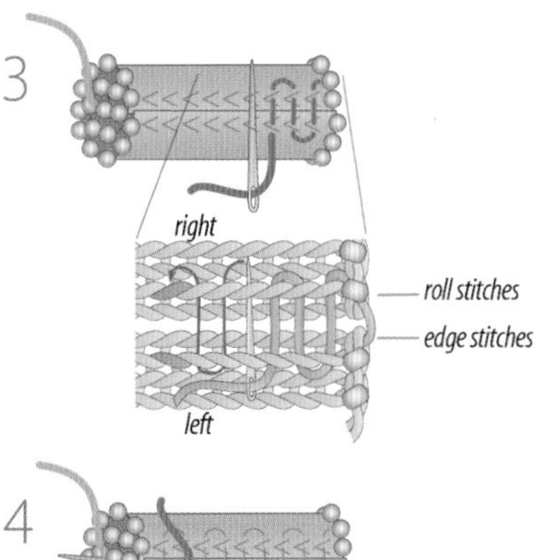

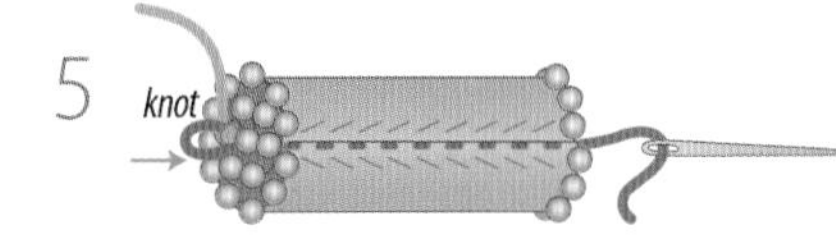

Size 6° Czech glass seed beads
750 in 956ME Matte Copper

INTERLACEMENTS New York 200
200 yds in 112 Woodlands

Rolled Bead

MAKE 19

Prepare

With beading needle, string 38 beads.

Knit

Leaving a 10" tail and using beaded long-tail cast-on, cast on 20 — 19 beads placed.

Rows 1–10 Work in stockinette, starting with a knit row.

Bind off using a beaded bind-off. Cut yarn, leaving a 15" tail.

Finish

1 With purl side facing, cast-on edge to your left, and bound-off edge to your right, roll the fabric from top to bottom. Knit side faces out and beads create a spiral on either end.

2 Align the column of knit stitches on the edge of the fabric (the edge stitches) with a column of knit stitches in the roll (the roll stitches). Thread the bind-off tail in a tapestry needle. Insert the needle under the top layer of the roll, then back out next to the first roll stitch.

3 Working from right to left, insert the needle under the outer leg of the first roll stitch, then the outer leg of the first edge stitch as shown. The two half stitches come together to create the look of a full stitch. Working from left to right, repeat with the second edge and roll stitches. Continue as established, working back and forth until all stitches from both columns have been joined.

4 Insert the needle into the roll, then out next to the cast-on tail.

5 Knot the cast-on and bind-off tails together. Thread the cast-on tail back through the center of the bead and out the opposite end. Trim each tail to approximately 7" long.

Wrapped Bead

MAKE 9 (USING FINISHED ROLLED BEADS)

Thread a 24" length of ribbon yarn in a tapestry needle. Leaving a 10" tail, insert the needle from the inside to the outside of the roll. Wrap the ribbon around the roll between the beaded ends, then insert the needle into the roll, through the center, and out next to the cast-on tail. Knot the cast-on and bind-off tails together, then weave the tails into the roll; trim.

Thread a 48" length of monofilament in a stole needle. String the beads, alternating rolled beads with wrapped beads, inserting the needle INSIDE the ribbon yarn tails on either side of the beads. Push the beads together along the monofilament, compressing the ribbon yarn tails between each bead. At each end of the strand, weave the ribbon tail back into the bead, then use monofilament tails to sew on the clasp.

WRAPPED BEAD

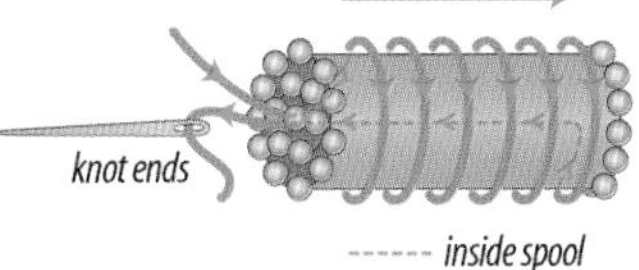

KBL Knit bead through stitch.

Beaded bind-off KBL every stitch EXCEPT the final stitch, keeping beads to the front of the work and making sure each bound-off stitch passes over both the stitch ahead of it AND the bead on that stitch.

WHAT IF...

You can also try stringing more of the glass beads between the rolled and wrapped beads. This option makes the piece a little dressier, I think.

Consider using a solid-colored yarn along with a great mix of glass bead colors.

gauge

6 stitches = 1"
finished length 35", including clasp

yarn

light weight
200 yds ribbon yarn

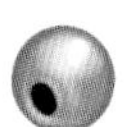

beads

750 size 6º Czech glass seed beads

needles

2.75mm/US2

and...

beading needle
tapestry needle
stole needle
beading monofilament
single-strand clasp

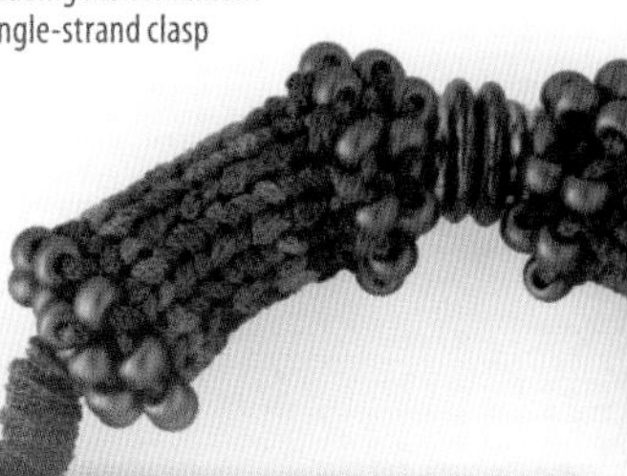

NOTES: intermediate

See page 160 for knitting abbreviations and techniques, and page 2 for beading basics.

Each of the 19 soft beads is created by working a small piece of bead-knit fabric, rolling it up, and then sewing it together to secure the shape. Ten of these rolls are used as is, while the other nine are wrapped with an additional length of the ribbon yarn.

Beads by the barrel

Beads by the barrel

Another soft bead, and yet another design that came about quite by accident (aka "playing with my knitting"). I had knit a small piece of beaded-stockinette fabric to use as a wrapper for a round wooden bead and was holding it in my hand while talking to a friend. As is natural for stockinette fabric, it rolled purl side out. Without really thinking about it, I started rolling the fabric the opposite way, with the beads on the inside. When I turned my attention back to the roll, I fully expected not to see any beads. Much to my surprise, there they were, peeking through the spaces between the now-visible knit stitches, and all lined up in perfect little rows! The pressure of all the beads rolled tightly to the inside pressed some beads through to the outside — there just wasn't enough room for all of them inside. And while it may seem like a waste of beads to knit them over the entire surface of the fabric when only a portion of them show through to the outside, the unseen beads support the shape of the rolled bead AND help make the outermost beads visible. I love surprises, don't you?

Size 6º Czech glass seed beads
947 in ME 956 Matte Copper

INTERLACEMENTS New York
200 yds in 311 Colorado Treasures

Rolled Bead
MAKE 9

Prepare

With beading needle, string ribbon with 95 beads.

Knit

Leaving a 10" tail, cast on 20.
Row 1 (WS) P1, **[SB, p2]** 9 times, SB, p1.
Row 2 K2, **[SB, k2]** 9 times.
Repeat Rows 1–2 for a total of 9 rows, end with Row 1.
Bind off in pattern, placing beads as in Row 2.
Cut yarn, leaving a 12" tail.

Finish

1 With purl side facing, cast-on edge to your left, and bound-off edge to your right, roll the fabric from top to bottom. Knit side faces out and beads create a spiral on either end.

2 Align the column of knit stitches on the edge of the fabric (the edge stitches) with a column of knit stitches in the roll (the roll stitches). Thread the bind-off tail in a tapestry needle. Insert the needle under the top layer of the roll, then back out next to the first roll stitch.

3 Working from right to left, insert the needle under the outer leg of the first roll stitch, then the outer leg of the first edge stitch as shown. The two half stitches come together to create the look of a full stitch. Working from left to right, repeat with the second edge and roll stitches. Continue as established, working back and forth until all stitches from both columns have been joined.

4 Insert the needle into the roll, then out next to the cast-on tail.

5 Knot the cast-on and bind-off tails together. Thread the cast-on tail back through the center of the bead and out the opposite end. Trim each tail to approximately 7" long.

With beading needle, string rolled beads onto both monofilament and ribbon, beginning and ending with 26 glass beads and adding 5 glass beads between each pair of rolled beads. Knot thread and ribbon to clasp; and thread tails back through glass beads to hide.

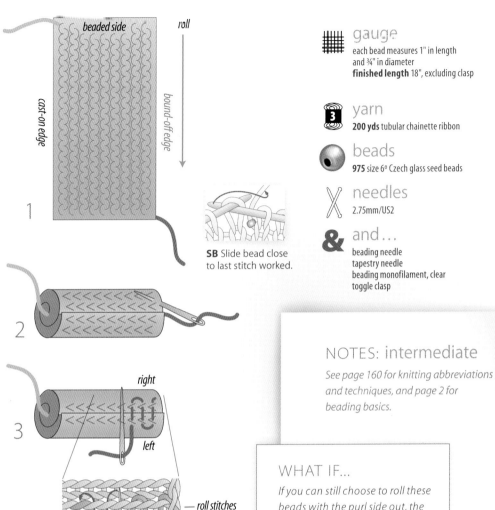

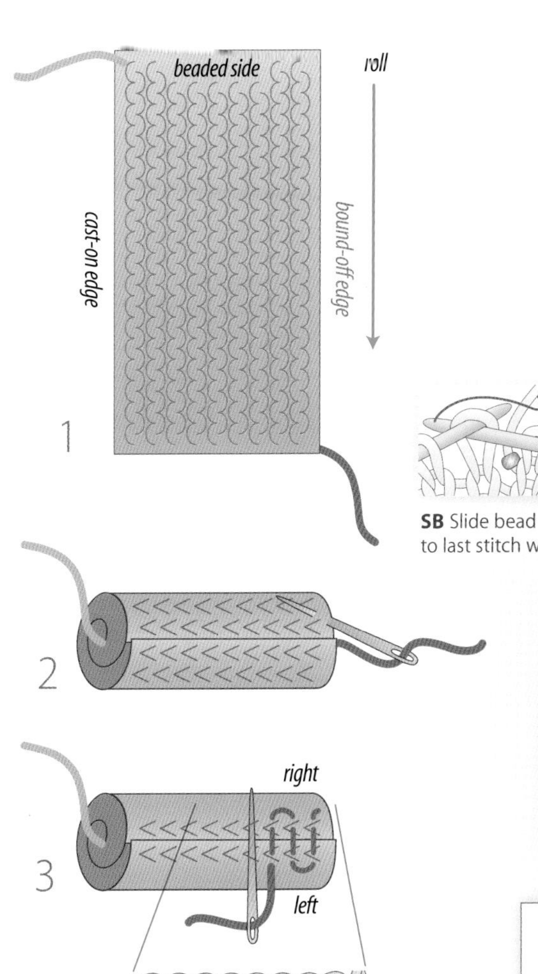

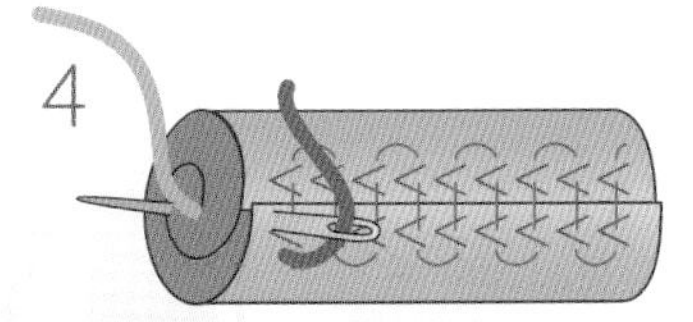

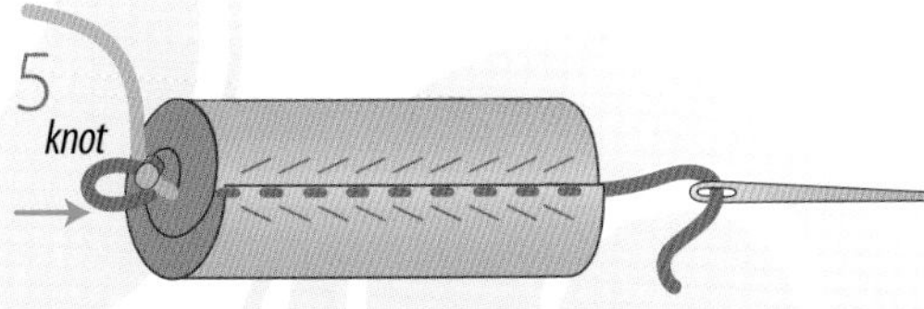

SB Slide bead close to last stitch worked.

gauge

each bead measures 1" in length and ¾" in diameter
finished length 18", excluding clasp

yarn

200 yds tubular chainette ribbon

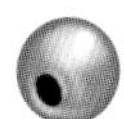

beads

975 size 6° Czech glass seed beads

needles

2.75mm/US2

and...

beading needle
tapestry needle
beading monofilament, clear
toggle clasp

NOTES: intermediate

See page 160 for knitting abbreviations and techniques, and page 2 for beading basics.

WHAT IF...

If you can still choose to roll these beads with the purl side out, the beads will be more prominent on the outside of the roll. Perhaps work half of the rolled beads each way—some with beads on the outside, some with beads on the inside—and then use them together on a necklace.

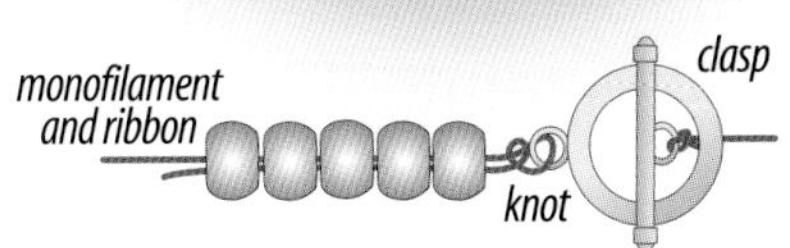

Links and loops

Golden links

When I first decided to try to create bead-knit jewelry, it helped to think of the components of more traditional jewelry. Bead-knit tubes and I-cord are great substitutes for chains. Beads, both hard and soft, are created with and without substructures (like wooden beads) to support the knit fabric. But what about links? In the next 2 projects you'll learn a fun way to make knit links, both with and without bead-knit accents. The technique that works best for me is working the links in the round. Double-pointed needles are NOT just for socks! And thanks to my daughter for naming the bracelet. Did I really let my children eat that sugary cereal? Well—not as much as they would have liked…

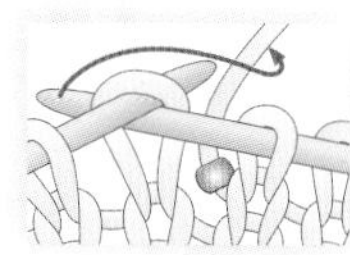

SB Slide bead close to last stitch worked.

Small link *MAKE 4*

Leaving a 10" tail, cast on 18 and divide evenly onto 3 double-pointed needles (dpn), join without twisting, and place marker to work in the round. Knit 5 rounds. Bind off. Cut yarn, leaving an 8" tail.

Finish link

Fold tube in half with purl side out; shape into a circle with fold along outer edge. With tapestry needle and cast-on tail, and using an overcast stitch, join cast-on and bound-off edges together. Weave in tails.

BERROCO Lumina
100 yds in 1620 Gold Coast

MIYUKI glass seed beads
320 Size 6° in 234 Sparkle Metallic Gold-lined Crystal
40 Size 8° in 234 Sparkle Metallic Gold-lined Crystal

Large link *MAKE 5*

With beading needle, string 24 Size 6° beads. Leaving a 10" tail, cast on 24 and divide evenly onto 3 dpn, join without twisting, and place marker to work in the round. Knit 2 rounds.

Bead round **[SB, k1]** 24 times.

Knit 2 rounds. Bind off. Cut yarn, leaving an 8" tail. Finish as for Small Link (beads are along outer edge of circle).

Finish

Joining links

Large bead link With beading needle, string 25 Size 6° beads onto silk thread. Join the beads into a circle through the centers of one large and one small knit link. Pass thread through beads a second time; knot and weave the tails back into the bead link. Join all links in this way, alternating large and small knit links (see drawing).

Small bead link With beading needle, string 20 Size 8° beads onto silk thread. Join the beads into a circle through the center of the large end link and the toggle clasp. Pass thread through the first 4 beads a second time; knot thread to clasp (see drawing). Thread tails back into bead link to hide; trim. Repeat at other end.

gauge
6 stitches = 1"
finished length 17", including clasp

yarn
fine weight
100 yds metallic yarn

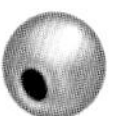
beads
350 size 6° Japanese glass seed beads
50 size 8° Japanese glass seed beads

needles
3.25mm/US3

and...
twisted-wire beading needle
tapestry needle
stitch marker
KREINIK Silk Serica in 2017 Very Dark Gold
toggle clasp

JOINING LINKS

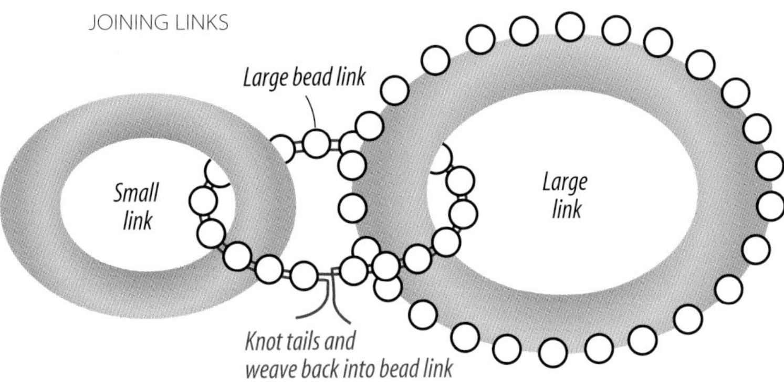

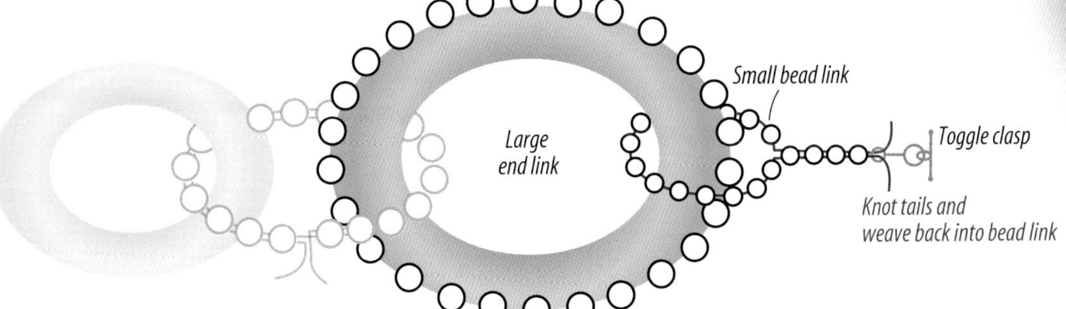

NOTES: easy +

See page 160 for knitting abbreviations and techniques, and page 2 for beading basics.

Each link or loop is constructed in the round, then joined with links of beads strung on silk thread (the necklace) or elastic cord (the bracelet, next page).

WHAT IF...

I love the metallic look of the yarns used in both of these projects, but when you see a project like this with lots of individual components, try to recognize what a great opportunity it presents to use up lots of little bits of stash yarns. That, in turn, gives you the opportunity to play with your color- and texture-combining skills—the necklace or bracelet equivalent of a crazy quilt, perhaps? I think I might have to make one of those!

Fruit loops

KATIA Gatsby Lux
35 yds each in 3811 Green/Turquoise (A)
AND 3807 Pink/Green (B)

OR PLYMOUTH YARNS Gold Rush
35 yds each of 2 colors

gauge

8 stitches = 1"

yarn

fine weight
70 yds metallic yarn, shown in 2 colors

beads

approximately 75 size 6º Japanese glass seed beads, shown in 3 colors
80 size 8º Japanese glass seed beads

needles

2.75mm/US2

and…

twisted-wire beading needle
tapestry needle
stitch marker
Stretch Magic Cord
fabric glue

Plain loop

MAKE 12 IN A AND 8 IN B

Leaving a 10" tail, cast on 18 and divide evenly onto 3 double-pointed needles (dpn), join without twisting, and place marker to work in the round. Knit 5 rounds. Bind off. Cut yarn, leaving an 8" tail.

Finish loop

Fold tube in half with purl side out; shape into a circle with fold along outer edge. With tapestry needle and cast-on tail, and using an overcast stitch, join cast-on and bound-off edges together. Weave in tails.

Beaded loop *MAKE 4 IN B*

With beading needle, string 18 Size 8º beads. Work as for Plain Loop EXCEPT:
Round 3: Bead round **[SB, k1]** 18 times.
Finish as for Plain Loop (beads are along outer edge of circle).

Finish

With beading needle, and alternating 3 colors of beads, string a length of elastic cord with enough size 6º beads to fit around your wrist comfortably when NOT stretched plus an additional inch to accommodate the space needed by the knitted loops. Run beaded cord through loops as follows: **[1 beaded loop, 5 plain loops (A, B, A, B, A)]** 4 times. Tie the elastic cord in a square knot; secure knot with a drop of fabric glue. When glue has dried, trim ends.

MIYUKI Size 6º glass seed beads
25 each in 143 Transparent Chartreuse
AND 2601 Sparkle Antique Rose-lined Crystal

MATSUNO Size 6º glass seed beads
25 in 320 Aqua/Teal-lined Crystal

TOHO Size 8º glass seed beads
72 in 553 Medium Dusty Rose

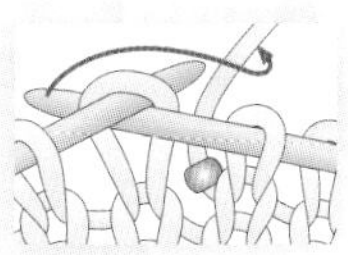

SB Slide bead close to last stitch worked.

SQUARE KNOT

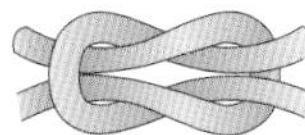

FONTY Serpentine
25 yds in 830 White

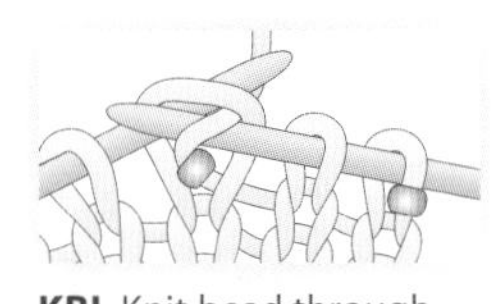

KBL Knit bead through stitch. On next round, knit stitch through back loop.

These ornaments resemble one of my jewelry-sized bead-knit beads—on steroids! Instead of a wooden bead underneath the knitting, I've used a Styrofoam ball—the kind easily obtained from your local craft store—and a glistening white ribbon yarn that reminds me of snow. This project provides a wonderful opportunity to practice the technique of knitting a bead through a stitch. I chose to have all the beads slant in the same direction so you can really get the hang of the technique. There are still plenty of challenges here. You'll be stringing beads of 2 different colors, so you will want to pay close attention to the stringing order.

WHITE ORNAMENT

Prepare

With beading needle, string beads following the White Ornament chart or Stringing Sequence.

Knit

Leaving a 24" tail, cast on 54 and divide evenly onto 3 double-pointed needles (dpn), join without twisting, place marker, and work the White Ornament chart in the round. Bind off. Cut yarn, leaving a 12" tail.

Finish

With tapestry needle and bind-off tail, cinch the bound-off edge tightly. Secure, then make a hanging loop of desired length. Secure and weave in tail. Insert Styrofoam ball.

With tapestry needle and cast-on tail, cinch the cast-on edge around the bottom of the Styrofoam ball. Secure, then thread remaining length in beading needle and create 3 beaded loops as follows: ***Short loop*** String **[2A, 1B]** 8 times, 2A, secure to bottom of ornament; ***Long loop*** String **[2A, 1B]** 12 times, 2A, secure; repeat short loop; secure. Weave tail between wrapper and Styrofoam ball; trim. Weave in cast-on tail and trim.

Cinch cast-on and bind-off of tubular wrapper around hole in wooden bead

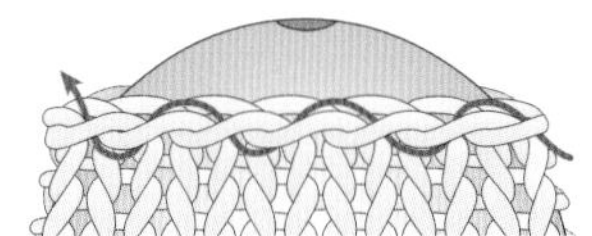

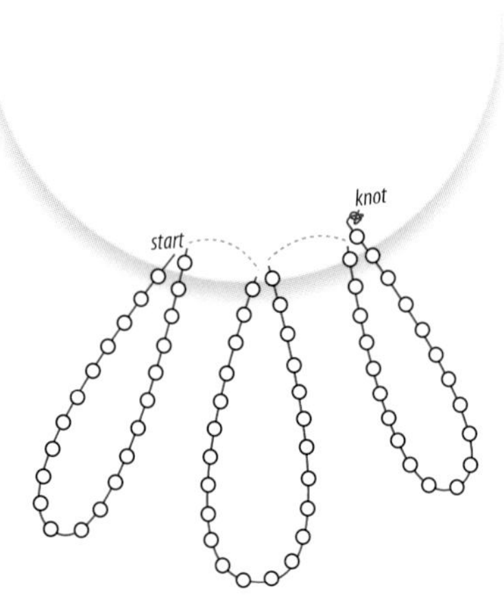

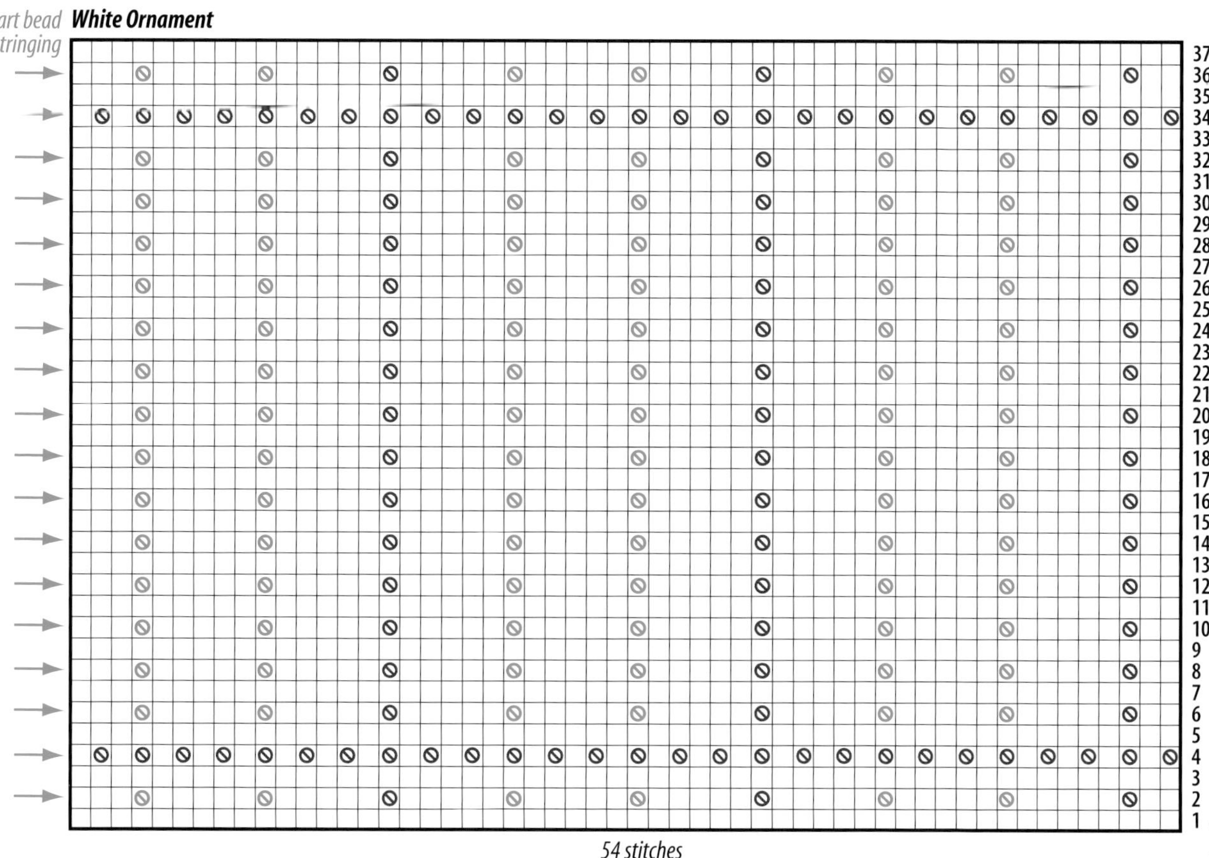

gauge

7 stitches = 1"

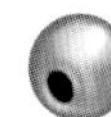

yarn

light weight
25 yds tubular chainette ribbon

beads

310 size 6° Japanese glass seed beads, shown in 2 colors

needles

3.25mm/US3

& and…

beading needle
tapestry needle
stitch marker
2½" Styrofoam ball

Stitch key

☐ *Knit on RS*

⊘ ⊘ *KBL with standard wrap. On next round, knit stitch tbl with bead to RS of work.*

→ *Direction of bead stringing*

Bead key

● *A*

● *B*

WHITE ORNAMENT stringing sequence

start → **[2A, 1B]** 3×, 27B, **[2A, 1B]** 42×, 27B, **[2A, 1B]** 3× *end*

NOTES: easy +

See page 160 for knitting abbreviations and techniques, and page 2 for beading basics.

WHAT IF…

Too many challenges? One way to simplify this project is to use a single color of beads. Or take 2 colors (or more?) and string them randomly. The end result can be uniquely your own.

MIYUKI Size 6° glass seed beads
158 in 26F Matte Silver-lined Olive (A)

TOHO Size 6° glass seed beads
130 in 329 Gold Lustered African Sunset (B)

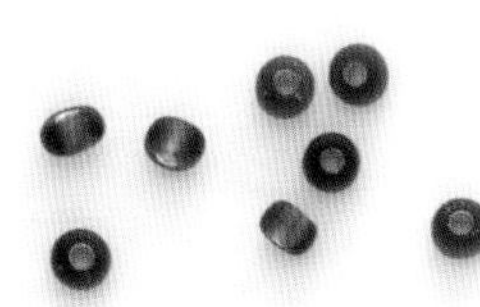

DEBBIE BLISS Baby Cashmerino
25 yds in 34 Cherry

In my basic bead-knitting class, I teach students ways to knit beads into stockinette fabric so the beads can appear in 4 distinct orientations—horizontal, vertical, diagonal left, and diagonal right. Given the small size of the beads we often work with, I am often asked, "Why should I care about orientation? Why does it really matter what direction the beads are facing?" The red ornament is a perfect illustration of how it can matter. I was able to use the slant of the beads to more accurately draw the beaded swirl and snowflake images into the knitting. On a garment, the slant of a bead can highlight a beautiful neckline or draw attention to the graceful line of a raglan shoulder. The more tools you have at your disposal as a knitter, the more options you have in your design process.

RED ORNAMENT

Prepare

With a beading needle, string 180 beads.

Knit

Leaving a 20" tail, cast on 45 and divide evenly onto 3 dpn, join without twisting, place marker, and work the Red Ornament chart in the round.
Bind off. Cut yarn, leaving a 12" tail.

Finish

With tapestry needle and bind-off tail, cinch the bound-off edge tightly. Secure, then thread the remaining length in a beading needle, string 33 beads, and secure tail to the fabric to create a hanging loop. Insert Styrofoam ball. With tapestry needle and cast-on tail, cinch the cast-on edge around the bottom of the Styrofoam ball. Secure, then thread remaining length in beading needle and create 3 lengths of beaded fringe as follows: string 17 beads, then thread needle back through the first 16 beads and secure; repeat with a 19-bead length and a 21-bead length. Weave tail between wrapper and Styrofoam ball; trim. Weave in cast-on tail and trim.

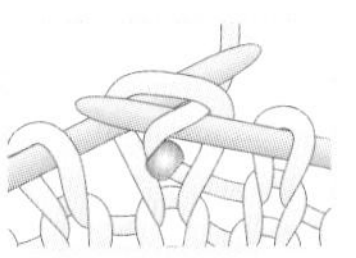

KBL Knit bead through stitch with standard wrap. On next round, knit stitch through back loop.

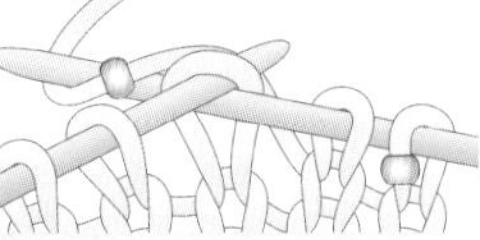

KBR Knit bead through stitch with reverse wrap. On next round, knit stitch in front loop — stitch twists because of reverse wrap.

MATSUNO Size 6º glass seed beads
270 in 563 Silver

Red Ornament

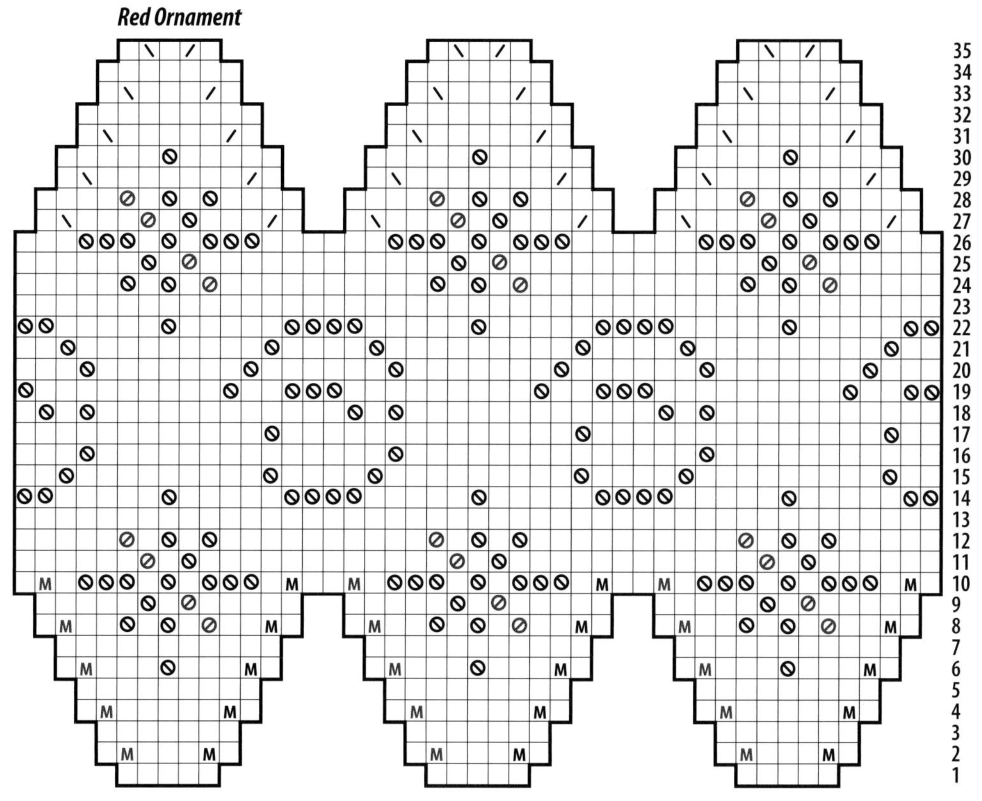

Stitch key

- Knit
- KBL with standard wrap. On next round, knit stitch tbl.
- KBR with reverse wrap. On next round, knit stitch through front loop; stitch twists because of reverse wrap.
- SSK
- K2tog
- M1R
- M1L

gauge

6 stitches = 1"

yarn

light weight
25 yds DK-weight yarn

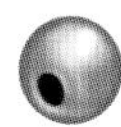

beads

290 size 6º Japanese glass seed beads

needles

3.5mm/US4

and...

beading needle
tapestry needle
stitch marker
2½" Styrofoam ball

NOTES: intermediate

See page 160 for knitting abbreviations and techniques, and page 2 for beading basics.

In order to shape the bead-knit-in-the-round fabric to the underlying Styrofoam ball (so the swirl and snowflake designs are clear), the fabric must be shaped — first with increases and then with decreases. Notice how the shape of the chart looks a lot like a world map taken from a globe.

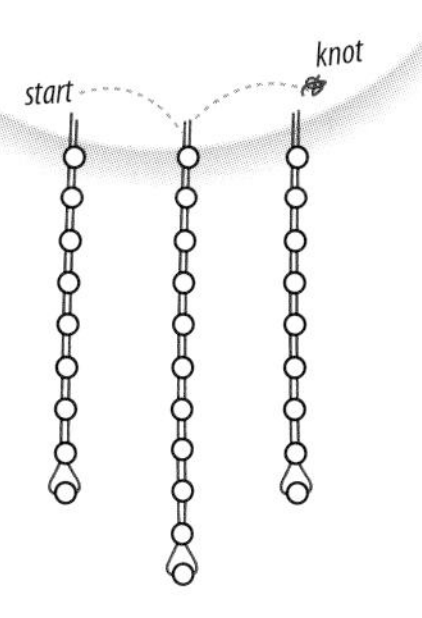

WHAT IF...

Once you understand how to use the different slants of the beads to your advantage, you can chart your own beaded design for an ornament. How much fun would it be to personalize an ornament with an initial and the year it was made, and then give it as a gift? Lots of wonderful possibilities exist!

Easter eggs

There is much truth in the old saying, "There's more than one way to skin a cat." Or, in this case, to wrap an egg! I was inspired to make these fun little projects when I went to the craft store to find the Styrofoam balls for my Christmas ornaments. Sitting on the shelf right next to the balls were Styrofoam eggs. Who could resist? Certainly not me. The peach egg is made with a flat piece of bead-knit fabric, grafted and cinched around the form. The blue/multi egg is worked in the round with a bit of shaping at the beginning, then gathered at the end after the form is inserted. What knitter wouldn't enjoy finding one of these trinkets in their Easter basket?

DEBBIE BLISS Baby Cashmerino
25 yds in 600 Dusty Pink (Peach egg)
OR 202 Baby Blue (Blue/multi egg, A)

FIESTA YARNS Gelato
10 yds in Stargazer (Blue/multi egg, B)

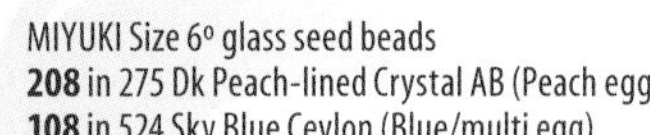

MIYUKI Size 6º glass seed beads
208 in 275 Dk Peach-lined Crystal AB (Peach egg)
108 in 524 Sky Blue Ceylon (Blue/multi egg)

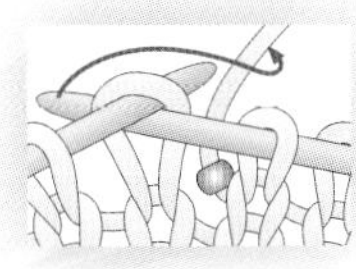

SB Slide bead close to last stitch worked.

gauge
6 stitches = 1"

yarn
light weight
25 yds DK yarn per egg

yarn
medium weight
10 yds rayon ribbon for blue/multi egg

beads
size 6° Japanese glass seed beads
240 for peach egg
120 for blue/multi egg

needles
3.25mm/US3
2.75mm/US2

3.25mm/US3

and...
beading needle
tapestry needle
2 2½" x 1⅞" Styrofoam eggs

PEACH EGG

Prepare

With beading needle, string 208 beads.

Knit

With straight needles, and leaving an 8" tail, cast on 18.

Row 1 (WS) K2, **[SB, k2]** 8 times.

Row 2 P1, **[SB, p2]** 8 times, SB, p1.

Row 3 Purl.

Row 4 Knit.

Row 5 Purl.

Row 6 Repeat Row 2

Repeat Rows 1–6 for a total of 47 rows, end with Row 5.

Bind off in pattern, placing beads as for Row 6. Cut yarn, leaving a 12" tail.

Finish

With RS facing, tapestry needle, bind-off tail, and using Zipper Graft, join cast-on and bound-off edges. Insert Styrofoam egg. Using cast-on and bind-off tails, cinch edge stitches around the ends of the egg. Secure and weave in tails between wrapper and Styrofoam egg; trim.

BLUE/MULTI EGG

Prepare

With beading needle, string A with 108 beads.

Knit

With A, cast on 6 and divide evenly onto 3 larger double-pointed needles, join without twisting, and place marker to work in the round.

Rounds 1, 3 Knit.

Round 2 **[Kf&b]** 6 times — 12 stitches.

Round 4 **[K1, kf&b]** 6 times — 18 stitches.

Rounds 5, 6 Knit.

Round 7 **[K2, kf&b]** 6 times — 24 stitches.

Rounds 8, 10 Knit.

Round 9 **[K1, kf&b]** 12 times — 36 stitches.

Round 11 P1, **[SB, p2]** 17 times, SB, p1.

Round 12 SB, **[p2, SB]** 17 times, p2.

Rounds 13–16 Repeat Rounds 11–12 twice.

Switch to smaller dpns and B.

Rounds 17-34 Knit.

Bind off. Cut yarn, leaving a 10" tail.

Finish

Slide Styrofoam egg, large end first, into knit tube. With tapestry needle and bind-off tail, cinch bound-off edge tightly around the top (small end) of the egg. Secure; weave tail between wrapper and Styrofoam egg; trim. Weave in cast-on tail and trim.

NOTES: easy +

See page160 for knitting abbreviations and techniques, and page 2 for beading basics.

WHAT IF...

Looking at the blue/multi egg, another real-life comparison occurred to me. Doesn't it look a bit like an acorn? So... change the colors to the warm shades of fall and make a few of these to hang on your front door with some great looking gourds come October. Or use them in a Thanksgiving centerpiece! Or...???

Finishing the hat…

At the conclusion of Stephen Sondheim's musical *Sunday In the Park with George*, the main character, the post-impressionist painter Georges Seurat, sings a song in which he both celebrates and bemoans the life of an artist. He sings of his sacrifice, his pride and his reward:

> *…however you live,*
> *There's a part of you*
> *always standing by,*
> *Mapping out the sky,*
> *Finishing a hat…*
> *Starting on a hat…*
> *Finishing a hat…*
> *Look, I made a hat…*
> *Where there never was a hat.*

NOTE: So you don't think this essay has been misplaced from a different book, it may help you to know that along with my passion for knitting I am absolutely crazy about musical theater, and this song has an important lesson to teach. Okay! Now back to our regularly scheduled program to see what this has to do with knitting…

Finishing. It's a word that has powerful meanings for me. One meaning relates to the concrete process of finishing a project: joining the pieces of knitted fabric, weaving in loose yarn ends, sewing on buttons or embellishments. I know there are many knitters out there who absolutely HATE finishing. Many rush through the process and some even gladly pay others to do it for them. Not me. I LOVE finishing. I'm always happy to discover a new technique that will help me finish a project beautifully. When you finish a project with attention to detail, you honor the investment of time and effort put into the creation of the pieces that comprise it. It's always time well spent.

Another meaning of finishing is related to the more concrete creative process that I am discovering. I start each new design with a small idea that may have been inspired in any number of ways. A series of iterations on that idea usually follows, with each swatch responding to a What if…? that makes it marginally different from the swatch that came before. So far, so good. But what comes next? When do I stop making marginal changes and expand the swatch into a full-sized project? In other words, how do I know when a new design idea is finished—ready to be realized? And once realized, how can I be sure that the resulting full-sized piece is finished? Might this process be ultimately frustrating because you may never know when you're done? What I'm learning is that maybe focusing so hard on whether or not something is finished is actually counter-productive!

It's called a creative PROCESS for a reason. My process involves taking lots of small steps. I love taking small steps, because it allows me to focus on one change at a time, and because it makes risk-taking—often a critical component of creativity—feel less scary. When a swatch sufficiently excites me, I try to use what I've learned from it to make a full-sized project. Does that mean I'm finished with it? Maybe yes and maybe no. At any time in the future, I can return to a design idea I've worked on before and use it to jump start a new series of swatches. And sometimes, no matter how many iterations I work, an idea goes nowhere that pleases me. But I keep all of my swatches, successful or not on my studio wall, calling them my UBO's—my Unidentified Beaded Objects. Because even failed UBO's have something to teach me. Learning what DOESN'T work is often just as important as learning what DOES.

If you decide that this process is one you'd like to try, I hope you'll consider the following. As your work develops, don't ever settle for less than you know you are capable of. Put aside the attempts that don't satisfy your vision or, at the least, present you with an exciting alternative path to pursue. Work each new step and move on to the next one be it a new idea, a new swatch, or a new project—only after you've learned what you need to learn from the immediate task at hand. It's the recognition of what you've learned with each step along the way, coupled with the sense of accomplishment you feel when you create something you can be truly proud of, that provides the closure. In the short term, you can move forward with confidence. In the long term, as you continue to keep your eyes and mind open, and to seek out new techniques and acquire new materials, the process can be repeated over and over again. If you believe there is always more to see, more to learn, and more to create, you will never be truly finished. And that's just fine, because along the way you will have the ongoing joy of:

Mapping out the sky,
—Finishing a hat...
Starting on a hat...
Finishing a hat...

Look! You made a hat.

Serpentine spirals *necklace (2009)*
Glass beads, fiber, Chinese turquoise/sterling silver clasp
Fascinated with spirals, but prior to discovering all-purl, spiral weaving to realize my spiral dreams.
Technique link: Beaded tubes

Welts

TECH TRIALS

NOTES

See page 160 for knitting abbreviations and techniques, and page 2 for beading basics.

SB Slide bead close to last stitch worked.

I'm always looking for ways to add dimension to my work, especially beading and/or knitting techniques that will add a third dimension to knit fabric. A knit-in welt is just such a technique. It's a close cousin to the hem, and also to the stand-alone knit tubes I use so often. As defined by June Hemmons Hiatt in *The Principles of Knitting*, "the major difference (from hems) is that welts are internal to the fabric rather than at the edge." I also like to exploit the fact that welts add a certain desired stiffness to the finished fabric. And of course, to my eye, they provide an ideal canvas for bead knitting or embellishment. Lots of "What if…?" possibilities here!

Plain and beaded welts — horizontal construction

A welt is a tubular form worked into a piece of fabric as it is being knit, by picking up stitches from a previous row and working them together with the stitches on the needle. Whether plain or beaded, the welt adds structure and great texture wherever it's used. The more rows incorporated into the welt, the flatter the finished welt will be.

Beaded welt, purl side out

Plain welt, purl side out

Plain welt, knit side out

String 24 beads. Cast on 17.
Knit 3 rows.
Next row (WS) Purl.
Work 7 rows in stockinette.
Welt row (WS) With smaller circular needle or dpn, pick up purl bumps 5 rows below stitches on needle — 17 stitches. **[P2tog (stitch from back needle with stitch from spare needle)]** to end. See drawings 1–2b — plain welt, knit side out.
Work 4 rows in stockinette.
Work 4 rows in reverse stockinette (purl on RS, knit on WS).
Next row (WS) Repeat Welt Row — plain welt, purl side out.
Work 4 rows in stockinette.
Beaded welt: Row 1 (RS) Purl.
Rows 2, 4 K1, **[SB, k2]** 8 times.
Row 3 P1, **[SB, p2]** 8 times.
Row 5 Purl.
Next row (WS) Repeat Welt Row — beaded welt, purl side out.
Work 4 rows in stockinette.
Knit 2 rows.
Bind off.

MAKE WELT

1

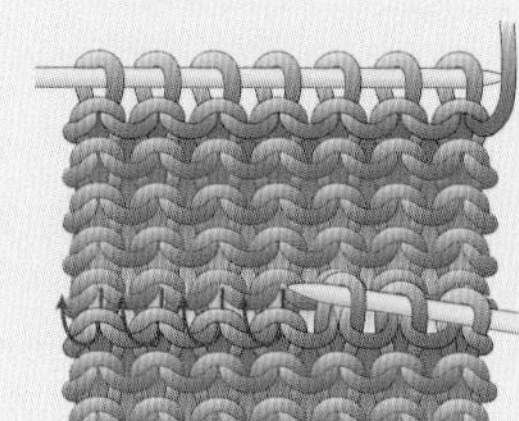

2a

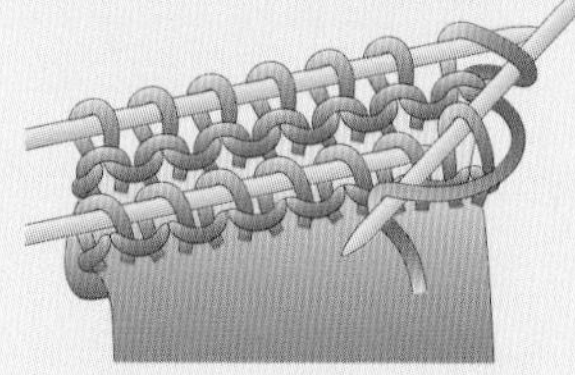

2b

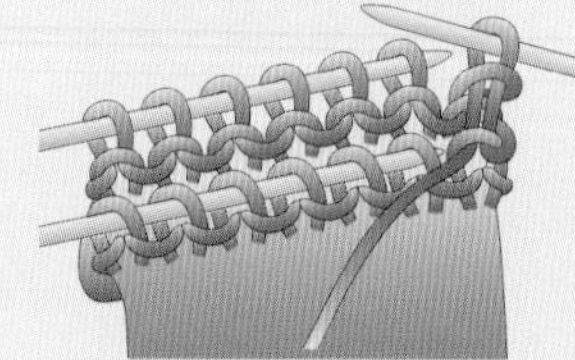

Hems

TECH TRIALS

If you appreciate quality finishing, knitting-in a hem is an invaluable technique for garments and accessories alike. Once you learn how to create a knit-in hem, it's hard NOT to think about using it every time you can. The traditional purl turning ridge of a stockinette hem is an ideal place to knit beads into your fabric—when folded, any bead-knit effects will lie along or hang from the bottom of the hem. You can also think of a hem as a stand-alone construction, since it has many of the same qualities and applications as a double-sided strap: it lies flat and inside there is a valuable empty space to conceal yarn ends or to weave beads into after the knitting is complete. If it's luxury and drama you're looking for, think about layering multiple hems, as in the Girly Pearls necklace in this section. While I often say I'm a fan of the *judicious* use of beads, sometimes more IS better!

WHAT YOU NEED

Any size 6° beads

Smooth sock- to DK-weight wool or wool-blend yarn in a solid, light color

Knitting needles in a size you would normally use for the yarn (usually US 3–5)

AND set of 4 double-pointed needles

Smaller circular or double-pointed needles

Fine beading thread

Beading needle

Waste yarn

Crochet hook

Plain and beaded hems—horizontal construction

The first samples show—from the right side and the wrong side—a plain stockinette hem with a purl ridge as the turning row. Knitting beads along this purl row is a wonderfully simple way to create a beaded edge. The turning row can also be worked with yarn-overs to create a picot edge. Beads can then be woven along the picot edge to create a bead-knit look without pre-stringing the beads.

Plain purl-ridge hem, RS

Plain purl-ridge hem, WS

Beaded purl-ridge hem

Beaded picot hem

Plain stockinette hem with purl-ridge turning row

With waste yarn and a temporary crocheted cast-on, cast on 16.

Row 1 (RS) With yarn, knit.

Row 2 P14, p2tog—15 stitches.

Rows 3–10 Work in stockinette.

Row 11: Turning row (RS) Purl.

Rows 12–20 Work in stockinette.

Remove waste yarn from cast-on, placing 15 stitches onto a spare double-pointed needle.

Hem: Row 21 Hold cast-on needle behind work and **[k2tog (stitch from spare needle with stitch from back needle)]** to end—15 stitches.

Rows 23–25 Work in stockinette.

Bind off.

Stockinette hem with beaded turning row

String 14 beads.

Work as above EXCEPT work Row 11 as follows:

Row 11: Beaded turning row P1, **[SB, p1]** 14 times.

Stockinette hem with beaded picot turning row

Work as above EXCEPT work Row 11 as follows:

Row 11: Picot turning row K2, **[yo, k2tog]** 6 times, k1.

Using fine beading thread and a stiff beading needle, weave beads into the picot hem in the spaces created by the yarn-overs.

Picot edge

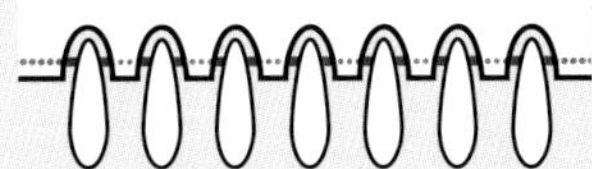

Weave thread through hem, stringing a bead onto needle at each picot yarn-over space.

Wired for wow

Wired for wow

This next project grew out of my desire to offer some jewelry designs that could be worked on somewhat larger needles. Size 4's may not seem large to you, but hey—it's all relative, right? After working on size 0, 1, and 2 needles, 4's felt like broomsticks! I also wanted to use one of my favorite fibers. It's called Corde', and it's a soutache—a fiber comprised of a cotton core wrapped with very fine rayon thread, and then hand dyed in an amazing array of colors. It has great body and provides extraordinary stitch definition, but this same body, combined with the thickness of the fiber, makes it all but impossible to string small glass beads onto it. This project illustrates how you can have the best of both worlds by alternating the heavier cord with a finer yarn used for stringing the beads. I've used the internal tubular space created by the welting to conceal sturdy but flexible copper wire, which allows the bangle to be opened and closed around the wrist without a clasp. Pretty cool, yes? Fun to make and easy to wear!

JUDI & CO. Cordé
40 yds in Thistle (A)
FILATURA DI CROSA New Smoking
10 yds in 07 White (B)

MIYUKI Size 4mm cube beads
35 each in 242 Sparkle Pewter-lined Crystal (AA)
AND 234 Sparkle Metallic Gold-lined Crystal (BB)

Prepare and knit

With A cord and cable cast-on, cast on 36 stitches. Slip cast-on stitches back onto right needle and turn work.

Row 1 (WS) With beading needle, string B with 35 AA beads.

With B, k1, **[SB, k1]** to end. Cut B, leaving an 8" tail.

Rows 2–10 With A, work 9 rows in stockinette, starting and ending with a knit row.

Row 11: Welt (WS) With smaller circular needle or dpn, pick up purl bumps 5 rows below stitches on needle — 36 stitches. **[P2tog (stitch from back needle with stitch from spare needle)]** to end. See drawings 1–2b, below.

Rows 12–31 Work Rows 2–11 twice more — 3 welts.

Row 32 Knit. Do not cut A.

Row 33 (WS) With beading needle, string B with 35 BB beads.

With B, k1, **[SB, k1]** to end. Cut B, leaving an 8" tail.

Row 34 With A, bind off. Cut A, leaving an 8" tail.

Finish

Insert a length of copper wire inside each welt. This is easier to accomplish if you first slide a knitting needle into the welt, then run the wire alongside the needle.

1 Use needle-nose pliers to bend back one sharp end of the wire.

2 Push bent end of wire back into welt (as shown). Use a wire cutter to trim wire ½" shorter than the total length of welt.

3 Bend cut end of wire and push into welt. Tack ends of welt and weave tails inside.

Bend and wrap the bracelet around the wrist to fit.

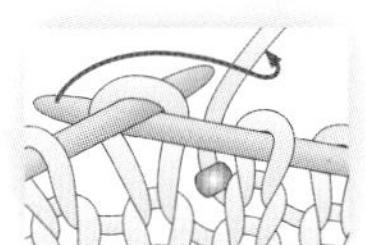

SB Slide bead close to last stitch worked.

gauge
4¾ stitches = 1"
finished length 7½"

yarn
medium weight
40 yds cord

yarn
fine weight
10 yds metallic yarn

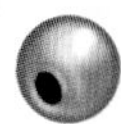

beads
85 size 4mm Japanese cube beads, shown in 2 colors

needles
3.5mm/US4

and...
beading needle
tapestry needle
smaller metal circular or double-pointed (dpn) needle
16-gauge copper wire
wire cutter
needle-nose pliers

MAKE WELT

1

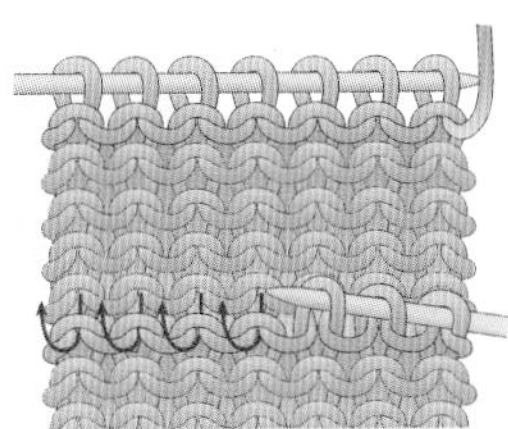

2a

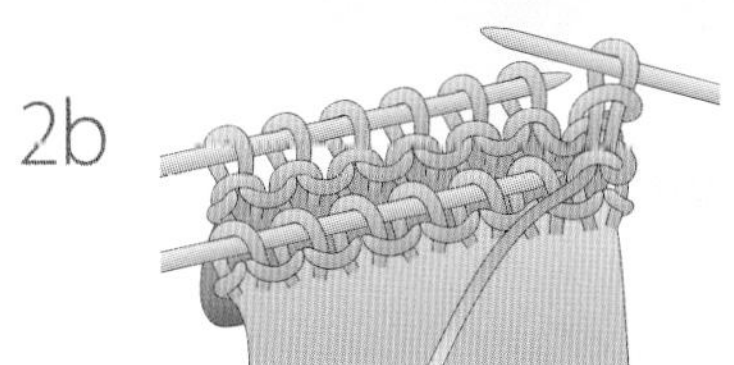

2b

INSERT WIRE

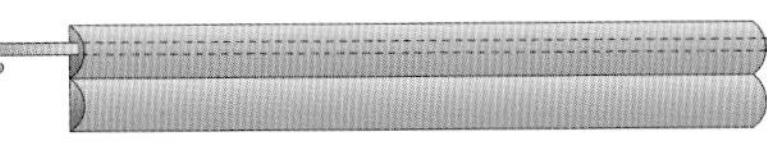

1 Bend end of wire

2 Push wire back into welt (farther than necessary) and cut other end.

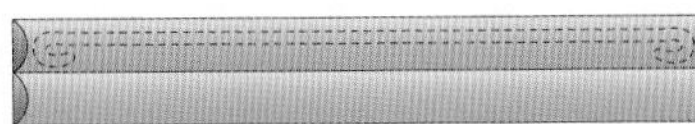

3 Bend wire and push into welt.

NOTES: easy

See page 160 for knitting abbreviations and techniques, and page 2 for beading basics.

Look for the 16-gauge copper wire in the electrical section of your nearest hardware store. It's a bit heavier and sturdier than the lighter wire sold in craft stores.

WHAT IF...

If you prefer, leave out the wire and stitch a closure on the ends of the bangle — maybe 2 magnetic clasps?

Try this pattern with a different chunky yarn of your choice. It just needs to have enough substance and be worked at a gauge tight enough to hold its shape. And if you don't care to string the beads onto metallic yarn, use another strong, fine-weight yarn. Experiment! There are lots of options with this one.

Granite cuff

This cuff is similar to the Welted Bangle bracelet, but includes some interesting variations. It gave me the opportunity to use another unique Judi & Co fiber called Disco. Due to its spongy, tubular construction, Disco has lots of stretch. It compresses easily, so the beads can be placed onto the yarn with a crochet hook, and I was able to work on relatively small needles, given the weight of the fiber. The firm tension this combination of needles and fiber produces maintains the shape of the cuff, and the stretch is helpful when it's time to work the closely placed welting rows. This yarn has some subtle bling, so you don't need many beads to give the bracelet lots of shine. Copper wire is again threaded into a couple of the welts to support the shape of the cuff, allowing it to be opened and closed securely over the wrist without the addition of a closure.

Knit

Leaving a 12" tail, cast on 42.

Work all rows in stockinette EXCEPT

Rows 6, 12 Work Welt Row, 4 rows below.

Row 20 Work Welt Row, 6 rows below.

Row 25 Work Bead Row.

Row 28 Work Welt Row, 6 rows below.

Row 33 Work Bead Row.

Rows 36, 44 Work Welt Row, 6 rows below.

Rows 50, 56 Work Welt Row, 4 rows below.

Bind off. Cut yarn, leaving an 18" tail.

Finish

Finish as for Wired for Wow, page 143.

JUDI & CO Disco
40 yds in Mulberry

WELT ROW (WS) With smaller metal circular needle or dpn, pick up purl bumps 4 or 6 rows below stitches on needle. **[P2tog (stitch from back needle with stitch from spare needle)]** to end. See drawings 1–2b, below.

BEAD ROW (RS) **[Place 1 bead onto the steel crochet hook. With hook, lift the first stitch off left needle and draw it through the bead; slip stitch back onto left needle and knit it]** to end. See drawings 1–4, right.

MAKE WELT

1

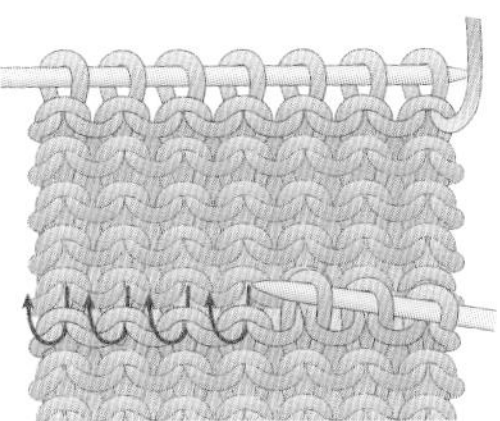

2a

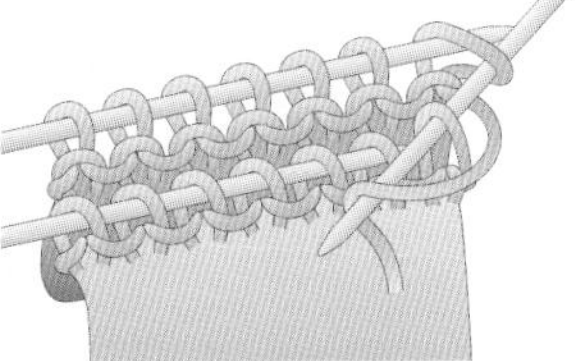

2b

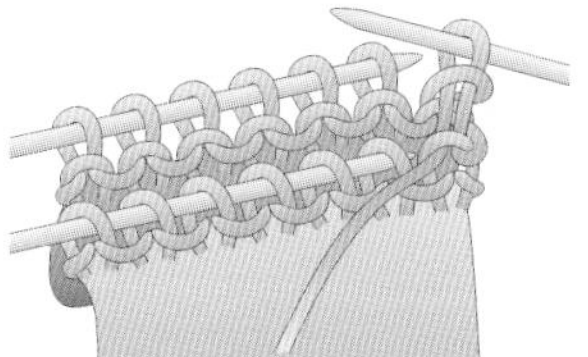

Miyuki Size 6° glass seed beads
84 in 451 Gunmetal

BEAD ROW

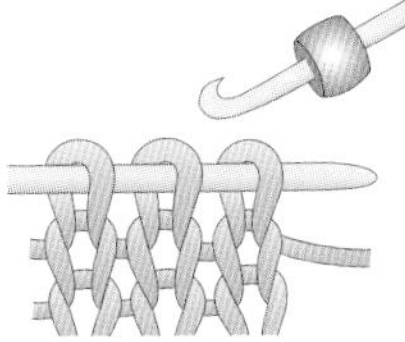

1 Place 1 bead onto crochet hook.

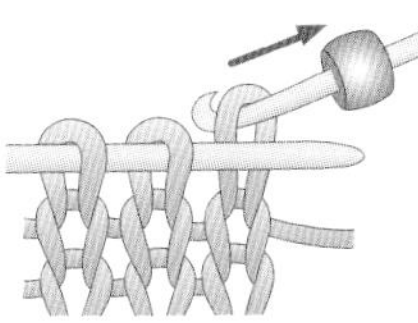

2 With hook, slip the first stitch off left needle and pull it through the bead.

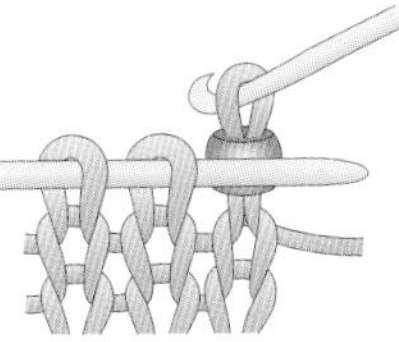

3 Slip stitch back onto left needle…

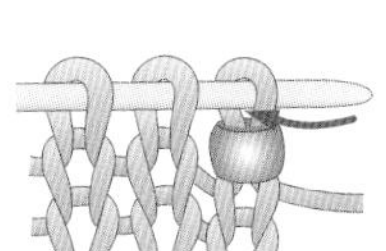

4 …and knit it.

gauge

6 stitches = 1"
finished length 7"

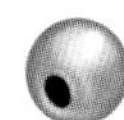

yarn

medium weight
40 yds tubular chainette ribbon

beads

90 size 6° Japanese glass seed beads

needles

3.75mm/US5

& and…

tapestry needle
1.5mm or smaller steel crochet hook
smaller metal circular or double-pointed (dpn) needle
16-gauge copper wire
wire cutter
needle-nose pliers

NOTES: easy

See page 160 for knitting abbreviations and techniques, and page 2 for beading basics.

WHAT IF…

I'd love to see this cuff made from one of the gorgeous rayon ribbon yarns available from Fiesta (Gelato), Prism (Quicksilver) or Interlacements (New York). They share the same technical construction as Disco, so they can be worked on needles small enough to achieve the firmness required for this cuff and still accommodate the size 6° beads. And their variegated colorways would be stunning knit up in this way.

You could leave the wire out of this cuff and use a clasp or button/loop closure instead.

Bead warmers

Bead warmers

Once I started to think of welts as a form of knitted tube, all kinds of ideas began to percolate. If I used the reverse-stockinette side of the knitted fabric as the outside of the welt, I could easily bead it. A review of my Idea Book—I try to write down every idea I have for a design—reminded me of an idea for winter jewelry (bead-knit pieces that can be worn with outerwear). This scarf and earwarmer are the result. Because the number of beads I wanted to use and the density of the welting would increase the weight of the knit fabric—especially with the number of welts I had in mind—a warm but lightweight yarn would work best. This soft and yummy worsted-weight alpaca is perfect! And I think the color and finish on these beads makes them look like just-fallen snow melting on the yarn: warm and frosty at the same time.

BASIC WELT (BW)
Row 1 (RS) Knit.
Row 2 Purl.
Rows 3–4 Knit.
Row 5 Purl.
Row 6 Knit.
Row 7 Purl.
Row 8, Welt Row (WS) With spare needle, pick up purl bumps 4 rows below stitches on needle to end. **[P2tog (stitch from back needle with stitch from spare needle)].**

BASIC WELT WITH BEADS (BWB)
Work as for Basic Welt, placing beads on Rows 5–7 as shown on Earwarmer or Scarf chart.

INC ROW
Row 3 of Welt K1, M1, knit to last stitch, M1, k1.

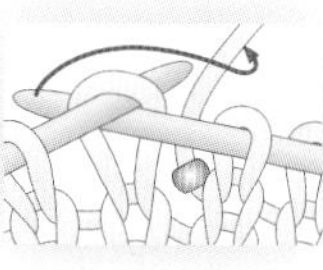

SB Slide bead close to last stitch worked.

EARWARMER
stringing sequence

start→ 61A, 1B, 3A, 1B, 1A, 1B, **[2A, 2B]** twice, **[1A, 1B]** 3 times, 8B, **[1A, 1B]** 5 times, 2B, 1A, 12B, 1A, 11B, 1A, 1B, 1A, 10B, 1A, 31B *end*

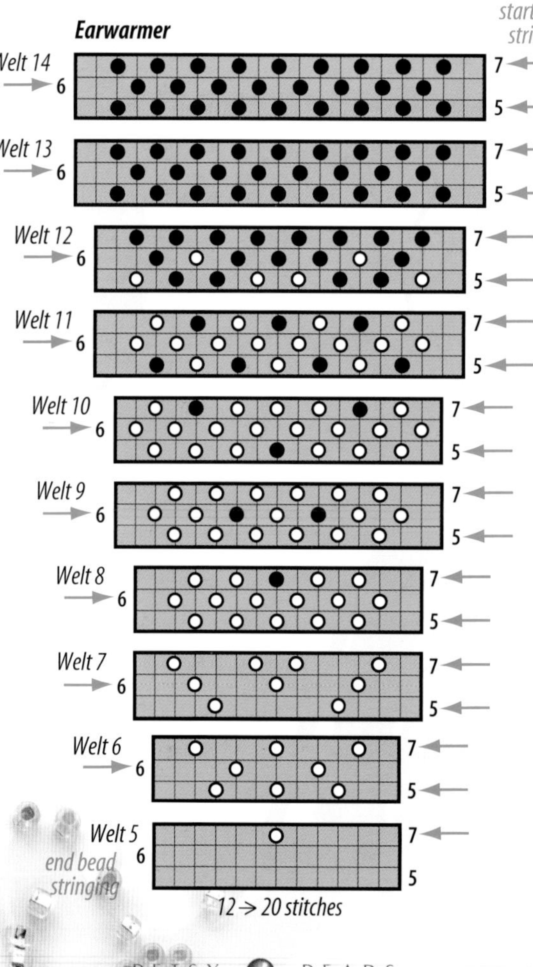

Earwarmer
MIYUKI Size 5º glass seed beads
82 283 Noir-lined Crystal AB (A)

MATSUNO Size 6º glass seed beads
90 64 Square-holed, Silver-lined Transparent Crystal (B)

Scarf
MIYUKI Size 5º glass seed beads
244 131S Silver-lined Crystal (A)
308 283 Noir-lined Crystal AB (B)

EARWARMER
MAKE 2

Prepare

With beading needle, string beads following Earwarmer chart or Stringing Sequence.

Knit

With waste yarn, and using a temporary crochet cast-on, cast on 11.
Row 1 (RS) With yarn, knit.
Row 2 P9, p2tog—10 stitches.
Rows 3–12 Work even in stockinette.
WELTS 1–3 Work Basic Welt (BW).
WELT 4 Work BW with Inc Row—12 stitches.
WELTS 5–6 Work Basic Welt with Beads (BWB).
WELT 7 Work BWB with Inc Row—14 stitches.
WELTS 8, 10, 12 Work BWB.
WELT 9 Work BWB with Inc Row—16 stitches.
WELT 11 Work BWB with Inc Row—18 stitches.
WELT 13 Work BWB with Inc Row—20 stitches.
WELT 14 Work BWB. Do not bind off; place stitches on spare knitting needle. Cut yarn, leaving a 24" tail.

Finish

Place the 2 halves RS together and, using a 3-needle bind-off, bind off.
Remove waste yarn from cast-ons, placing 9 stitches from each piece on 2 knitting needles. Make any necessary adjustments in length by removing or adding rows to one or both halves. With tapestry needle and 24" tail, and using stockinette graft, join.

NEW ERA FIBER/MEISCHAY ELITE
Worsted Alpaca in White
75 yds for Earwarmer
150 yds for Scarf

SCARF

Prepare

With beading needle, string beads following Scarf chart or Stringing Sequence.

Knit

With waste yarn, and using a temporary crochet cast-on, cast on 15.

Row 1 (RS) With yarn, knit.

Row 2 P13, p2tog—14 stitches.

WELT 1 Work Basic Welt (BW) beginning on Row 3.

WELTS 2–10 Work BW.

WELT 11 Work BW with Inc Row—16 stitches.

WELTS 12–18 Work BW.

WELT 19 Work Basic Welt with Beads (BWB), with Inc Row—18 stitches.

WELTS 20–26 Work BWB.

WELT 27 Work BWB with Inc Row—20 stitches.

WELTS 28–32 Work BWB.

Bind off. Cut yarn.

Remove waste yarn from cast-on, placing 14 stitches on a knitting needle.

With beading needle, string beads and work as for first half of Scarf, EXCEPT purl Row 2.

Finish

With tapestry needle, weave in ends.

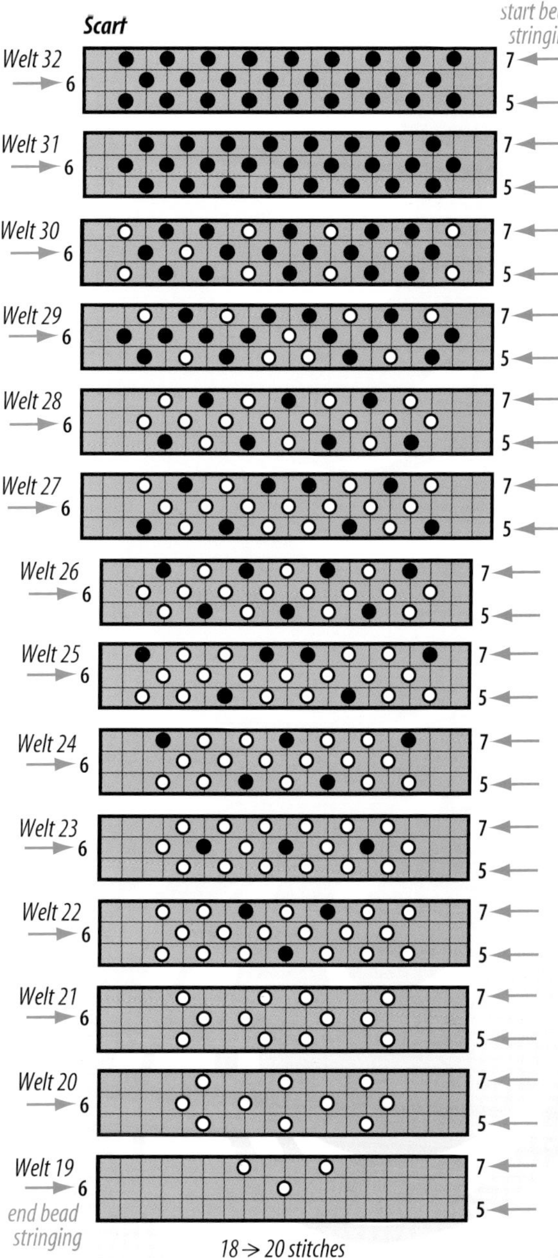

Stitch key

- Purl on RS, knit on WS
- SB, p1 on RS
- SB, k1 on WS

Bead key

- ● A
- ○ B

SCARF stringing sequence

start → 51A, 1B, **[2A, 1B, 1A, 1B]** twice, 2A, **[2A, 1B, 1A, 1B]** twice, 2A, 2B, 1A, 1B, 2A, 1B, 1A, 1B, 4A 1B, 5A, 1B, 1A, 2B, **[1A, 1B]** 5 times, 8B, **[1A, 1B]** 5 times, 2A, 1B, 1A, 8B, 1A, 1B, 1A, 2B, 1A, 1B, 1A, **[1A, 1B]** 4 times, 8B, **[1A, 1B]** 4 times, 1B, 2A, 2B, 1A, 7B, **[2B, 1A]** 5 times, 8B, **[1A, 1B, 1A, 9B, 1A, 1B]** twice, 1A, 11B, 1A, 28B *end*

gauge

5 stitches = 1"
finished length 19" for earwarmer, 35" for scarf

yarn

medium weight
75 (150) yds for earwarmer (scarf)

beads

90 (260) Size 5º Japanese glass seed beads for earwarmer (scarf)
100 (330) Size 6º Japanese glass seed beads for earwarmer (scarf)

needles

5mm/US8

and...

beading needle
tapestry needle
spare knitting needle, same size or smaller
waste yarn
crochet hook

NOTES: intermediate +

See page 160 for knitting abbreviations and techniques, and page 2 for beading basics.

The earwarmer is worked in 2 pieces that are grafted together on both ends.

The scarf is worked one half at a time, from the middle outward toward the beaded ends, so only half of the beads need to be strung at a time.

WHAT IF...

If you don't feel up to stringing this many beads in order while following the charted design, just string the beads in random order and place them as the spirit moves you. They will surely look like a dusting of early winter snow.

Girly pearls

Girly pearls

I think pearls are so beautiful! I grew up during a time when the best-dressed women wore them and lots of little girls dreamed of owning them. Later in life, my father gave me a beautiful pearl necklace for a special birthday. It was only natural for me to want to find a way to use pearls with knitting. One of the challenges presented by pearls is that the holes drilled through them are very, very small, preventing them from being strung on most knitting yarns. So how to work pearls into knitted fabric? I solved this problem by first creating a picot-edged hem. I then used a strong but fine thread to weave the pearls into the yarn-over spaces between the picots, with one pearl peeking through each yarn-over. Not actual bead knitting, but a great bead-knit look. Traditional pearls—youthful, new, and hand-knit.

223 Top-drilled, Drop Freshwater Pearls

ALCHEMY YARNS Silken Straw
150 yds in 42m Silver

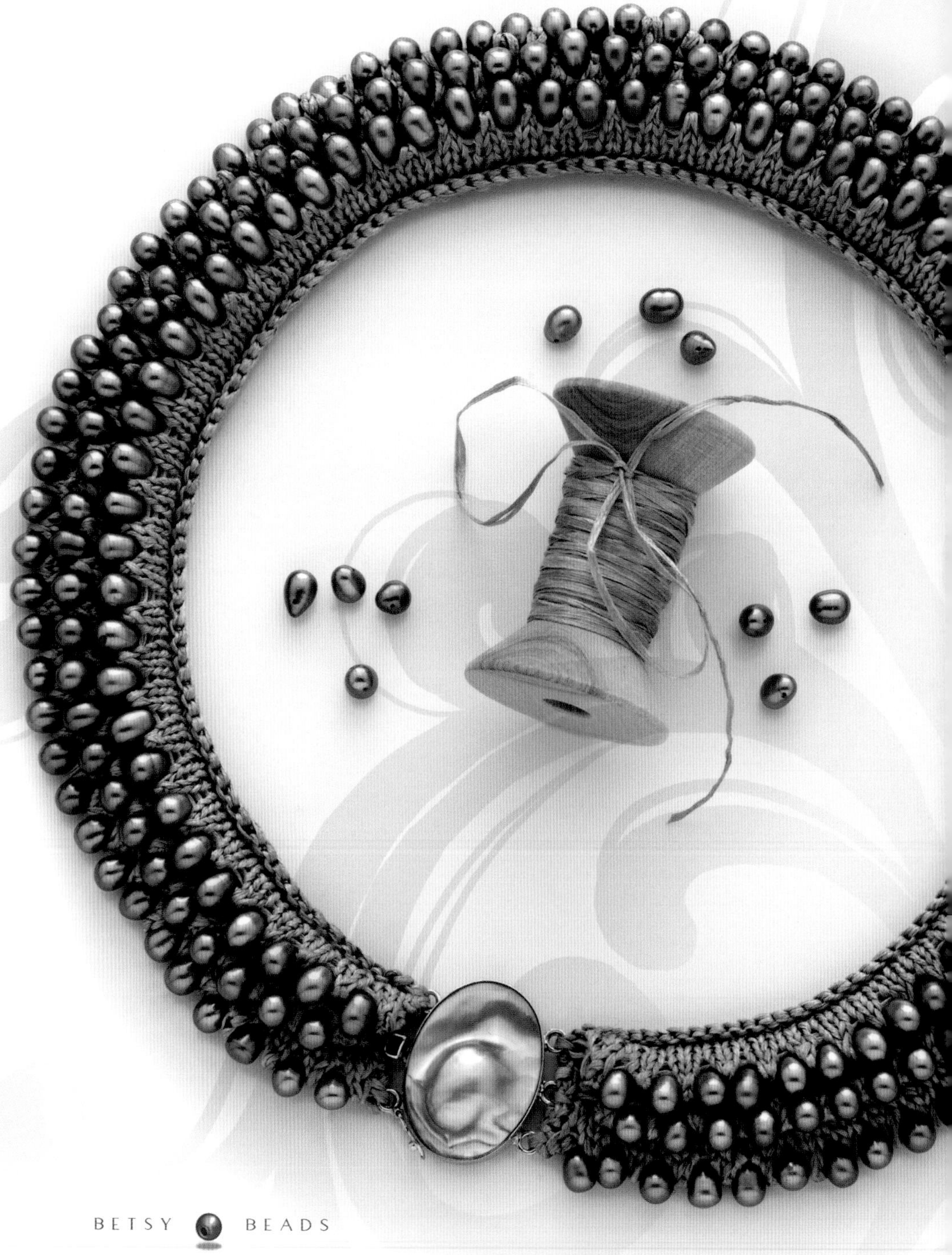

Bottom layer

With waste yarn, and using a temporary cast-on (see Notes), cast on 168.

Row 1 (RS) With silk, knit.

Row 2 Purl to last 2 stitches, p2tog — 167 stitches.

Rows 3–6 Work in stockinette.

Row 7: Picot (RS) K2, **[yo, k2tog]** to last stitch, k1.

Rows 8–12 Work in stockinette.

Remove waste yarn from cast-on, placing 167 stitches onto a spare circular needle.

Row 13: Hem (RS) Hold cast-on needle behind work and **[k2tog (using 1 stitch from each needle)]** to end.

Rows 14, 16 Purl.

Row 15 (RS) **[K8, SSK]** 8 times, then **[k8, k2tog]** 8 times, k7—151 stitches.

Cut yarn, leaving a 4½-yd tail. Place stitches on a spare circular needle.

Middle layer

With waste yarn, and using a temporary cast-on, cast on 152.

Work Rows 1–12 as for Bottom layer.

Remove waste yarn from cast-on, placing 151 stitches onto a spare circular needle.

Work Rows 13 and 14 as for Bottom layer.

Row 15: Join layers Place Middle layer on top of Bottom layer and, using the 4½-yd tail, knit the stitches from both needles together. Do not turn work.

Row 16 Using the working yarn from Middle layer, k9, **[SSK, k8]** 7 times, **[k2tog, k8]** 7 times, k2—137 stitches. Place stitches on a spare circular needle.

Top-drilled pearls

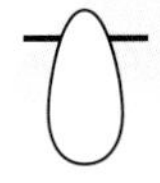

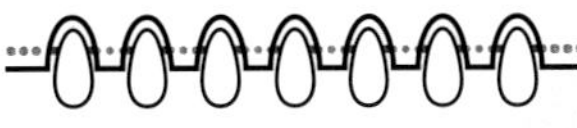

Thread monofilament through hems, stringing a pearl at each yarn-over space.

Placing pearls

67
74
82

Top layer

With waste yarn, and using a temporary cast-on, cast on 138.

Work Rows 1–4 as for Bottom layer.

Row 5: Picot (RS) K2, **[yo, k2tog]** to last stitch, k1.

Rows 6–8 Work in stockinette.

Remove waste yarn from cast-on, placing 137 stitches onto a spare circular needle.

Row 9 Hold cast-on needle behind work and **[k2tog (using 1 stitch from each needle)]** to end.

Row 10: Join layers Place Top layer on top of joined Bottom and Middle layers and, using a 3-needle bind-off, bind off purlwise.

Finish

Placing pearls

Using a very fine beading needle, thread monofilament through bottom of each hem, stringing one pearl onto the beading needle at each yarn-over space — 67 pearls in Top layer, 74 pearls in Middle layer, 82 pearls in Bottom layer. Secure monofilament at each end and weave tails inside hem.

With tapestry needle and yarn tails, attach 3-strand clasp.

WHAT IF...

If pearls are not your thing, consider substituting any top-drilled drop bead.

You can change the number of layers—1, 2, 4? Try a single pearled hem with fewer rows of stockinette for a knit variation on the traditional pearl necklace.

gauge

7½ stitches = 1"
finished length 18", excluding clasp

yarn

fine weight
150 yds 100% silk

beads

240 top-drilled drop pearls

needles

2 2.75mm/US2

and...

very fine beading needle
tapestry needle
2 spare circular needles, same size or smaller
beading monofilament
waste yarn
crochet hook
3-strand clasp

NOTES: easy

See page 160 for knitting abbreviations and techniques, and page 2 for beading basics.

Using waste yarn and a temporary crochet cast-on is VERY important.

The 3 hemmed layers of this necklace are worked separately and then joined. The pearls are woven into the hems afterwards.

Your yarn choice does not have to be suitable for stringing beads.

The Silken Straw feels very stiff, but becomes wonderfully supple and soft when worked, while maintaining great stitch definition.

Struggling with the 'A' words

I have always struggled with what I call the 'A' words: Art, Artist, Artistic.

I've always wondered how someone gets to be an Artist. Who determines what Art is? And I've certainly never thought of myself as Artistic. On the other hand, I've always thought of my sister as an Artistic person. She was an Art History major in college, she managed an Art gallery, and she's married to an amazingly gifted sculptor. She has a seemingly effortless way of making everything in her life beautiful.

As a way of understanding why people turn out the way they do, she has a concept she calls "The Born House," a place where all soon-to-be-living creatures wait prior to birth. It is here they are assigned the attributes that will in large part determine the life they live and the kind of person they will be. Parents, teachers, family and friends can do only so much, she reasons. Here in The Born House I've imagined some higher being looking around and designating as Artists some small percentage of the folks waiting to be born. The rest of us are told we will have to find something else to do. Believing this made it easy to accept not being Artistic. Being one of the chosen was a gift from the powers that be, not something you could cultivate or nurture. It was this gift that destined you to become an Artist and to make Art. I contented myself with other gifts. I can always find a parking place and I have great hair.

It has taken me 60-odd years and writing this book to find out just how wrong I've been.

Here is what I now believe:

I've been debilitatingly obsessed with A words, when in truth they are no more than words, labels assigned by others. If you labor to make something where before there was nothing, you are, by definition, being creative. Whether, as a result of your work, you are described as Artistic or your work is called Art is not something you can control or should worry about. The act of creation is the important part.

I've spent way too much time devaluing my technical strength as a knitter, allowing myself to feel less than those who are deemed Artists. No one produces Artistic work without some level of technical expertise. With that expertise can come the confidence to explore creative ideas. If you never stop

Reveille *necklace (2006)*
Glass beads, vintage brass bugle beads, fiber, vintage brass clasp
Scores of vintage bugle beads follow the twist of the knit stitches from which they are suspended.
Technique link: Beads knit between stitches

seeking to learn more and see more, you will always have new tools and ideas with which to create the next evolution of your work.

Work to please yourself first. You can't please everyone, so why try? Why allow that to be the driving force behind your creative decisions? If, in the end, YOU are proud of what you create, however it is received, you can be content.

And lastly, if you have the choice, work at what you love. For me, it has always been the process of knitting—the click of the needles, the feel of the yarn passing through my fingers, the way my shoulders drop and my breathing slows when I've settled into my favorite knitting spot. It is the knitting itself that brings me enormous pleasure. What the knitting produces is a bonus.

It's been quite a journey, coming to understand and then making peace with what I both have and haven't learned. I still don't know the answers to those big questions about what Art is or why some people are called Artists or Artistic. But more importantly, I have learned that I don't need those answers in order to work in a creative way. It is so liberating to let go of old perceptions—hang-ups really—especially when many were just excuses for not trying things I was afraid of. Now I can just do the work. And learn more. The path remains challenging, marked by steps both forward and back. But the journey is filled with joy, it is never boring, and it continues.

Techniques

ABBREVIATIONS

BO bind off
CC contrast color
cn cable needle
dpn double-pointed needle(s)
" inch(es)
inc increas(e)(ed)(es)(ing)
k knit(ting)(s)(ted)
KBL knit bead on left arm
kf&b knit in front and back of stitch
KBR knit bead on right arm
M1 Make one stitch (increase)
MC main color
mm millimeter(s)
p purl(ed)(ing)(s) or page
RS right side(s)
SB slide bead between stitches
sl slip(ped)(ping)
SSK slip, slip, knit these 2 sts tog
st(s) stitch(es)
tbl through back of loop(s)
tog together
WS wrong side(s)
yd(s) yard(s)
yo yarn over (UK yarn forward)
X times

Cast-ons

LONG-TAIL CAST-ON, KNIT

Make a slip knot for the initial stitch, at a distance from the end of the yarn, allowing about 1" for each stitch to be cast on.

1 Bring yarn between fingers of left hand and wrap around little finger as shown.

2 Bring left thumb and index finger between strands, arranging so tail is on thumb side, ball strand on finger side. Open thumb and finger so strands form a diamond.

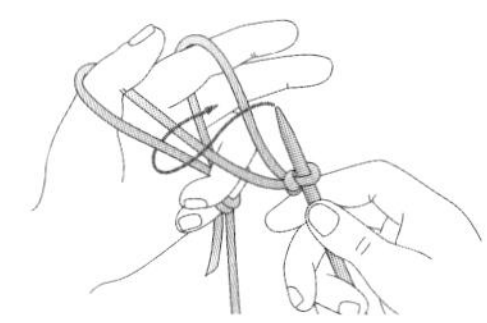

3 Bring needle down, forming a loop around thumb.

4 Bring needle **under** front strand of **thumb loop**…

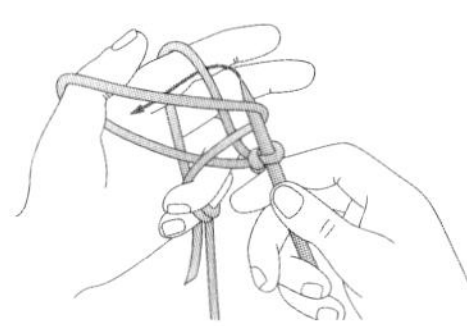

5 …up over index finger yarn, catching it…

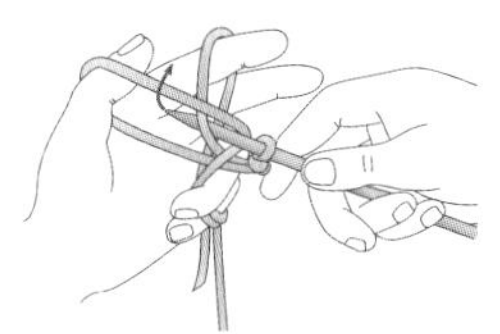

6 …and bringing it **under** the front of **thumb loop**.

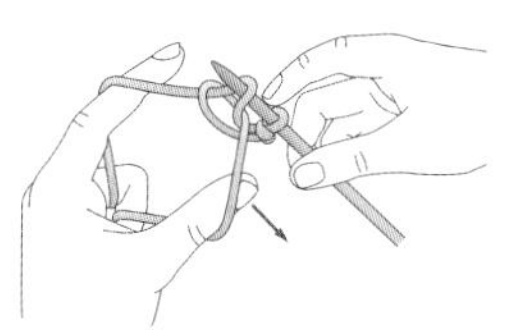

7 Slip thumb out of its loop, and use thumb to adjust tension on the new stitch. One knit stitch cast on.

TEMPORARY CROCHET CAST-ON

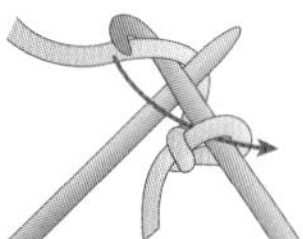

1 With waste yarn and leaving a short tail, make a **slipknot** on crochet hook. Hold hook in right hand; in left hand, hold knitting needle on top of yarn and behind hook. With hook to left of yarn, bring yarn through loop on hook; yarn goes over top of needle, forming a stitch.

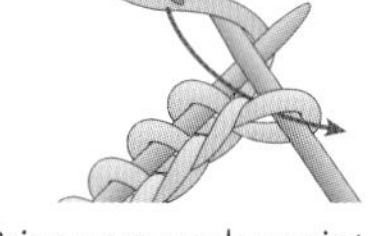

2 Bring yarn under point of needle and hook yarn through loop forming next stitch.

Repeat Step 2 until 1 stitch remains to cast on. Slip loop from hook to needle for last stitch.

CABLE CAST-ON

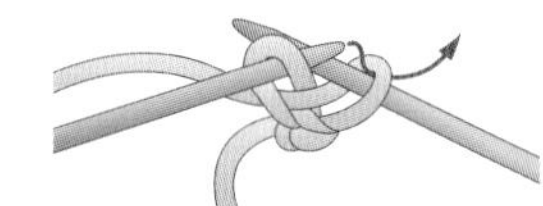

1–2 Work as for Steps 1 and 2 of KNIT CAST-ON, page 161.

3 Insert left needle in loop and slip loop off right needle. One additional stitch cast on.

4 Insert right needle *between* the last 2 stitches. From this position, knit a stitch and slip it to the left needle as in Step 3.

Repeat Step 4 for each additional stitch.

PICKING UP LOOPS FROM A TEMPORARY CAST-ON

Temporary cast-ons use waste yarn to hold the loops that form between stitches under the needle. When this waste yarn is removed, these loops can be placed on a needle.

There will be 1 fewer loops than cast-on stitches. Casting on 1 extra stitch and decreasing 1 on Row 2 of the pattern, results in the same number of stitches and loops for the graft.

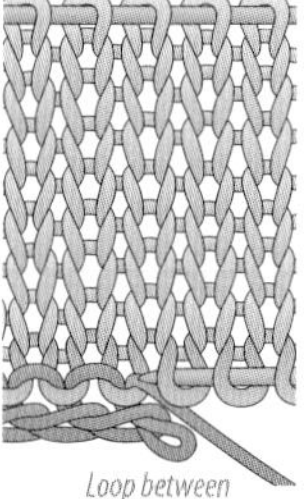

Cast-ons

KNIT CAST-ON

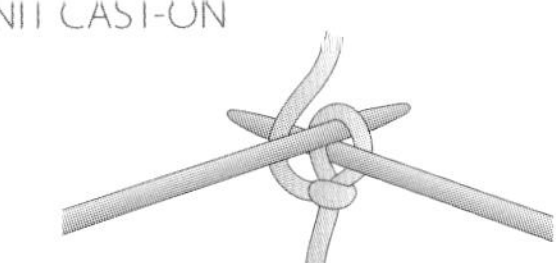

1 Start with a **slipknot** on left needle (first cast-on stitch). Insert right needle into slipknot from front. Wrap yarn over right needle as if to knit.

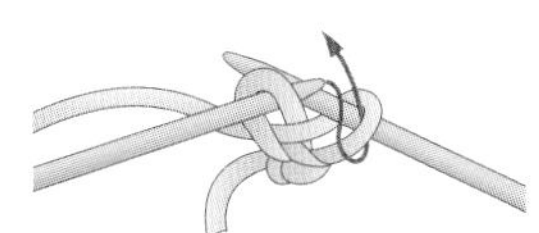

2 Bring yarn through slipknot, forming a loop on right needle.

3 Insert left needle under loop and slip loop off right needle. One additional stitch cast on.

4 Insert right needle into the last stitch on left needle as if to knit. Knit a stitch and transfer it to the left needle as in Step 3.

Repeat Step 4 for each additional stitch.

Increases

MAKE 1 (M1) **M**

KNIT

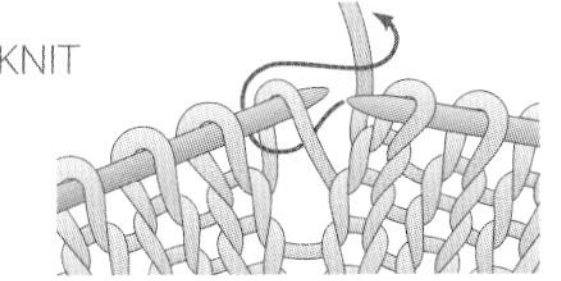

For a *left-slanting* increase (M1L), insert left needle from front to back under strand between last stitch knitted and first stitch on left needle. Insert needle into loop **at back** of needle...

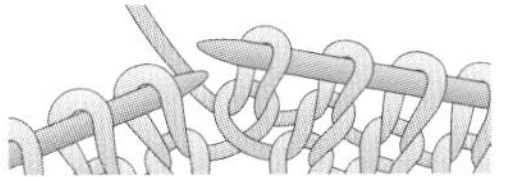

and knit, twisting the strand.

For a *right-slanting* increase (M1R), insert left needle from back to front under strand between last stitch knitted and first stitch on left needle. Insert needle into loop **at front** of needle...

and knit, twisting the strand.

KNIT INTO FRONT AND BACK (KF&B)

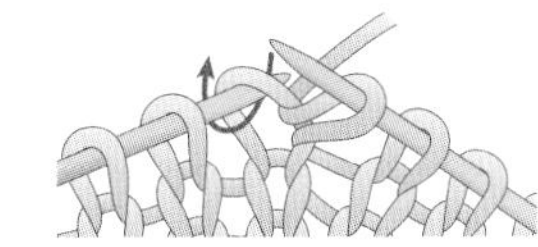

1 Knit into the front of next stitch on left needle, but do not pull the stitch off the needle.

2 Take right needle to back, then knit through the back of the same stitch.

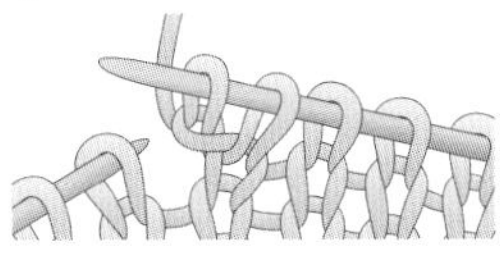

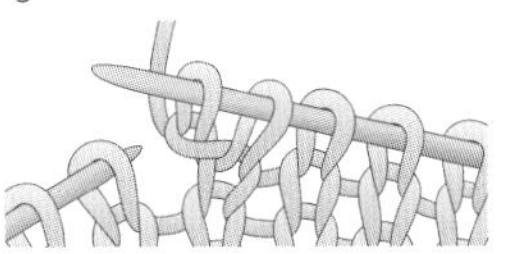

3 Pull stitch off left needle. Completed increase: 2 stitches from 1 stitch. This increase results in a purl bump after the knit stitch.

Decreases

SSK **** ***A left-slanting single decrease.***

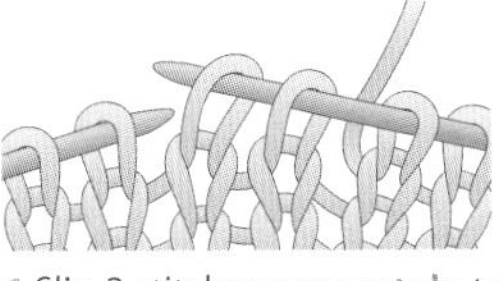

1 Slip 2 stitches **separately** to right needle as if to knit.

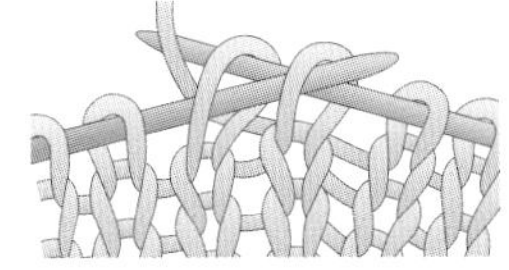

2 Slip left needle into these 2 stitches from left to right and knit them together: 2 stitches become 1.

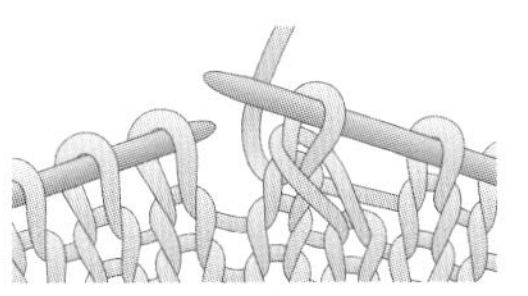

The result is a left-slanting decrease.

K2TOG **/**

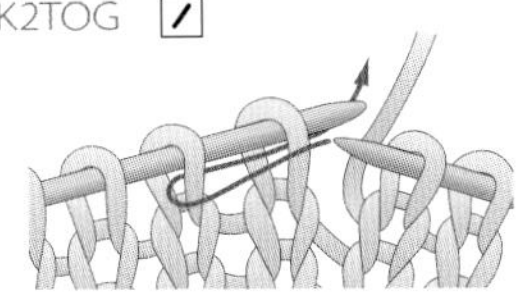

1 Insert right needle into first 2 stitches on left needle, beginning with second stitch from end of left needle.

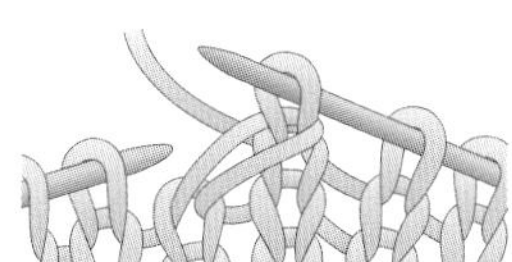

2 Knit these 2 stitches together as if they were 1. The result is a right-slanting decrease.

P2TOG **/**

1 Insert right needle into first 2 stitches on left needle.

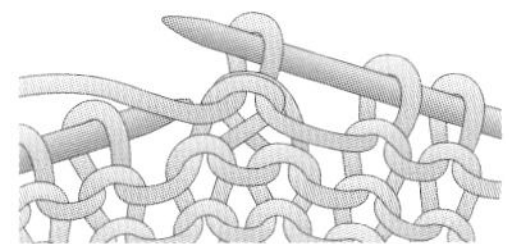

2 Purl these 2 stitches together as if they were 1. The result is a right-slanting decrease.

TECHNIQUES INDEX

3-needle bind-off	page 162
Abbreviations	page 160
Attaching fringe	page 76
Beaded cast-on	page 9, 118
Beaded bind-off	page 9, 119
Bind-off in pattern	page 162
Cable cast on	page 160
Crochet cast on	page 160
Graft in stockinette	page 163
I-cord	page 162
K1 tbl	page 162
K2tog	page 161
KBL	page 8
KBR	page 8
Kf&b	page 161
Knit cast on	page 161
Long-tail cast-on	page 160
M1L	page 80
M1R	page 80
Make 1	page 161
Make welt	page 145, 147
Mattress stitch	page 163
P1 tbl	page 162
P2tog	page 161
Pick up & knit (PUK)	page 162
SB	page 7
SSK	page 161
Yarn over	page 162
Zipper graft	page 49, 61
Working from charts	page 163
Working with DPNs	page 162

Bind-offs

3-NEEDLE BIND-OFF

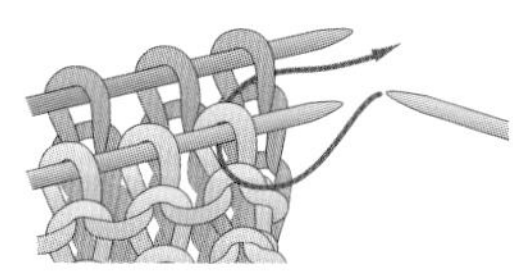

Bind-off ridge on wrong side

1 With stitches on 2 needles, place **right sides together**. * Knit 2 stitches together (1 from front needle and 1 from back needle, as shown); repeat from * once more.

2 With left needle, pass first stitch on right needle over second stitch and off right needle.

3 Knit next 2 stitches together.

4 Repeat Steps 2 and 3, end by drawing yarn through last stitch.

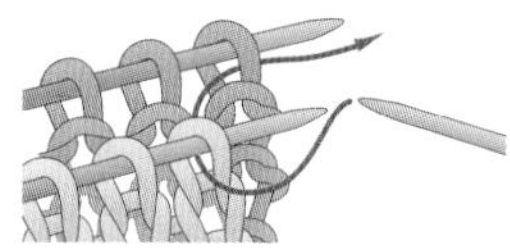

Bind-off ridge on right side

Work as for ridge on wrong side, EXCEPT, with **wrong sides together**.

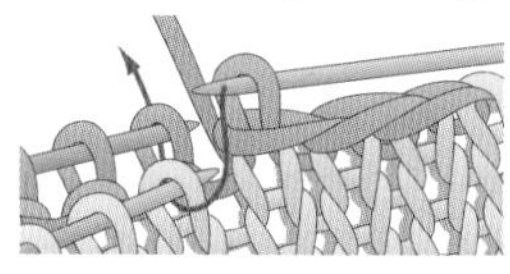

OVERHAND KNOT

BIND-OFF IN PATTERN

As you work the bind-off row for fabrics other than stockinette and garter stitch, knit or purl the stitches and place beads as the pattern requires.

BIND OFF KNITWISE

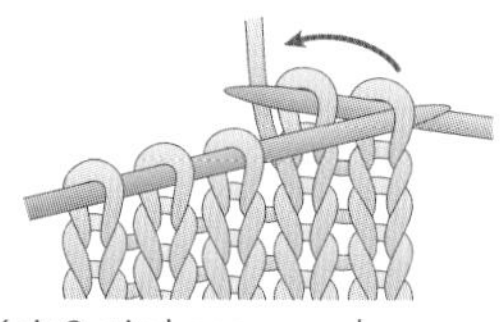

1 Knit 2 stitches as usual.

2 With left needle, pass first stitch on right needle over second stitch…

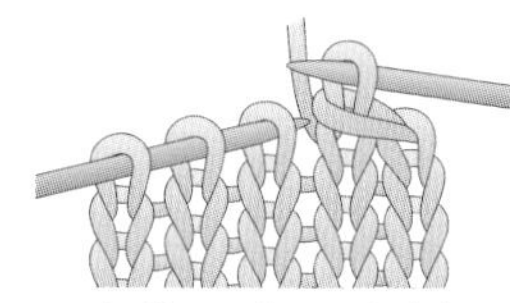

…and off needle: 1 stitch bound off (see above).

3 Knit 1 more stitch.

4 Pass first stitch over second. Repeat Steps 3–4.

TIPS

• Since 2 stitches must be on the right needle before you can bind off 1 stitch, to bind off 10 stitches, you must work 11 stitches. Only count stitches as bound off when they have been pulled off the right needle.

• Usually the bind-off should be as elastic as the rest of the knitting. To avoid binding off too tightly, bind off with a larger needle or use Suspended Bind-off.

BIND OFF PURLWISE

Work Steps 1–4 of **Bind off Knitwise** EXCEPT, purl the stitches instead of knitting them.

Extras

WORKING WITH 3 DOUBLE-POINTED NEEDLES (DPNS)

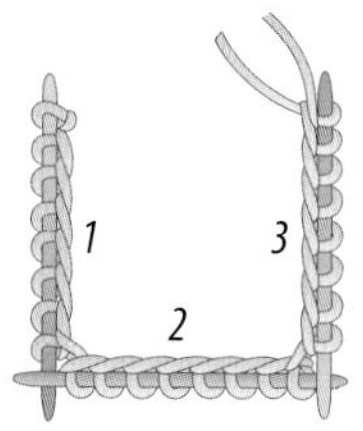

Cast stitches onto 1 dpn.

1 Rearrange stitches on 3 dpns. Check carefully that stitches are not twisted around a dpn or between dpns before beginning to work in rounds.

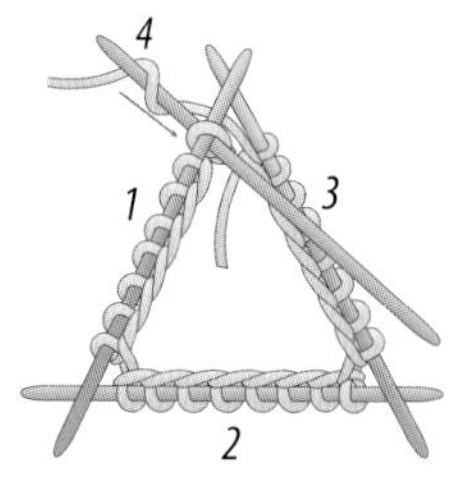

2 With a 4th dpn, work all stitches from first dpn. Use that empty dpn to work the stitches from the 2nd dpn. Use that empty dpn to work the stitches from the 3rd dpn—one round completed. Place a marker between first and second stitch of first needle to mark beginning of round.

Notice that you work with only 2 dpns at a time. As you work the first few rounds, be careful that the stitches do not twist between the needles.

I-CORD

Make a tiny tube of stockinette stitch with 2 double-pointed needles:

1 Cast on 3 or 4 sts.

2 Knit. Do not turn work. Slide stitches to opposite end of needle. Repeat Step 2 until cord is the desired length.

PICK UP & KNIT (PUK)

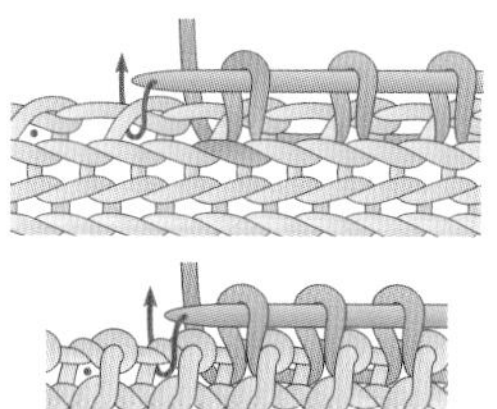

With right side facing and yarn in back, insert needle from front to back in center of edge stitch, catch yarn and knit a stitch. (See stockinette above, garter below.)

KNIT THROUGH BACK LOOP (K1 TBL)

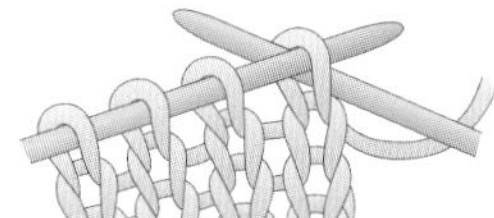

1 With right needle behind left needle and right leg of stitch, insert needle into stitch…

2 …and knit.

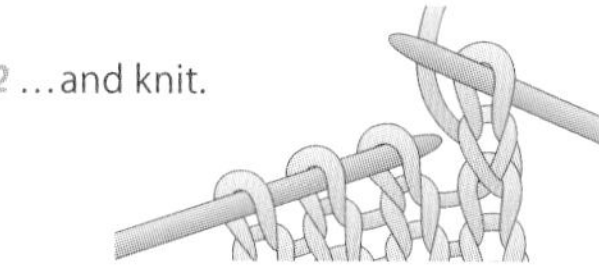

PURL THROUGH BACK LOOP (P1 TBL)

1 With right needle behind left needle, insert right needle into stitch from left to right…

2 …and purl.

YARN OVER (YO)

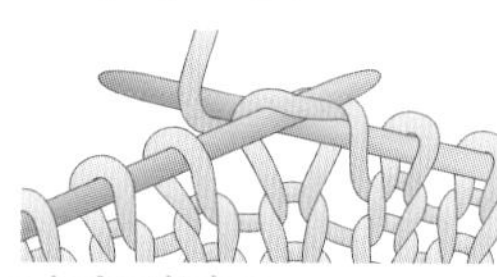

Between knit stitches

Bring yarn under the needle to the front, take it over the needle to the back and knit the next stitch.

Extras

GRAFT IN STOCKINETTE

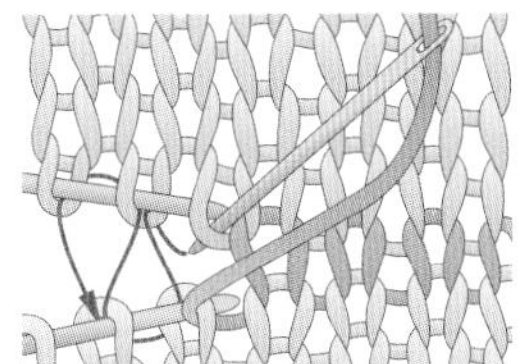

ON THE NEEDLES

1 Arrange stitches on 2 needles as shown.

2 Thread a blunt needle with matching yarn (approximately 1" per stitch).

3 Working from right to left, with right sides facing you, begin with Steps 3a and 3b:

3a Front needle: bring yarn through first stitch as if to purl, leave stitch on needle.

3b Back needle: bring yarn through first stitch as if to knit, leave stitch on needle.

4a Front needle: bring yarn through first stitch as if to knit, slip off needle; through next stitch as if to purl, leave stitch on needle.

4b Back needle: bring yarn through first stitch as if to purl, slip off needle; through next stitch as if to knit, leave stitch on needle.

Repeat Steps 4a and 4b until 1 stitch remains on each needle.

5a Front needle: bring yarn through stitch as if to knit, slip off needle.

5b Back needle: bring yarn through stitch as if to purl, slip off needle.

6 Adjust tension to match rest of knitting.

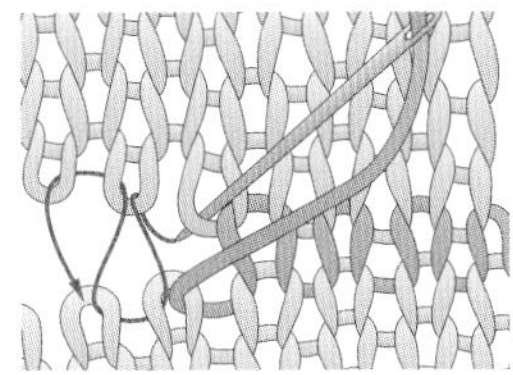

OFF THE NEEDLES

1 Place stitches on holding thread, remove needles, block pieces, and arrange as shown.

2 Thread a blunt needle with matching yarn (approximately 1" per stitch).

3 Working from right to left, with right sides facing you, begin with Steps 3a and 3b:

3a Lower piece: bring yarn from back to front through first stitch.

3b Upper piece: repeat Step 3a.

4a Lower piece: bring yarn from front to back through previous stitch worked, then from back to front through next stitch.

4b Upper piece: repeat Step 4a.

Repeat Steps 4a and 4b until 1 stitch remains on each piece.

5a Lower piece: bring yarn from front to back through stitch.

5b Upper piece: repeat Step 5a.

6 Remove holding thread and adjust tension to match rest of knitting.

OTHER USES

Finished edges

Align stitches as shown. Graft over finished edges. Adjust tension.

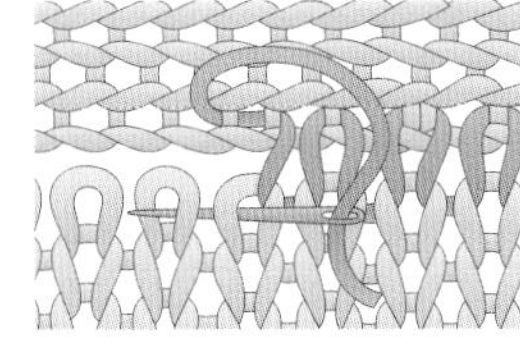

Graft live stitches to rows

Compensate for different stitch and row gauges by occasionally picking up 2 bars (as shown above), instead of 1.

GRAFTING
An invisible method of joining live stitches. Useful at underarms, mitten tips, sock toes, and hats; also called Kitchener stitch.

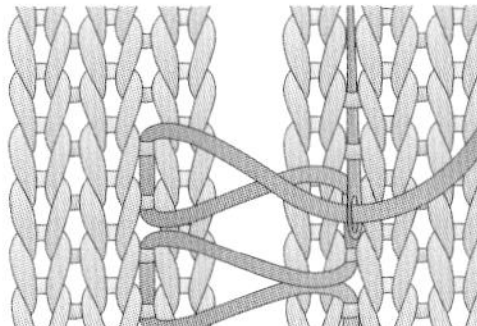

Mattress stitch seams are good all-purpose seams. They require edge stitches (which are taken into the seam allowance).

MATTRESS STITCH

1 Place pieces side by side, with right sides facing you.

2 Thread blunt needle with matching yarn.

3 Working between edge stitch and next stitch, pick up 2 bars.

4 Cross to opposite piece, and pick up 2 bars.

5 Return to first piece, work into the hole you came out of, and pick up 2 bars.

6 Return to opposite piece, go into the hole you came out of, and pick up 2 bars.

7 Repeat Steps 4 and 5 across, pulling thread taut as you go.

WORKING FROM CHARTS

Charts are graphs or grids of squares that represent the right side of knitted fabric. They illustrate every stitch and the relationship between the rows of stitches.

Squares contain knitting symbols.

The stitch key defines each symbol as an operation to make a stitch or stitches.

The pattern provides any special instructions for using the chart(s) or the key.

The numbers along the side of charts indicate the rows. A number on the right marks a right-side row, which is worked leftward from the number. A number on the left marks a wrong-side row that is worked rightward. Since many stitches are worked differently on wrong-side rows, the key will indicate that. If the pattern is worked circularly, all rows are right-side rows and worked from right to left.

Bold lines within the graph represent repeats. These set off a group of stitches that are repeated across a row. You begin at the edge of a row or where the pattern indicates for the required size, work across to the second repeat line, then repeat the stitches between the repeat lines as many times as directed, and finish the row.

YARN WEIGHTS

	1	2	3	4
	Super Fine	***Fine***	***Light***	***Medium***
Also called	Sock Fingering Baby	Sport Baby	DK Light- Worsted	Worsted Afghan Aran

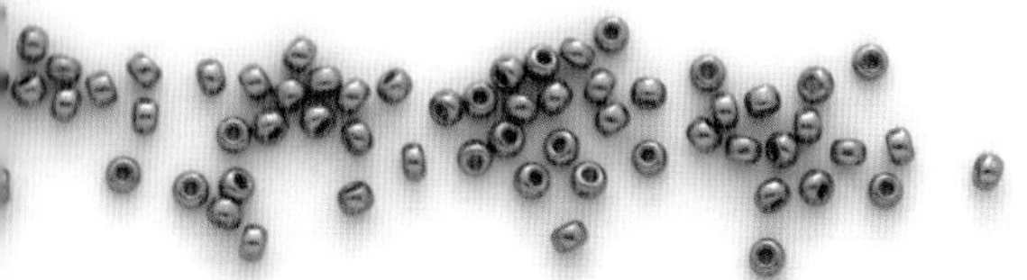

Resources

Beads, Findings & Tools

What follows are just some of the (mostly) online sources for purchasing the beads, findings, and tools you may need for the projects in this book. As always, if you are fortunate enough to have a local retail bead or craft store, please look there first.

Japanese bead company websites

For great general information about these wonderful glass beads

MIYUKI
www.miyuki-beads.co.jp/english/seed/index.html

MATSUNO
www.mgb.co.jp/

TOHO
www.tohobeads.net

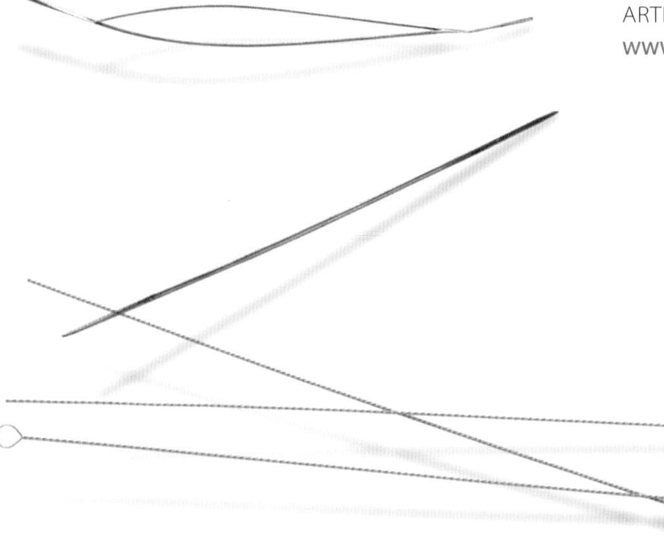

Retail sources

CARAVAN BEADS
www.caravanbeads.net

915 Forest Ave, Portland, ME 04103
(800) 230-8941 or
(207) 761-2503

What's special:
Miyukis, great website, customer service

This is my favorite online source for Miyuki beads. The website is extremely user-friendly with a great search engine, there are pictures of every bead and the owner truly understands the meaning of the words "customer service."

BLUE SANTA BEADS
www.bluesantabeads.net

1165 West Baltimore Pike, Media, PA 19063,
(610)-892-2740

What's special
Miyukis, Tohos & Matsunos, clasps, endless loop earring findings, customer service

This is MY local bead store and I'm so lucky to have it. While the shopping part of their website is still a work in progress, they have a huge variety of the beads I use most often, including Miyuki, Toho and all the Matsuno beads. If you call them they will check for and ship just what you need.

ARTBEADS
www.artbeads.com

11901 137th Ave KPN, Gig Harbor, WA 98329,
(866) 715-2323 or (253) 857-3433

What's special ***Tohos & Mag-lok clasps***

Good source for Toho beads and a good search engine. Otherwise, lots of everything — findings, tools and even some instructional info for jewelry making.

BELLO MODO
www.bellomodo.com

Online only (360) 357-3443

What's special ***Miyukis & Tohos***

Carry both Miyuki and Toho beads.

FUSION BEADS
www.fusionbeads.com

3830 Stone Way, Seattle, WA 98103,
(888) 781-3559 or (206) 782-4595

What's special
Japanese & great Czech glass beads

A fun, not overly busy-looking site with lots of information. They carry glass beads of all sorts — Czech, Japanese, and others but don't identify their Japanese beads by maker. Still I see lots of materials I'd like to work with here.

FIRE MOUNTAIN GEMS
www.firemountaingems.com

No retail outlet but you can tour their location in Grants Pass, OR (800) 355-2137

What's special
Wide range of beads & supplies, volume discount pricing

They carry limited amounts of Miyuki beads and do have Matsuno beads (not easy to find online). Lots and lots of everything else.

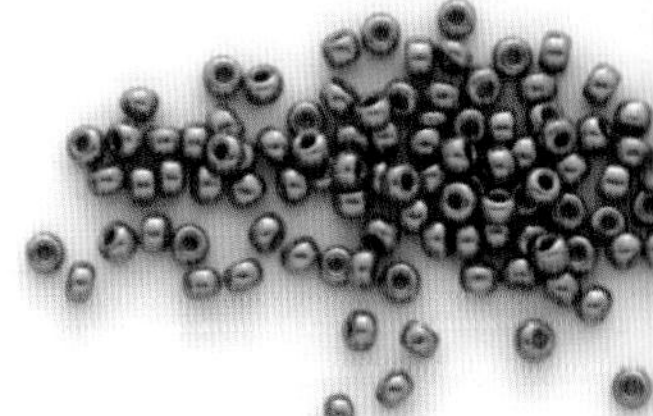

WOODWORKS LTD
www.craftparts.com

Online only. (800) 722-0311

What's special **wooden beads for wrapping**

Go to the section entitled "Beads & Spools, Wood" and you'll find all of the wooden beads I use under knitted wrappers — different size rounds and large oval "rice" beads. For smaller quantities of these beads, do an online search for Lara's Crafts or find their wood products at your local craft store (like Michaels or A.C. Moore). Look in the Wood Products section, not the Beading section.

A GRAIN OF SAND
www.agrainofsand.com

Online Only. (704) 660-3125

What's special
incredible clasps, rare and vintage beads

If you are looking for one-of-a-kind clasps and unique beads to distinguish your projects, you must check out this site. Prepare to spend a while looking through their offerings. Make sure to register for their newsletter for special deals and notices.

M&J TRIMMING
www.mjtrim.com

1008 Sixth Ave (between 37th & 38th),
New York, NY 10018,
(800) 965-8746 or (212) 391-6200

What's special
paillettes (large sequins), Stash Buster belt buckle

A wonderful site for inspiring notions of all kinds including Paillettes (Large Sequins). If I ever get to the retail store, I might never leave. Find the Stash Buster buckle in the Buckles and Closures section.

HOBBY LOBBY
www.shophobbylobby.com

Retail stores nationwide. (800) 888-0321

What's special **pailletes (large sequins)**

I have purchased large-hole paillettes here but they are not always in stock. They do seem to have the smaller-hole paillettes and you can use a standard hole punch to make these usable for knitting projects.

CARTWRIGHT'S SEQUINS
www.ccartwright.com

Online only. Contact by emailing from website.

What's special
large-hole paillettes (large sequins)

Many colors of large-hole paillettes

UMX FASHION SUPPLIES
www.umei.com

Online only. (800) 921-5523

What's special **suspender clips**

Find a wide variety of sewing/finishing notions. Find the suspender clips I used here: www.umei.com/suspender-clips-s.htm

CREATE FOR LESS
www.createforless.com

Online Only. (866) 333-4463

What's special
big-eye & twisted-wire beading needles

While you can find Big Eye and Twisted Wire Beading Needles at many craft stores, this is a good online source for needles and a wide range of craft supplies with frequent discounts. They call Twisted Wire needles "collapsible eye" needles.

RIO GRANDE
www.riogrande.com

Online and Catalog Sales. (800) 545-6566

What's special **findings, needles**

Perhaps the largest jewelry-making supplier in the US. Order their catalogs for endless hours of browsing pleasure.

TWISTED SISTAH BEADS
www.twistedsistahbeads.com

Online or shows only. (267) 254-4845

What's special
Miyukis, beading needles, Czech pressed glass, search engine, customer service

Friendly service and great selection of beads and beading supplies. Often at shows, including Stitches. Check website for show schedule.

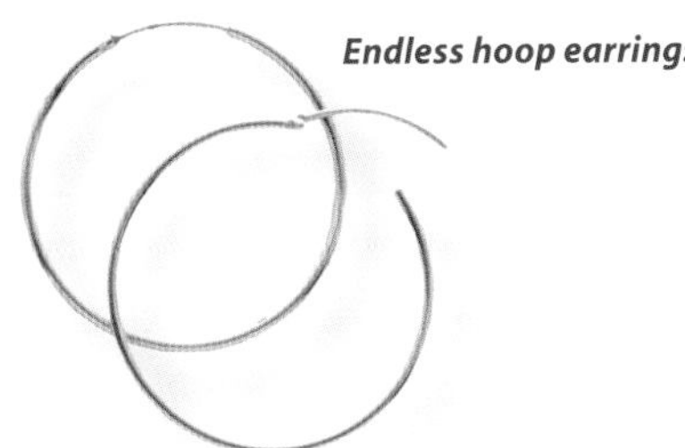

Endless hoop earrings

Colophon:
MAGICAL MOMENTS

(Opposite page, counterclockwise, from top) Years in the making —Morning Glories; and the all-purl I-cord that inspired it; Betsy's yarns; Betsy's knitting teacher, mom Nancy.

(This page, counterclockwise from bottom left) Betsy's beads, Betsy's bracelets, Betsy beads, Betsy's studio.

Betsy's studio on the second floor of her spacious Philadelphia home resembles a gallery filled with dazzling polychrome bangles, bracelets, necklaces, belts, and earrings.

They fill black velvet stands on the mantle and on top of bookcases lined with storage cases of beads, they hang on gray walls, door and drawer knobs, and they rest on Betsy's beading tray, on an ottoman in front of her favorite Pompeian red leather chair.

Betsy, standing by the fireplace, points to a square crystal vase full of fibers. "Every time I finish a piece," she says, "I take a snippet of the yarn I used and throw it in here. It's my memory jar. I like to be reminded of the pieces that came before. And truthfully, I like the way all the yarns look!"

On her studio door, a long cork board is covered with more memories, what Betsy laughingly calls her UBO's—her Unidentified Beaded Objects. They are Magical Moments: tiny swatches of bead knitting that represent a "Eureka!" discovery in the *Betsy Beads* journey.

She removes a push pin, takes a tiny swatch of blue knitting covered with red, gold, and ceramic beads (see photo, top of next page) and settles into her comfortable chair.

"You'll laugh," she says, "because it's so unbelievable. But this is what started it all—and it happened at STITCHES!"

That's where I first met Betsy Hershberg myself, as a student in my Shooting Your Stuff photography class.

I love sharing photography with my students, imparting to aspiring shutterbugs the importance of allowing the viewer to see every stitch. Photographing their work—scarves, shawls, sweaters, hats, stockings—with my students gamely modeling, is all part of the fun.

How could I have imagined then, looking at Betsy's 'stuff'—an exquisitely beautiful knit-bead bracelet—that, one day, I'd be looking through my macro lens at a book's worth of *Betsy Beads?*

Years later, here I am, in her sunny studio, photographing her work and, with my tape recorder at hand, asking Betsy: how did all of this happen?

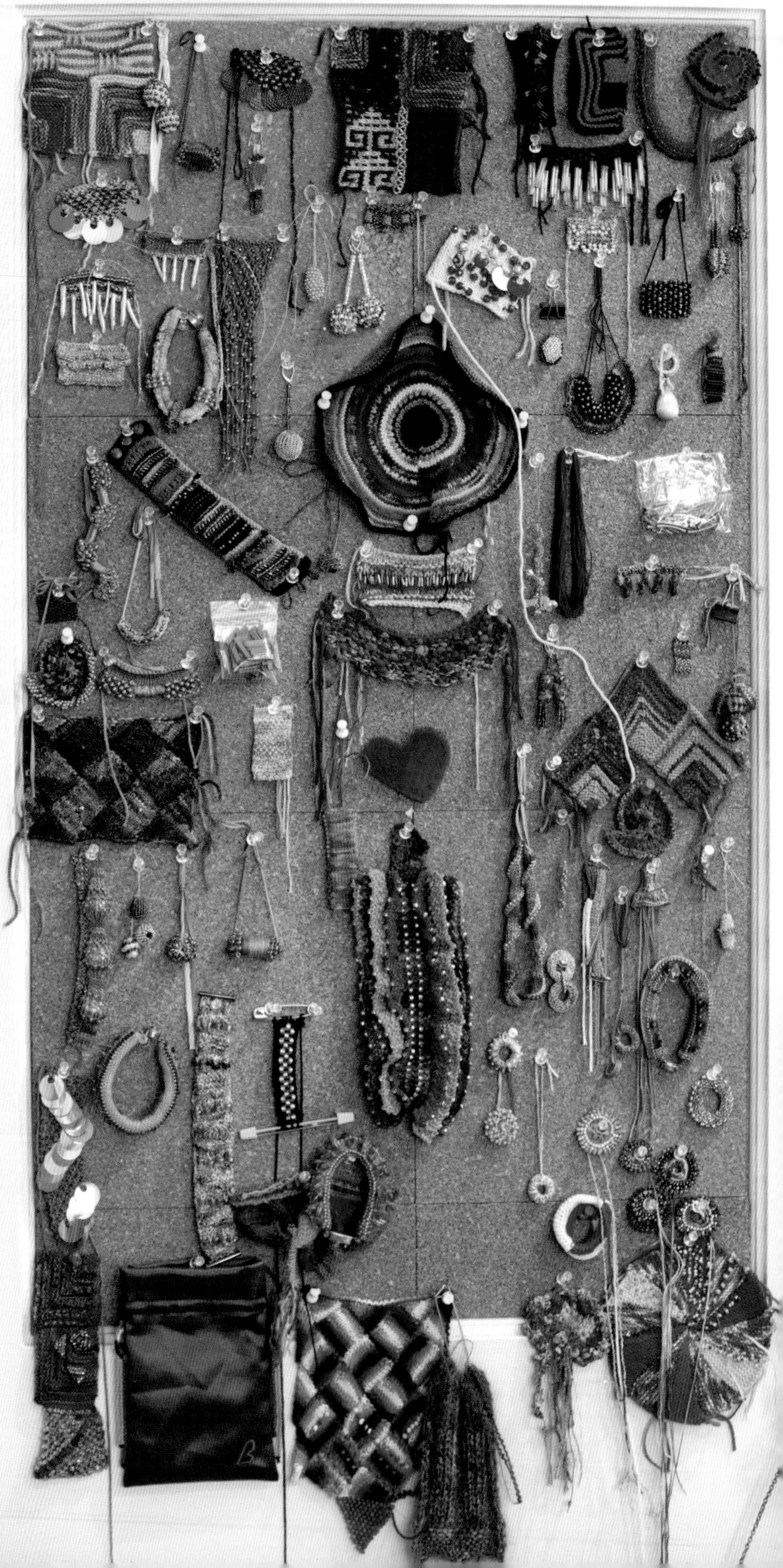

But Betsy, who, besides being a gifted designer and author, has an eye for photography, begins talking about the book photos.

"What you do," she says, "is the way I try to shoot my own work; what I want people to see. The level of detail that you have been able to show, in such an artistic way!"

High praise, indeed. But aren't we here to talk about *Betsy?*

"I have to tell you," she continues, "it's not just close-up, after close-up, after close-up. It's where you place the piece in the frame and your use of depth of field that draws the eye to just where I want someone to look.

"And your choice of backgrounds? Such an accurate reflection of the intent of the piece. For an everyday piece that I don't want people to take too seriously, you choose jellybeans! How much fun is that?

"I really appreciate this because occasionally people will say about my work, 'Oh, it's really beautiful; but I don't dress up like that.' So your fun shots reinforce what I have been trying to do—get people to think differently about how to think about and wear my work. Yes some pieces are meant to be dressy, but the majority you should feel comfortable wearing with a T-shirt and a pair of jeans.

"I try to use interesting materials to create works that are accessible and show my love of detail and my respect for finishing. I want people to enjoy my work, have fun making it, and *really* have fun wearing it. So, thank you for making those photos so beautiful *and* so much fun."

What looks like a lot of fun to me are all those little swatches hanging on her UBO corkboard. And I wonder out loud, if this tiny blue swatch—and close-ups of her key Magical Moments—wouldn't make a great Colophon?

"This is freaky," Betsy says. "Not only do we have the same eye, but you're inside my head! What a great way for knitters to understand the evolution of my work and the creative process I use. What a great way to tell this story."

Lily Chin's class sampler

"It all began at STITCHES, in 2002 in Valley Forge. I was an hour late for Lily Chin's basic bead knitting class because there was an accident on the Pennsylvania Turnpike.

"Besides being pathologically organized, I'm pathologically on time. It makes me crazy to be late! So I ran in huffing and puffing, and of course, Lily was well into her class.

"Lily does such a great job teaching. She's inspirational and quite the entertainer. She demonstrates with humongous needles that look like broomsticks, uses Cheerios for beads, marine cord for yarn. She had lots of samples, great handouts, and I was easily able to catch up.

"Five hours later, this tiny sampler was the result! But something more important happened in the class that triggered my knitting brain, and I became obsessed with the possibilities for combining beads and fiber.

"This little class swatch is a perfect illustration of why you shouldn't focus on perfection when you start something new. Look at it: it's just a tumble of beads and techniques, such a small little nothing. Everybody laughs when I show it to them, when I tell them I took a six-hour class and this is what I walked out with. Of course it's funny, but this little swatch is iconic for me, the seed for all the work that I have done since. I always tell Lily how grateful I am. What she shared with me opened up this whole other place in my head, propelled me forward, and got me so excited that I couldn't *not* pursue it.

"I'd been knitting since I was eight, but I had never put a bead in anything, and now all I wanted to do was play with beads and yarn."

Koigu tunic

"I tell my students to start with what they're passionate about. Back then, for me, it was mitered squares. Shall I show you the first piece that I put beads into? It'll also make you laugh. I'm usually quite adventurous when choosing knitting projects, but my personal style is often understated. So it wasn't about

What started it all—the sampler from Betsy's first bead-knitting class.

There are 156 mitered squares in Betsy's first knit-bead tunic—and only 45 beads.

"Only I know," Betsy says, "that there are beads in my first piece of bead knitting, the Koigu tunic. I always have to point them out to people!"

Mitered Square 1: If small beads don't fit on your yarn, string them on a fine carry-along thread.

Mitered Square 2: Inspired by bead-artist Valerie Hector, experimenting with surface embellishments — bead weaving (triangles) and couching (spiral).

Mitered Square 3: Seeing the fiber through crystal clear beads.

throwing 7,000 beads on my tunic: adding a little bead in the center of a square is what felt right. As a result, while the tunic is made up of 156 mitered squares, I only used about 45 beads in the whole thing! My left-brained self is just more comfortable with taking small steps, making one small change at a time.

"The Koigu yarn is so beautiful and the beads so small, no one ever notices that they're there. But *I* do, and that's what was important."

Mitered Square 1: Beads on a carry-along yarn

"The next step was to use more beads — more than one to a mitered square! — and see what happens. So I went on eBay and ordered odd lots of beads. For very little money, I could get a box filled with a million different kinds: seed, trade, ceramic, wood, acrylic — so I had all kinds to play with. Also, notice that all of my first bead samples were done with wool, not the fibers I use most today, because I was using yarn from my stash.

"These little mitered squares with their short changes of color cried out for little beads. I remembered Lily suggesting that if small beads didn't fit on your yarn, you could put them on a finer carry-along yarn and knit the two yarns together. I pulled up three beads at a time — assuming a single bead wasn't going to show at all — and learned that while they wouldn't sit flat in the knitting, they added texture to the fabric. I also learned that experimenting in this way had a lot to teach me."

Mitered Square 2: Surface embellishment

"Shortly after Lily's class, I met the extraordinary bead artist Valerie Hector at a local craft show. She was very encouraging about my ideas for working with beads and yarn. Her book, *The Art of Beadwork*, piqued my interest in off-loom bead weaving and using beads for surface embellishment along with knitting them into the fabric."

"I love teaching myself, learning how to do new things. These embellishments, the two little triangular swags, are my first attempt to take a bead-weaving technique and use it as an embellishment.

"The technique used for the little spiral is called couching: I embroidered a string of beads into a spiral on top of the knitting as another experiment in surface embellishment."

Mitered Square 3: See-through beading

"I think of myself first, last, and always as a knitter: that's who I am, that's what I want to do, that's what I want to show. With bead weaving, all you see are the beads, but for me, the yarn is really important. Even when I want to create something that is very heavily beaded, I still want to see the yarn.

"If I used clear beads, in a very heavy beading pattern, what kind of an effect would I get? Would I still be able to see the color and the wonder of the yarn? You *can* see the yarn through these clear beads, but I left a little line of stitches — in the center, where the miter decreases are — to show off the yarn even more.

"This was the swatch that led to the Double Play bracelet. I used clear beads that show the fiber in two different ways: allowing it to be the focus, and letting the bead be the focus. When they spiral together, you get the best of both worlds.

"For eighteen months I did not make a finished anything. I was in an absolute frenzy of wanting to learn. I played with different techniques — mosaics, mitered squares, circular knitting, different stitch patterns — trying to figure out how to combine beads with knitted fiber.

"I thought about 'wool art,' a canvas that I could work on with very fine yarns and small beads. I did a couple of pillows, but I didn't really connect with them. Still my left-brained self longed for something concrete to which to apply all of these new-found ideas. I would sit down, do a little something, put it away; do a little something, put it away.

"When my youngest child left for college, I went to work two days a week at a yarn store in my neighborhood. The store was owned by an extraordinary craftswoman who had done every needle art you can imagine. I had been buying yarn in her store for years and showing her some of the things I'd been making. She sensed something in me that I didn't even know was there. She subtly encouraged me to try designing, occasionally suggesting I take home a yarn that wasn't moving, to see what I could come up with.

"When someone does that — gives me a challenge, something to think about — then all of a sudden the gears start turning. There's a purpose, something I can focus my energies on. There's nothing I love more!"

No-bead-knitting bracelet

"The ideas just kept coming, and when I started playing around with I-cord, I realized that jewelry could be a possibility. It seemed like such an obvious connection!

"But how could I get beads into it? I was producing scads of I-cord on a machine, so there was no way to knit-in the beads. I tried sewing the I-cords together with beads, using an overcast stitch, with a couple of beads on each stitch. Stitching together three different colors of I-cord allowed me to change the look of the bracelet by turning to reveal another I-cord.

"The focus of your photo — the bead-woven focal piece — was simply a way to solve the problem of how to finish the bracelet: now that I had three pieces of I-cord sewn together, they looked pretty funky on the ends. I needed to hide the ends and turn this into a bracelet. A circular bead-woven piece was the answer.

"Looking back, it's interesting to me that there is no true bead knitting in my first piece of jewelry. It's just knitting and beads combined. But I loved the result and now years later I've expanded on this technique and used it for the Twofers Bracelet."

Bead sampler bracelet

"This early little bracelet started out as yet another sampler, an experiment with varied bead-knitting techniques. I just cast on stitches with thin yarn strung with tiny beads, and knitted a strip. It was only afterwards that I decided to turn the strip into a bracelet. I still love these little beads, the changing yarn colors, and the vintage button closures."

Bead-knit bead wrappers

"It's important to understand that you're likely going to make a bunch of strange or unsatisfying things before you make something you love. So I ask students to keep an open mind and not be afraid to make things that are not going to look fabulous the first time around. It's an important part of the creative process.

"So I figured the least I could do is share one of *my* first, less-than-satisfying, efforts. It's my first attempt at creating a bead-knit wrapper for a wooden bead.

"Photos A and B (lower right) show the same bead: but ***A*** shows the nicely knitted part, and ***B*** shows the disaster hiding on the other side. I had no idea of how to graft the edges of this little piece of bead-knit fabric together to make the wrap seamless. In time, the Zipper Graft was born, but only after many more adventures like this one!

"I think you have to be working on things in order to figure out *how* to make things work. You start with an idea, a technique, you work with it to find out what the problems are, and then try to solve them. It's pretty concrete. Each and every step has something to teach you."

Beaded cast-on/bind-off strap

"I was playing with cast-ons and bind-offs, trying to figure out ways to use beads in both of these techniques and discovered a wonderful component as a result. The only reason there are so few rows between the beads in this sample is that I was only interested in the beaded parts and didn't want to work many rows in between. I started with the knitted cast-on and then I only knit two rows. I was in a hurry to get to the bind-off! It was only after I figured out how to work the beaded bind-off that I noticed that I had created a terrific-looking strap with beads on either edge. Later it became the strap of the Byzantine Gold Handbag design that appeared in the Summer 2007 Issue of *Knitter's Magazine*."

The first piece of jewelry — no bead knitting, but bead weaving.

Early bead knitting sampler, later turned into a bracelet.

Knit wrapper for wooden beads — before development of zipper graft.

Beaded cast-on/bind-off strap

A "Wow!" moment — the inside-out bead tube.

First laddered I-cord sample

Tubular bead wrapper — a new way to wrap a bead of an odd shape, with no need for grafting.

The circular gold link.

"What If…" Link — embellishing a golden link with ribbon wrapping.

Bead-knit wrapper folded in half

"I clearly spent a lot of time playing with bead-knit wrappers! I cannot stress enough how important it is to play with these little swatches even after they are finished. One day I took a beaded wrapper and folded it in half — knit side out, beads to the inside. Lo and behold, compressing the beads into the tight space inside the fold forced them to subtly peek out between the stitches. Although no finished project resulted from this sample at the time, the idea resurfaced years later and you can see a similar effect in the Beads by the Barrel necklace."

First laddered I-cord sample

"I find I-cord to be endlessly fascinating. This I-cord variation turned out to be another great surprise. Traditionally, I-cord is worked with all knit stitches. But I wondered: what would happen if you changed the stitch pattern? What if I worked 5 stitches as k1, p3, k1?

"When I did that, the I-cord flattened from a round tube into a strap with two very distinct and very interesting sides. The front side presented a little purl cushion where beads could be knit between stitches, but the back side was really interesting! It had ladders of yarn across it, which just screamed for beads. I decided this was a unique way to use I-cord.

"Usually you try to pull firmly on the working yarn to close the back of the I-cord and create a tube. With this stitch pattern, the back stayed open. That's what it wanted to do. So instead of lamenting the difference, I tried to find a way to exploit it, use it to create a completely different look. That nice piece of yarn with nothing on it seemed a perfect place for these wonderful, matte finish, half-inch long bugle beads. The next step?

"I realized that by increasing the number of knit stitches in the I-cord, I would have a longer ladder of thread across the back and could use either longer beads or multiple smaller beads that would help keep the piece flat and open. Both the Ladder 72 bracelet and the Chiaroscuro belt are the products of this wonderful "What if…?".

Tubular bead wrapper

"My original bead wrappers are ninety degrees opposite of this one. For those I made a flat piece of fabric, wrapped it around the bead, grafted the bind-off to the cast-on, and cinched the ends together around the holes.

"But as I was making all of this I-cord in the round, it occurred to me that I could make a small piece of I-cord, stuff the bead inside the tube, cinch the ends, and be done! I wouldn't have to graft anything.

"This little bead is the very first tubular bead wrapper. Because of the unique shape of this little bead — wider at the center — I just had to put beads around its equator. You'll find this type of construction in the Four Seasons necklace and earrings as well as the Silver Orbit earrings."

Golden link

"When I made another short tubular bead wrapper, I took it off the needles and played with it, discovering that it easily flattened into a circular link! You see how one thing leads to another? It was easy to identify the row that was the outside edge of the link, the circumference — it was the center row of the tube. The next time around, I added beads to that row to get a beaded outer edge for the link. Then all I had to do was to stitch together the cast-on and bind-off edges of the tube that were now at the center of the link, to secure it. It's so magical. You can see these links in the Golden Links necklace and the Fruit Loops bracelet."

A "What if…?" link

"Trying a different yarn and then embellishing the link by wrapping yarn around it were the next iterations. I really never assume something is finished; it's always just waiting for the next "What if…?". But those next steps don't always come right away. Look how this later version shows the color variation in the ribbon yarn. And because it's wrapped, it has a firmer shape than the flat golden link. I haven't used this in a finished piece yet, but I think it's just a matter of time."

Drop bead drapes

"Hems are a relatively new fascination of mine. Here I placed a series of drop bead drapes along the turning row of a hem. If you make these little dangly drops with regular beads, they can't nestle next to each other, and you end up seeing the yarn on which they're strung. But the shape of the drop beads allows them to take the curve and make a beautiful drape."

Bead weaving in a picot hem

"While I love stringing and knitting beads, I recognize that not everyone does. So I love finding ways to give knitters an alternative for creating a bead-knit look without actually bead knitting. A picot hem is perfect for this. It offers both a little open space between the picots and an open area inside the hem where you can weave thread in and out of the spaces between the picots, adding a bead — or in this case, a beautiful blush stick pearl — in each space. A bead-knit look with no pre-stringing! This is the technique used in the Girly Pearls necklace."

All-purl I-cord spiral

"This last swatch illustrated my favorite magical moment of all — so far! I can't tell you how many years I tried to develop a technique that would allow I-cord to spiral on its own! I tried so many ideas, but none of them worked. Finally my I-cord stitch experiments paid off. What if, instead of all knit stitches, I used all purls? And Eureka! I discovered that when you do I-cord with all purls, it spirals naturally! How cool and unexpected was that? Sometimes you have to stop looking so hard for something but remain open to recognizing it when it appears. I used this simple technique for the Keep It Simple Spiral Necklace, the first project in the book, and it inspired my one-of-a-kind necklace called Morning Glories (pictured at the beginning of the Colophon). All I can think now is, what haven't I discovered yet? And how much fun is it going to be to find out?"

It's after four o'clock, and the arrival of Betsy's mom Nancy Fineberg means putting on my photographer's hat for a mother-daughter shot. It's forty-seven degrees outside, but you wouldn't know it as Nancy and Betsy smile for the camera (see page 166).

"My mom," Betsy says, "has been such an inspiration for me in my life, in my work, and in this book."

"I think it's fabulous," says Nancy, "especially since Betsy didn't start out this way. She was talented, but focused in a different direction. And all of a sudden, this appears, seemingly from nowhere.

"Betsy comes from a craft background in the family, but her thoughts, where they come from, I don't know. She tells me she gets up in the middle of the night knowing what she's going to do, the beads she's going to use, the colors. It's unbelievable. I love everything she does; I love *her*!"

"How can you not be successful," Betsy says, "when you grow up with a mother who constantly tells you, 'There isn't anything you can't do if you want to.' So now I encourage other knitters to be fearless, to try things for themselves. I want to empower them, knowing full well that I don't have all the answers. They have to ask their own questions and find their own answers."

As I wave goodbye, I stop my van, and lower the window to ask one last question: what is Betsy thinking about when she wakes up in the middle of the night these days? Another book?

"You and my husband!" Betsy says, laughing. "He says *Betsy Beads Again* would make a great title!

"Actually, I've always been fascinated with the work of a man in California who, with what he calls a music animation machine, makes music visual, creating animated cartoons that illustrate every note and rhythm of the music.

"It totally fascinates me, because I love music, played piano for twelve years as a child, and all those little notes sure look like beads to me. Someday I'm going to bead-knit Bach's Toccata and Fugue in D minor!"

— Alexis Yiorgos Xenakis
Sioux Falls, South Dakota, December 2011

Drop beads make the perfect drape on a beaded hem.

A picot hem with stick pearls.

After years of trying to create a naturally spiraling tube, "Eureka!" — the all-purl I-cord.

Acknowledgements

Wow. It's finished.

So many friends and family members believed I could do this long before I did. They've supported, pushed, pulled, cajoled, advised, suggested, questioned—done anything and everything they could to help me continue moving forward.

Much love and gratitude to:

My wonderful students and especially that first diehard group at the yarn store. Did they know then that I wasn't always sure I had something to teach them? Do they know now that they taught me at least as much as I taught them? I hope so. Special thanks to Tiania Warner and Sandy DeLeo. They'll understand.

Brenda Brown, my knitting angel. At first a customer at the store, then a student and friend, and forever a valued confidante and supporter the likes of which I would wish for everyone. Her knitting skills are extraordinary, her generosity is boundless, and her smile lights up the world.

Close friend and true artist Leslie Pontz for taking my work seriously long before I did. I'm not sure she'll ever know just how much her support means to me.

Valerie Hector, a remarkable bead artist and educator, who took time away from selling her extraordinary work at a crafts show to really listen to a total stranger and who encouraged me to explore my as yet unfocused ideas about bead knitting.

My fellow teachers. Your jaw-dropping technical skills, your spectacular designs and your devotion to teaching inspire me every time we are together as well as the days in between. Special thanks to Susanna Hansson, Elise Duvekot, Myra Wood, Gwen Bortner, JC Briar, Beth Whiteside, and the inimitable Fiona Ellis for their early support and ongoing enthusiastic generosity of spirit.

My XRX family. Karen, Denny, Carol, Greg, Sarah, Ginger, Lisa, Mavis, Molly, Jason—this company truly IS a family. To Rick Mondragon, for actually reading email from an unknown knitter with dreams and for helping find a way to say "Yes!" to all of them. To Natalie Sorenson for skillfully crafting the look of this book, pulling together and presenting so much information, so many materials, and so many gorgeous photos in such an artful way. To Elaine Rowley, an extraordinary editor who brings a unique combination of literary and needlework skills to an often daunting process. Endless thanks to you for filtering the complicated facets of my work and making them accessible and beautiful at the same time—no mean feat. To Alexis Xenakis, photographer and artist extraordinaire. You made me an early promise that I thought would be impossible to keep. I was wrong. You and your camera have illuminated my work in ways I never could have imagined. And to Benjamin Levisay—a true friend and a man of his word. This doesn't happen without you.

And most importantly, this book came to be because I have the best family in the world. I can't name them all but they are always there for me. I must recognize the best sister a girl could ask for, Dulcie Flaharty, and her husband David for their open hearts and keen artistic eye; my husband Ted, supportive from the start, challenging me to recognize my gifts beyond my technical comfort zone; my talented and inspiring children Daniel and Jessica, who lead by example, successfully pursuing their own creative passions every day; and last, but always first, my incomparable mother Nancy Fineberg. Thank you. You all make me believe that anything is possible.